S·O·C·I·A·L

W·O·R·K

W·I·T·H

CHILDREN

A·N·D

ADOLESCENTS

PAULA ALLEN-MEARES

University of Michigan

Longman *Publishers USA*

**Social Work with Children
and Adolescents**

Longman, 10 Bank Street, White Plains, N.Y. 10606

Associated companies:
Longman Group Ltd., London
Longman Cheshire Pty., Melbourne
Longman Paul Pty., Auckland
Copp Clark Longman Ltd., Toronto

Senior acquisitions editor: David Shapiro
Sponsoring editor: David J. Estrin
Development editor: Susan G. Alkana
Production editor: Linda Moser/The Bookmakers
Cover design: Susan J. Moore
Production supervisor: Richard Bretan

Library of Congress Cataloging-in-Publication Data
Allen-Meares, Paula
    Social work with children and adolescents / by Paula Allen-Meares.
        p.   cm.
    Includes bibliographical references and index.
    ISBN 0-8013-0211-0
    1. Social work with children—United States.   2. Social work with
    teenagers—United States.   I. Title.
    HV741.A566   1994   94-3705
    362.7'0973—dc20   CIP

1 2 3 4 5 6 7 8 9 10-CRS-9897969594

The interests of childhood and youth are the interests of mankind.

William James, in Tryon Edwards (ed.), *The New Dictionary of Thoughts: A Cyclopedia of Quotations* (1956). New York: Standard Book Company, p. 73.

Contents

List of Tables and Figures

Tables

Figures

Foreword

This book is a significant accomplishment because it presents readably and elegantly a broad perspective on social work with children and adolescents. It is never easy to present the essential content of any subject without sacrificing breadth or depth, the trick seems to be in the way the subject matter is thought about and organized in a book. Paula Allen-Meares has done it exactly right here.

Modern social work is about practice that derives from social policies; is steeped in specific, relevant knowledge; and is appropriately evaluated. The transactional person-in-environment view of case phenomena permits social workers to assess their child and adolescent clients in real-world contexts and includes knowledge of their development and their (competent) coping styles. Simultaneously, it includes knowledge of families, neighborhoods, schools, and other significant institutions in their environments. Just as important as explanations of lifestyles and behaviors are the diverse cultures reflected as aspects of ethnicity, class, and gender. This book covers all these topics and even more about the particular problems of child abuse and of adolescents in the current society. In other words, the author has constructed a kind of tour de force in her successful effort to paint the broadest picture of social work with children and adolescents, while at the same time providing essential knowledge about their life situations.

It is important to note the style of writing in this book. Addressed to students of social work, it is written as if for colleagues, with respect for the reader's intelligence and curiosity. The accompanying reading lists are current and evocative, and there is no attempt anywhere to leave the reader with the impression that the subject is closed, that more research is not needed, that deeper knowledge and greater experience will not make the social worker with children and adolescents more skillful. In other words, this book offers the reader a collegial journey through a complex subject, helping him or her along the way to comprehend the "state of the art."

Carol H. Meyer, DSW
Columbia University

Preface

This book offers a transactional framework that notes the importance of environmental conditions in providing direct and indirect services to children and adolescents. It is imperative that social work practitioners add to their array of frameworks a point of view that places intervention on behalf of children and adolescents, including work with their families, into a larger environmental perspective. Practitioners need to pay more attention to environmental conditions that place children and adolescents at risk of poor functioning. Emotionally sick children are often found in sick environments. This book is not intended to be a child welfare text, and thus it does not cover in any depth topics such as adoption, foster care, or the family preservation movement. These topics are well addressed in other texts. Instead, this book focuses on select target groups of children and adolescents not discussed in most child welfare texts. It can be used as a primary text in child and adolescent courses and as a supplementary text for select child welfare courses that embrace the concepts of environmental pathology, children at risk, and prevention—exceedingly important concepts that we need to think about and act upon as practitioners.

The book incorporates research, theoretical concepts, case illustrations, and practice directions in simple language. It is designed for advanced undergraduate students interested in a more complete view of practice with this group. Graduate students who have not been exposed to this content would benefit from this book as well.

I wish to acknowledge the contributions of Professors Elizabeth Segal, Nora Gustavsson, Venessa Hodges, and Betty Blythe, who wrote some of the chapters, and Kathleen Moroz and Gail Folaron who provided helpful suggestions and advice. Much appreciation is extended to Professors Stephen Schinke and

Constance Shapiro, for their review of the book, and Emeritus Professor Lela B. Costin, who read the initial prospectus of the book and encouraged its development; to the University of Illinois at Urbana-Champaign for a research grant and support; and to Jeannette Ingram, Liz Hoisington, and Barbara Cressman for typing the various drafts. I am also grateful to the following reviewers who read the manuscript and provided helpful suggestions:

Rosalie Anderson Ambrosino, University of Texas—Austin

Richard Barth, Univesity of California—Berkeley

Carol Bennett, University of South Florida

Jerry Brandell, New Mexico State University

Monit Cheung, University of Houston

Richard Dangle, University of Texas—Arlington

Kay Hoffman, New Mexico State University

John F. Longres, University of Wisconsin—Madison

Eldon Marshall, Indiana University

Christopher Peters, University of Kansas

Rhonda Reagh, Wright State University

Joan Robertson, University of Wisconsin—Madson

Alvin Sallee, New Mexico State University

Cheryl Springer, New York University

Arlene Rubin Stiffman, Washington University

I especially wish to thank my family for their patience and support. It is because of them that this book is finally a reality.

Introduction

S*ocial Work with Children and Adolescents* is divided into four parts. The first explains a transactional perspective for assessing and interviewing children and adolescents so as to target both the individual and the environments in which he or she functions. Too often in practice we forget that children and youths are largely defined by their environments. This framework is also useful for determining whether the desired outcome or target of change is the child or adolescent, the environment, or both. Further concepts from the ecological perspective and systems concepts undergird it. Included are some of the fundamental developmental considerations to be observed when assessing and interviewing.

The second part introduces the reader to federal programs and policies and to those family and cultural variables that directly affect children and adolescents and their families as well as the practice of social work. It also provides a brief summary of developmental theories.

The third part describes the current status and characteristics of select at-risk groups of pupils and discusses appropriate interventions. Though many groups of children are at risk and deserve our attention and concern, the authors selected those that appear to be the most widely discussed.

Some may question why we have included chapters on case management and the evaluation of practice in the fourth part. Case management, coordination of services, and the evaluation of practice are, in our opinion, required knowledge areas. Practitioners must know and understand the fundamental aspects of managing and coordinating limited resources, and they must demonstrate to funders that social work intervention produces beneficial results. Today's funders are interested in hard data.

Throughout the book case material is integrated to accentuate the complicated situations that involve children and adolescents, as well as to demonstrate the application of key concepts.

part I

A Conceptual Framework for Social Work Practice with Children and Adolescents

Before the practitioner can intervene to assist children and adolescents, their situations must be comprehensively assessed. The most informative approach is to conduct a comprehensive analysis of the context in which the child lives—family, community, school—and his or her degree of social, cognitive, emotional, and physical functioning and readiness. Unfortunately, practitioners too often draw upon a disease or medical model and thus localize the problem within the child or adolescent. This model has dominated social work practice for far too long. It ignores contributors to the problem that are essentially located in the transactions and interactions of the child, family, and environmental circumstances. The medical model directs attention to the child and often the family but ignores the other systems that could be at fault and thus need to be assessed. Further, this model leads to a piecemeal, narrow assessment process. Practitioners need a comprehensive framework for assessment that takes into account the complexities of environments (family, school, community, racial and ethnic group) in which the child exists and the child's developmental readiness. Such a framework must also include knowledge of child and adolescent development. In other words, not only concern for age-appropriate behaviors but also a transactional perspective that draws other environments or aspects of the child's microcosm into the assessment (family, peer group, school, community, racial or ethnic group) is required. Once a particular system is identified that appears to contribute to the client's poor functioning, the practitioner must determine the appropriate assessment procedures. For example, the practitioner may want to assess family functioning along the following dimensions: family composition, history, how the family responds to crisis, its structure, atmosphere, problem-solving skills, strengths, and communication patterns, and the like. During this process, it is important to keep in mind that the outside world affects family functioning (e.g., employment opportunities, racism, and sexism). The practitioner may want to observe the interactions of a child with peer groups in his or her community, visit the child's classroom, and interview significant others who comprise various settings in which the child functions.

Generic and cross-cutting skills that the practitioner brings to the assessment process include interviewing, collecting data, communicating, integrating information, taking the appropriate professional action, and evaluating outcome.

This section provides a transactional framework for conducting assessment that draws upon ecological and systems concepts, as well as an overview of child and adolescent development.

chapter 1

A Transactional Framework: Assessment and Intervention

A transactional view of infants, children, and adolescents leads the practitioner away from blaming and away from treating either the individual or the environment, or both. Because economic, family, cultural, and political factors influence the lives of our children, we must assess our clients more broadly and thus enlarge our view of potential targets of intervention. It is therefore fitting that the individual and his or her transactions with key environments is the primary domain of social work. The environment plays a critical role in development. For example, Gaussen and Stratton (1985) argue that an infant's competence is not only a biologically inherent quality, but also a function of the infant in a particular environment. They suggest that to assess the complex relationship between infants and their environments, a systems perspective must be included.

Honig (1986) offers an illustration of the importance of the environment by showing how the characteristics of a child and family reflect stressors, such as a death in the family, the birth of a sibling, or a divorce. She found that when mothers were instructed to act depressed and look solemn, babies showed disorganization and distressed behavior. Infants of nondepressed mothers showed more frequent positive facial expressions and vocalization. These data suggest that the stress of maternal personality disorders may be communicated to the infant. Environments full of positive feedback and containing loving responding adults appear to be urgent needs for infants.

Other environmental family characteristics associated with children's psychiatric disorders include severe marital discord, low social status, overcrowding or large family size, psychiatric disorder of a parent, and care through a local authority such as foster care (Rutter, 1979). In one study the presence of one of these characteristics did not increase children's chances for psychiatric disorder, but when two or more were present, problems doubled. When four or more of the risk factors occurred together, children's psychiatric problems were ten times as likely to occur (Rutter, 1979). In another study, children of low socioeconomic status showed such symptoms as fearfulness, less cooperation, greater timidity, and more depression than their counterparts (Sameroff & Seifer, 1983). Violence within the community and the larger society causes considerable acting out among our youth. Inappropriate parenting and poor parenting skills increase the chances of malperformance and other problems in infancy, childhood, and adolescence. For example, a parent who handcuffs a five-year-old child to a bed to solve behavior problems can cause further behavioral problems.

This chapter develops the ecological perspective and systems concepts, which together form a useful conceptualization of social work's central domain. More important, they provide a comprehensive approach for assessment and intervention. Combining systems concepts with the ecological perspective is consistent with contemporary thinking in that it acknowledges that characteristics of children and adolescents interact with various aspects of their immediate environments in either a dysfunctional or a functional manner.

THE ECOLOGICAL PERSPECTIVE AND SYSTEMS CONCEPTS

From the beginning of the profession, the mission of social work has been to improve the transactions and interactions between persons and their natural environment (Allen-Meares & Lane, 1987). The combined ecological perspective and systems concepts thus offer the profession a unified perspective for practice that takes note of its integrative tendency, the tendency to perceive the parts of the person in a situation as a whole.

According to Rappaport,

> The ecological viewpoint should be regarded as an orientation emphasizing relationships among persons and their social and physical environment. Conceptually the term implies that there are neither inadequate persons, nor inadequate environments, but rather the fit between persons and environments may be in relative accord or discord. (1977, p. 2)

A value of the ecological perspective is that it provides a comprehensive view of the person in an environment or situation; thus it can encompass a variety of intervention models and approaches. It enables the practitioner to assess consistencies, strengths, and conflicts or tensions. When combined with systems concepts, it becomes a metatheory.

According to Max Siporin,

> Ecological systems theory is such a general metatheory, one that provides for the many, and at times contradictory, purposes and activities of social workers. It constitutes an essential element of the generic core of social work knowledge, of its common person-in-situation and dialectical perspective, and of its basic helping approach. It supports the social work assessment and interventive focus. (1980, p. 4)

It is recognized that the environment imposes major constraining, deterministic influences on individual behavior, produces generalized effects on broader systems of responses in the individual, and instigates behavior directly. According to Lewin (1936), behavior is a function of both the person and the environment. Barker (1968) and associates expanded the concept of environment to include the psychological environment (the world as a particular person perceives it and is otherwise affected by it) and the ecological environment (the objective, preperceptual context of behavior or the real-life settings within which people behave). According to B. F. Skinner (1974) it is important to recognize the social environment and its special features, observable stimuli that act as determinants of behavior in social episodes. The environment is thus a complex set of discriminable stimuli. It is real, it can be measured, it exists in its own right, and it signals the reinforcement possibilities that influence behavior (Wicker, 1974).

The ecological perspective offers the following advantages:

1. Helps the practitioner gain a larger, more unitary and comprehensive unit of attention, a holistic and dynamic understanding of people and the sociocultural physical milieu.
2. Permits multiple perspectives, ways of thinking about parts and wholes.
3. Encourages a theoretically and technically eclectic approach.
4. Helps the practitioner identify which actions to take in order to alter intersystemic relationships and thereby optimize its goodness.
5. Encourages a multifactoral approach and stimulates the use of varied repertoire of assessment instruments and helping interventions.

Systems theory represents a general conceptual approach to human interaction and grouping. Social systems consist of persons or groups of persons who interact and influence one another's behaviors. Systems theory accordingly stresses the need to view the immediate system as an environment or social situation within which a person must operate. It provides the practitioner with some key concepts useful for assessing that environment or situation.

Siporin (1980) suggests that systems theory refers to a cognitive construction of reality necessary for the understanding of and operation within the intervention situation. Buckley defines a system as "complexes of elements or components directly or indirectly related in a causal network, such that each component is related to at least some others in a more or less stable way within a particular period" (1967, p. 41).

Key Ecosystems Concepts

Concepts derived from the ideas discussed here include the following:

1. The environment is a complex environment-behavior-person whole, consisting of a continuous, interlocking process of relationships.
2. There is mutual interdependence among person, behavior, and environment.
3. Systems concepts can be used to analyze the complex interrelationships within the ecological whole.
4. Behavior is recognized to be site specific.
5. Assessment and evaluation should be made through direct observation of the undisturbed natural organism–environment system.
6. The relationship of the parts within the ecosystem is orderly, structured, lawful, and deterministic.

Other important concepts related to the ecological perspective include the following:

1. *Natural Habitat.* The place where the organism (person) lives or the place where one would find it (See Balgopal & Vassil, 1983, p. 25 for a discussion of concepts).
2. *Ecological niche.* The position or status of an organism within its community.
3. *Ecosystem.* The basic functional unit of ecology, including both organisms and environment.
4. *Transactions.* Negotiations with a variety of systems with which the person has been or may be engaged. Refers to the interdependent and resonating aspects of parts in a system (Balgopal & Vassil, 1983, pp. 30–34).
5. *Interaction.* The process whereby an entity connected with other entities in a sequence of action and reaction.
6. *Holism.* The person-environment configuration. Includes the totality of the situation.
7. *Adaptation.* The accommodations and compromises of the organism (person) over time.
8. *Competence.* The repertoire of skill abilities a person is able to use. Skills change and grow as the person acquires new information and encounters new experiences.

There is much to be learned about the transactions between people and environments. Applied behavior-analysis research has helped focus attention on environmental events as determinants of behavior (Ballard, 1986). Finc (1985) contends that the systems–ecological perspective can be used to underscore the nature of a disruptive child's relationship within and across settings.

For example, the adolescent is a member of a system (family) that exists within a larger context—community and society (Patterson & McCubbin, 1967). Each of these systems (family, community) is characterized by demands (stressors and strains) and capacities (resources, coping behaviors). Each strives to achieve adaptation through reciprocal relationships where the demands of one unit are met by the capabilities of another to bring about a "balance" in functioning, which is achieved when there is a minimal discrepancy between demands and capabilities to meet those demands. "Adaptation calls for 'fit' at each systemic interface individual-to-family, family-to-community" (Patterson & McCubbin, 1967, pp. 166–167). For example, applying these concepts to adolescents struggling to establish identity implies that they must simultaneously fit within the family and within the community (peers and schools). Stress or distress can result when the adolescent's needs differ from or exceed the family's capabilities to meet them. This situation is frequently called "misfit," "poor fit," or imbalance.

In a study of 74 low socioeconomic families, both abusive and nonabusive, Conger, McCarthy, Yang, Lahey, & Kropp (1984) examined intersecting sets of ecological and personal variables that were believed to predict child abuse. When a mother's values were found to be authoritarian and she had a negative perception of her child, demographic factors associated with maternal abuse were the child being the firstborn, economic distress, more than one child, less education, and lower occupational status.

THE TRANSACTION BETWEEN INDIVIDUALS AND ENVIRONMENTS FRAMEWORK (TIE)

Drawing upon the ecological perspective and systems concepts, in conjunction with the TIE framework, permits the inclusion of specific areas of the person and environment in the assessment process, a process that also directs intervention (Monkman & Allen-Meares, 1985). A fundamental aspect of social work is the assessment of the person in environment. In 1917 Mary Richmond wisely stated,

> The four processes which lead to social diagnosis are 1) the first full interview with a client, 2) the early contacts with his immediate family, 3) the search for further insight and for sources of needed cooperation outside the family unit, 4) the careful weighing in their relation to one another of the separate items of evidence thus gathered and their interpretation. By interpretation is meant the attempt to derive from all of the evidence as exact a definition as possible of the client's social difficulties—the act of interpretation is the act of diagnosis. (p. 17)

Assessment is the bridge between what is happening in a practice situation and the intervention needed to change it. For example, when a child becomes a social worker's client, it is necessary to collect information about the child's situation from key persons—parents or guardians, teacher, relatives—in the child's environments. The worker may also collect data by observing the child in key situations and environments. This effort could be either highly structured or random. Furthermore, the worker may review existing records (e.g., psychological reports, medical records, family assessment data, and the like). Of course, it is important for the worker to place existing records in perspective and to avoid accepting such information at face value.

After these data are collected, the worker begins the integration and interpretation. From this process emerges an intervention plan or strategy to help the child or adolescent either achieve healthy social functioning or change some aspect of his or her environments.

Monkman and Allen-Meares (1985) offered the Transaction between Individual and Environments as a framework for looking at the child or adolescent and his or her situation. The framework takes into consideration the dual focus of social work person in environment. It moves social work practice beyond the primary objective of targeting the person to look at the various aspects of the environment.

TIE Concepts

The TIE Framework, which uses an ecological perspective and systems concepts, is applicable to a variety of client populations. A discussion of components comprising the framework follows (see Figure 1.1).

Coping Behavior.   Coping behaviors are directed toward the environment, purposeful efforts of the individual to exert some control over his or her own behavior. In practice, according to this framework, social workers deal essentially with three categories of coping behaviors: (1) surviving, (2) affiliating, and (3) growing and achieving. These categories set priorities for social work practice. For example, it is virtually impossible for a practitioner to help a child develop social skills when his or her survival needs (food, clothing, medical care) are not being met.

Thus coping behaviors for surviving enable a person to obtain and use resources and enable him or her to continue life or activity. Subcategories of surviving behaviors are capacities to obtain food, shelter, clothing, medical treatment, and transportation. Coping behaviors for affiliating enable persons to unite in close connection to others in their environments. Subcategories include the capacity to develop and maintain intimate personal relationships and the ability to use organizations and their structures (e.g., clubs, family, school). Coping behaviors for growing and achieving enable persons to pursue intellectual and social activities useful to themselves and others. Subcategories of coping behaviors for growing and developing include cognitive, physical, economic, and

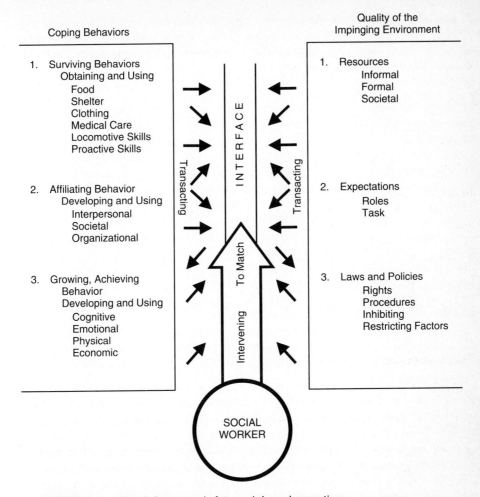

FIGURE 1.1   TIE: A framework for social work practice

From "The Specialization of School Social Work and a Model for Differential Levels of Practice," by Marjorie M. Monkman in *Differential Levels of Student Support Services and Programs: Crisis, Remedial and Developmental Approaches.* C. Dean Miller (Ed.). Copyright © 1982. Minnesota Department of Education. Reprinted with permission.

emotional functioning. This is particularly relevant to the focus of this book. Developmental theories unique to children and adolescents are discussed in Chapter 3.

Children and adolescents cope just like adults, though their styles and skills may not be as well developed. For example, there are basic ways to conceptualize coping functions: (1) coping may involve direct action to eliminate or reduce demands or to increase resources for managing demands; (2) coping may be used to redefine demands so as to make tasks more manageable; and (3) coping may be used to manage the tension felt as a result of demands. For children and adolescents, coping skills develop through personal experiences, vicarious experiences (e.g., as a result of observing family, peers, and others), perceptions regarding their own vulnerability, and social persuasion from peers, family, and others (Werner & Smith, 1982).

Information and Coping Patterns.   Information for coping includes knowledge of specific events, resources, or situations. It may also include information about self. Coping patterns are the cognitive, behavioral, and affective capacities of the individual. These capacities interact to form patterns and become a part of the individual's history. For example, a child is a product of his or her environment, genetics, and family circumstances. Coping patterns are not static; they can change over time. However, it is essential to acknowledge that coping patterns can be constructive or destructive as a child or adolescent attempts to exert control over his or her environments. For example, to control an abusive parent (a parent who uses extreme physical force), a child may lie or blame others. This behavior can become generalized to other situations when the child fears punishment, even though the punishment is appropriate. Specifically, the child may lie to his or her teachers and to others to avoid the consequences of inappropriate behaviors. Although such coping patterns are destructive, the child may use them to avoid brutal beatings from parents. Thus coping patterns may be a response to the present environmental situation or they may be patterns of behavior developed in response to expectations and feedback from a past or present environment.

Quality of Environments.   According to the TIE Framework, the environment consists of those qualities and characteristics of the situation with which the client is in direct contact or transaction. The environment may be flexible, stressful, restrictive, resourceful, supportive, deprived, inflexible, emotionally empty, or dysfunctional. Physically, the environment could be dirty, dense (e.g., crowded or heavily populated, lacking privacy), spacious, or clean. In some instances, these environmental characteristics can operate to undermine functioning. In social work practice with children and adolescents, practitioners inspect not only the clients' capacities to obtain what they need from the environment for surviving, affiliating, and growing or achieving but also the environment's degree of responsiveness. If the sanitary conditions of the home are substandard, an infant can encounter digestive problems or repeated illness. If the environment is stressful and too many expectations are imposed, a child can develop tics.

Each client must be viewed as an individual. Though practitioners can draw generalizations from what they read about various client situations and environments, they must not lump cases into a grouping and thus ignore the client's unique circumstances and characteristics.

Important dimensions of environment include resources, institutions, expectations, and laws and policies. Unlike the categories of coping behaviors, the categories of environments do not have priorities of their own. It is clear that the major value is the person—in this case the infant, child, or adolescent. Resources are people (e.g., family, peer group), organizations (e.g., social services), or institutions (e.g., church) that can be drawn upon to support or help as needed. *Informal resources* are support, advice, and concrete services. In one study it is reported that bereaved adolescents (14 to 19 years old) whose siblings had died suffered enduring grief reactions, but with time the suffering decreased (Balk, 1983). A strong factor in the resolution of bereavement for this group was the quality of parent–child relationships after the death. With appropriate environmental support and response, bereavement can be overcome with time, and psychopathology can be minimized. *Formal resources* are organizations or formal associations that promote a particular interest on the part of their members. *Societal resources* (e.g., schools, hospitals, social service programs, courts, or police departments) are structured service institutions. In social work practice, the resources needed to help a child either do not exist or are unavailable at a specific time (e.g., some agencies have waiting lists). Thus, the worker is often left to pursue other options.

For example, a social worker may have to change the expectations of those significant others who comprise the child or adolescent's environment. The worker may not be able to locate an alternative educational program for a child with a learning disability, but instead may be forced to work with the existing educational staff to change their expectations of the child and to supplement instruction with new learning materials. Expectations are patterned performances and normative obligations grounded in established societal structures. Expectations can involve roles and tasks, and they may be resource specific.

Laws and policies are binding customs or rules of conduct. For example, child abuse must be reported to an appropriate authority. This law protects the child and simultaneously determines the social worker's responsibilities and tasks. As discussed in Chapter 4, laws and policies govern individual behaviors and dictate institutional policies, practices, and programs.

Thus, the TIE Framework forces practitioners to view the child or adolescent's coping behavior with environmental characteristics as a fundamental aspect of the principle of ecological change.

Another contribution of this multifaceted framework is the assumption that a complete diagnostic view must involve description of the child or adolescent's symptoms in the context of overall developmental level. In turn, this is viewed in the context of caregiver or environmental characteristics (e.g., functioning, nurturing, deprivation), as is evident from the earlier discussion of the TIE Framework and systems and ecological concepts.

The framework requires a parallel analysis of the child or adolescent's specific characteristics and the caregiving environments. Such an analysis forces the practitioner to assess the level of functioning of the primary caregiver as a key figure in the immediate environment. Greenspan, Nover, and Scheuer (1984) offer a scale that quantitatively rates the functioning of the primary caretaker from one to ten in terms of degree of impairment. A rating of ten indicates severe psychopathology within the caregiver system. Specifically, ten indicates such characteristics as ego deficits or problems in reality testing and organization of perception and thought.

The previous discussion of level of functioning of the primary caretaker accentuates the need on the part of practitioners to use some planful approach to assess various environments and persons with whom the child interacts. The following case illustration accentuates the important role of the primary caretaker.

CASE ILLUSTRATION: DONNA—12 MONTHS OLD

Donna, a white, 12-month-old girl, receives monthly early intervention sessions to monitor her development in all areas. She lives with her mother, father, and five-year-old brother, Travis. Services were initiated after the death of her 3-year-old sister, Sally, in a home accident. As a result of the accident, Travis suffered severe burns to his legs, hands, and face. Sally was involved in a preschool special education program before her death. Before sustaining his injuries, Travis had been scheduled for screening by the school district to determine if he had special education needs.

Donna's mother, Marlene, is 21 years old. She received special education services for the severely language and learning disabled from elementary school through high school. She quit high school in her third year because of an unplanned pregnancy. *Marlene is quiet, often looks depressed, and holds her head down when spoken to.* She rarely makes eye contact. She says that Donna is smarter than Sally was, and she is not sure why Donna needs this program, yet she comes each month and calls if she is going to miss it. She loves her children. She provides them with food and clothing, but she does not talk to them very much.

Donna's father Tom, age 28, has a high school degree and works seasonal jobs. Donna's parents do not think she has any special needs. Child assessment revealed that Donna is approximately 6 months delayed in personal, social, and communication development. Qualitative concerns exist about fine and gross motor development.

Donna receives health care through the Department of Public Health. Extended family members assist with financial needs. Travis receives treatments for his burns in a large Chicago hospital 35 miles from home. Before Sally's death, Marlene received birth control services and counseling from a "Parents Too Soon" program; but these services were discontinued because of her age. Marlene pursued her GED but gave up because of learning difficulties. Homemaker services were also being investigated, but efforts to do so were discontinued at the parent's request. Donna's mother has expressed an interest in obtaining a job.

SOURCE: Prepared by Kathy Moroz, Assistant Professor, University of Vermont, Burlington.

Because Donna's primary caretaker appears to be depressed and has language and learning disabilities, Donna's development is being retarded. When she is placed in a stimulating environment (for example, with her babysitter who has two young children), she tends to react more actively, smile more frequently, and respond more quickly to conversations.

Eco-Map. The eco-map is a tool for visually depicting the transactions between a client and key environments. It is derived also from ecosystems concepts, and much has been written about its value and purposes. Much of this discussion is credited to the thinking of Ann Hartman (1978). By employing an eco-map, the practitioner can locate dysfunctional and functional exchanges (transactions) between the infant, child, or adolescent and his or her environments. For example, an eco-map pictures the child or adolescent and his or her family in life space. It is a simple paper-and-pencil simulation tool that helps with assessment, planning, and intervention. According to Hartman, it "maps in a dynamic way the ecological system, the boundaries of which encompass the person or family in life space" (p. 467). It is a picture of the important nurturant or conflict-laden connections between family or person and other systems (e.g., school, hospital, church, social services).

Instructions for drawing an eco-map are as follows:

1. The family system, household, or client is drawn in a large circle in the center of the map. Males and females comprising the family are identified by geometric shapes, such as a square to depict a male and a circle to depict a female. Each person's age is entered into the geometric figure, and the offspring are identified in essentially the same way.
2. Circles are made to represent other systems or institutions with which the family has exchanges (schools, extended families, hospitals, churches, and the like).
3. Both the connections and the quality of the relationships between the family or client and these other systems are illustrated by lines and arrows. A straight line with arrows reflecting reciprocal exchanges means that the transactions between the family and a system are positive (or healthy). A dotted line could imply a tenuous connection, and a jagged line could represent conflict or stress. The flow of energy is represented by drawing arrows (e.g., —>, <—>, <—).
4. In developing the eco-map, the practitioner relies on the clients' reports and perspectives about what is going on in his or her life space. The worker shares the map with the client to make him or her an active participant in the process.

Figure 1.2 is an eco-map depicting the quality of relationships and transactions of a family. This drawing represents a family receiving resources and support from social welfare. Though the father is employed, there are tenuous ties between him and his work. There are stressful ties between the mother and the extended family. Sue, age five, and Jill, age seven, are both experiencing difficulty in school. Though the arrows indicate that the school is directing

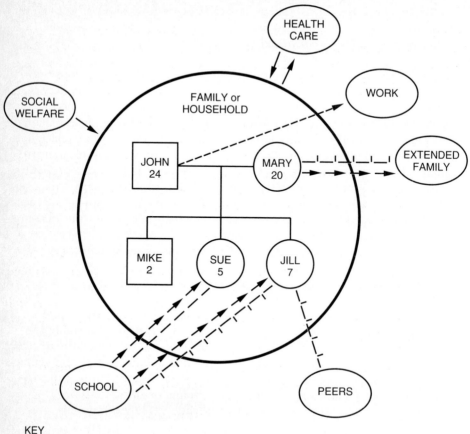

KEY

The ➤ shows the direction and flow of energy
The — — means a strong positive exchange
The --- means a tenuous relationship
The —I—I means no relationship

FIGURE 1.2 Eco-map

considerable energy toward both children, the quality of the relationship could be characterized as stressful. Also, Jill is not developing friendship patterns, a behavior atypical of her stage of development.

The eco-map can also be used to assess changes in clients' life spaces. By asking clients to recall perceptions of past relationships between them and various systems, as well as the current situation, changes can be identified. The eco-map can also be used as a recording tool.

Genogram.   The genogram (Hartman, 1978) is also a pencil-and-paper simulation of a family. It focuses on the family tree and includes more social data. It depicts as many as three or four generations and records major generational stresses, genealogical relationships, family events, losses, migrations and dispersals, alignments, and communication patterns. Geometric symbols similar to those used on an eco-map are used to depict males and females. Ages and dates of marriages and deaths are important in the construction of the genogram. Deceased family members are represented by X's. Dotted lines identify households. Sometimes the occupations of family members, current place of residence, and facts about the health and psychological history are included. The demographic data help the practitioner to understand the development of the family over time. They can give the worker insight into the crises and stresses the family has coped with and the ways it has adapted.

Assessment of Stress.   An important aspect of the practitioner's work with children and adolescents is the assessment of stresses that have occurred within a family (here broadly defined to encompass a variety of structures).

Figure 1.3 is a list of indicators that could either result from stress or contribute to stress for most households and hold some negative consequences for children and adolescents in particular.

Other Tools.   Other useful tools consistent with the TIE Framework are included here. The Child Home Behavior Checklist (Wahler & Cormier, 1970) includes a set of behaviors performed daily by most children and the ways the children react to them. For example, doing chores is one behavior, and a child's response to this task can range from "always has to be told" to "has to keep things in order." The Child–Community Behavior Checklist (Whaler & Cormier, 1970) is similar to the Child Home Behavior Checklist, but it focuses on behaviors that a child or youth would exhibit in the community environment and the ways he or she responds.

Geographic Maps (Munger, 1991) are useful in gathering information about how a child or youth functions within a specific group (for example, how he or she might function on the school playground with peers).

The Community-Interaction Checklist (Munger, 1991) provides information about persons with whom the family interacts and notes the degree of friendliness.

To discover whether or not those individuals with whom a child's family interacts are potential resources for the family when it experiences difficulty, the Network Orientation Scale (Tolsdorf, 1976) is very helpful. The identification of environmental resources that can be included in the service plan is one form of intervention. The Personal Network Map (Tolsdorf, 1976) is closely related to the Network Orientation Scale, but it includes both intimate and nonintimate social contacts, and focuses on the strengths and weaknesses of such contacts or relationships.

Life Event (occurred within last 12 months)	Mean Value	Your Score
1. Death of spouse	100	_____
2. Divorce	73	_____
3. Marital separation	65	_____
4. Jail term	63	_____
5. Death of close family member	63	_____
6. Personal injury or illness	53	_____
7. Marriage	50	_____
8. Fired at work	47	_____
9. Marital reconciliation	45	_____
10. Retirement	45	_____
11. Change in health of family member	44	_____
12. Pregnancy	40	_____
13. Sex difficulties	39	_____
14. Gain of new family member	39	_____
15. Business readjustment	39	_____
16. Change in financial state	38	_____
17. Death of close friend	37	_____
18. Change to different line of work	36	_____
19. Change in number of arguments with spouse	35	_____
20. Mortgage over $10,000	31	_____
21. Foreclosure of mortgage or loan	30	_____
22. Change in responsibilities at work	29	_____
23. Son or daughter leaving home	29	_____
24. Trouble with in-laws	29	_____
25. Outstanding personal achievement	28	_____
26. Secondary wage earner begins or stops work	26	_____
27. Begin or end school	26	_____
28. Change in living conditions	25	_____
29. Revision of personal habits	24	_____
30. Trouble with boss	23	_____
31. Change in work hours or conditions	21	_____
32. Change in residence	20	_____
33. Change in schools	20	_____
34. Change in recreation	19	_____
35. Change in church activities	19	_____
36. Change in social activities	18	_____
37. Mortgage or loan less than $10,000	17	_____
38. Change in sleeping habits	16	_____
39. Change in number of family get-togethers	15	_____
40. Change in eating habits	15	_____
41. Vacation	13	_____
42. Christmas	12	_____
43. Minor violation of the law	11	_____
TOTAL		_____

Score of 300 or more indicates an extreme amount of energy is being used for social readjustment behavior; score of 299–150 indicates an excessive amount of energy is being used for social readjustment behaviors; score of 149–11 indicates a moderate amount of energy is being used for social readjustment behaviors.

FIGURE 1.3 The social readjustment rating scale

From "The Social Readjustment Rating Scale" by T. Holmes and K. Rohe in *Journal of Psychosomatic Research, 11.* 1967, pp. 213–218. Copyright © 1967. Reprinted by permission of Pergamon Press.

Other environmental assessment measures include the Youth Support Inventory (Barth, 1983) and the Community Support Systems Assessment (Garrison & Podell, 1981), to name a few.

SUMMARY

The transactional framework and concepts derived from systems and the ecological perspective focus attention on assessment, as well as targets of intervention. In practice, efforts are often directed at the child or adolescent rather than the environment. Of course, making certain that the child or adolescent is safe and free from harm and receives basic life needs (food, shelter, medical care, etc.) should have the highest priority. Moreover, in setting priorities, short-term and long-term goals and objectives; barriers that stand in the way of goal attainment; the roles of facilitators, supporters, and resources; and ways to document the impact of intervention are all important. Chapter 12 contains a discussion of different practice evaluation approaches helpful in ascertaining whether intervention is making a difference.

QUESTIONS FOR DISCUSSION

1. In the case of Donna describe and discuss the interactions and transactions between the baby and the family environment. What resources should be added to the family environment to enhance the functioning of the baby? Apply ecological and systems concepts as you think about and discuss the case.
2. Why are the ecological perspective and systems concepts useful and complementary to social work?
3. Give examples of infant, child, or adolescent cases that illustrate dysfunctional transactions or interactions between the children and the environment.
4. Is the perspective advocated in this chapter useful for developing preventive strategies? If so, explain why and give examples.
5. Review the TIE Framework, and discuss additional implications for assessment and outcome.

ADDITIONAL READINGS

Field, T., Philip, M. & Schneidermon, W. (1992). *Stress and coping in infancy and childhood.* HIllside, N.J.: Erlbaum Associates.

Lee, E. (1983). A social systems approach to assessment and treatment for Chinese-American families. In M. McGoldrick, J. Pearce, & J. Giordana, eds., *Ethnicity and family therapy.* New York: Guilford Press.

Konopka, G. (1980). Coping with the stresses and strains of adolescence. *Social Development* 4: 1–17.

Moos, R. H., & Billings, A. C. (1982). Conceptualizing and measuring coping resources and processes. In L. Goldberger & S. Brezritz, Eds., *Handbook of stress*. New York: Free Press.

McCubbin, H., Needle, R., & Wilson, M. (1985). Adolescent health risk behaviors: Family stress and adolescent coping as critical factors. *Family Relations* 34: 51-62.

Zeanah, C. (1993). *Handbook of infant mental health*. New York: Guilford Press.

REFERENCES

Allen-Meares, P., & Lane, B. (1987). Grounding social work practice in theory: Ecosystems, *Social Casework* 68: 515-521.

Anderson, R., & Carter, I. (1978). *Human behavior in the social environment: A social system approach*. Chicago: Aldine.

Balgopal, P., & Vassil, T. (1983). *Groups in social work: An ecological perspective*. New York: Macmillan.

Balk, D. (1983). How teenagers cope with sibling death: Some implications for school counselors. *School Counselors* 31: 150-158.

Ballard, K. (1986). Child learning and development in context: Strategies for analyzing behavior–environment interactions and a proposal for research into everyday experiences. *Educational Psychology* 6: 123-137.

Barker, R. (1968). *Ecological psychology: Concepts and methods for studying the environment of human behavior*. Stanford, Calif.: Stanford University Press.

Barth, R. (1983). Social support networks in services for adolescents and their families. In J. Whittaker & J. Gabarino, eds., *Social support networks: Informal helping in the human service*, pp. 299-331. New York: Aldine.

Buckley, W. (1967). *Sociology and modern systems theory in social work*. Englewood Cliffs, N.J.: Prentice Hall.

Conger, R., McCarthy, J., Yang, R., Lahey, B., & Kropp, J. (1984). Perception of child, child rearing values, and emotional distress as mediating links between environmental stressors and observed maternal behavior. *Child Development* 55: 2234-2247.

Finc, M. (1985). Intervention from a systems ecological perspective. *Professional Psychology Research and Practice* 16: 262-270.

Garrison, J., & Podell, J. (1981). Community support systems assessment for use in clinical interviews. *Schizophrenia Bulletin* 7: 101-108.

Gaussen, T., & Stratton, P. (1985). Beyond the milestone model: A systems framework for alternative infant assessment procedures. *Child-Care, Health and Development* 11: 131-150.

Greenspan, S., Nover, R., & Scheuer, A. (1984). A developmental diagnostic approach for infants, young children and their families. *Early Child Development and Care* 16: 85-148.

Hartman, A. (1978). Diagrammatic assessment of family relationships. *Social Casework* 58: 465-476.

Honig, A. (1986). Stress and coping in children, part 2: Interpersonal family relationships. *Young Children* (July): 47-58.

Lewin, K., (1936). *Principles of topological psychology*. New York: McGraw-Hill.

Monkman, M., & Allen-Meares, P. (1985). The TIE Framework: A conceptual map for social work assessment. *Arete* 10: 41-49.

Munger, R. (1991). *Child mental health practice from the ecological perspective.* Lanham, Md.: University Press of America.

Patterson, J., & McCubbin, H. (1987). Adolescent coping style and behaviors: Conceptualization and measurement. *Journal of Adolescence* 10: 163–186.

Rappaport, J. (1977). *Community psychology: Values research and action.* New York: Holt, Rinehart & Winston.

Richmond, M. (1917). *Social diagnosis.* New York: Russell Sage Foundation.

Rutter, M. (1979). Protective factors in children's responses to stress and disadvantage. In M. W. Kent & J. A. Rolf, eds., *Primary prevention of psychopathology* (vol. 3.): *Social competence in children.* Hanover, N.H.: University Press of New England.

Sameroff, A. J., & Seifer, R. (1983). Familial risk and child competence. *Child Development* 54: 1254–1268.

Siporin, M. (1980). Ecological-systems theory in social work. *Journal of Sociology and Social Welfare* 7: 507–532.

Skinner, B. F. (1974). The social environment. In R. Moose & P. Insel, eds., *Issues in social ecology: Human milieus,* pp. 536–566. Palo Alto, Calif.: National Press Books.

Tolsdorf, C. (1976). Social networks, support, and coping: An exploratory study. *Family Press* 15: 407–418.

Wahler, R., & Comier, M. (1970). The ecological interview: A first step in out-patient child behavior therapy. *Journal of Behavior Therapy and Experimental Psychiatry* 1: 279–289.

Werner, E., & Smith, R. (1982). *Vulnerable but invincible: A longitudinal study of resilient children and youth.* New York: McGraw-Hill.

Wicker, A. (1974). Processes which mediate behavior–environment congruence. In R. Moos & P. Insel, eds., *Human milieus,* pp. 601–615. Palo Alto, Calif.: National Press Book.

chapter 2

Growth and Development of Children and Adolescents

The reader might ask why a knowledge of child and adolescent development is required. It's importance can be underscored on several counts: Without adequate knowledge of child and adolescent development, for example, it would be extremely difficult to assess whether age-appropriate behaviors have been attained. The development of such behaviors is intimately tied to the availability of health services, emotional security, quality of nurturing, the availability of basic necessities (e.g., food, shelter, etc.), and the opportunity to experience and explore the environment.*

It is essential to begin with a definition of critical stages of development. The successful completion of one stage is often required for the inception of the next. Each stage includes specific developmental tasks. Their resolution and successful completion depends upon a variety of factors often beyond the child or adolescent's control. Though the focus here is on the child or adolescent, the extremely important role of infancy and early development must be recognized. Understanding the continuum of development is a prerequisite for assessment. Case material highlights this point, as well as others.

Development is determined by a variety of factors—biological or genetic— and a host of environmental conditions. Social workers see the individual not only as a product of maturation and learning but also as part of a social system. Thus there are considerable cultural variations in a child's life experiences, and each child must be viewed within his or her context. The practitioner may expect variance in development among children.

---

* The discussion of development in this chapter is derived from several sources: Mussen, P., Conger, J., & Kagan, J. (1980) *Essentials of child development and personality,* New York: Harper & Row; Specht, R., & Craig, G. (1982) *Human development: A social work perspective,* Englewood Cliffs, N. J.: Prentice-Hall; and Rogers, D. (1981) *Adolescent and youth,* Englewood Cliffs, N.J.: Prentice-Hall.

STAGES OF DEVELOPMENT

The following discussion addresses the stages of development—infancy and the importance of prenatal care, middle childhood, and adolescence (the adolescent period is discussed in terms of early adolescence and late adolescence). Factors and conditions that place children and adolescents at risk are highlighted.

Prenatal

Among many genetically determined disorders leading to mental retardation are phenylketonuria, Down's syndrome, Turner's syndrome, and Klinefelter's syndrome. Prematurity may also affect the physical and psychological development of the child; the more premature the infant, the more likely that developmental delays will occur.

A tragic consequence of drug, alcohol, and tobacco use during prenatal development is their effects on the fetus. For example, fetal alcohol syndrome, a disorder produced by heavy maternal drinking, can result in severe retardation of intrauterine growth, premature birth, heart defects, and a variety of other abnormalities.

Infancy

During the first years of life, an infant grows and develops in a number of different ways. The development of locomotor skills and sensorimotor coordination follows a predetermined course. Infants are attracted to color and movement; and by about eight to ten months of age, they develop a capacity for memory. They can differentiate their caretakers, vocalize, and smile. Attachment relationships are characterized chiefly by two components—the interaction with a significant other that occurs daily and the infant's association of that person with warm and positive feelings stemming from relief of discomfort. By age two, children are fairly well coordinated, and language development and skills steadily increase. These children are still subject to separation anxiety.

Preschool Years

During this period (three to five years) the child's skeletal, muscular, and nervous systems change rapidly. Sentences are longer and more complex. Aggression may be the target of socialization, particularly when the child is frustrated. Conscience development becomes evident as the child moves to internalize certain standards and to model significant adults in the environment. Fears are prevalent (e.g., fear of darkness, sleep, and strangeness). Role models are also viewed as essential in the development of prosocial behaviors (Helms & Turner, 1981).

The following signs or behaviors might signal a problem: has poor muscle control (falls a lot, has trouble controlling arms and legs); drools all the time, shows signs of seizures; refuses to eat; does not point, wave, or imitate others; withdrawn; does not talk; or has trouble following simple directions.

Middle Childhood

This period (6-12 years) is characterized by rapid physical development; and cognitive skills also increase at a rapid rate. The child's competence in memory and conceptual thinking or recognition develops. At this age, children can categorize complicated systems of objects and respond quickly to problems by engaging in a problem-solving process. The emergence of executive functioning—increase in implementation or generality of perceptions, memory, reasoning, reflection, and deduction—also occurs. Parents continue to play a key role in development. A child's overall self-concept is influenced by the family. Relationships with siblings and friends may also have significant effects on the child's personality.

Psychological problems during middle childhood may include phobias, tics, anxiety reactions, obsessions and compulsions, psychosomatic symptoms (stomach aches, headaches, sleeping problems). It is important to explore the quality of the parent–child relationship (both father and mother), the social environment, the expectations placed upon the child, and the health of the child when trying to identify factors contributing to malperformance.

During middle childhood, the child has exposure to a variety of persons who influence development (e.g., peers, teachers, family, classmates). Conformity behavior increases as children strive to be more like their immediate models. Success and failure in the classroom takes on more importance.

Adolescence

Blos (1962) suggests six phases specific to the adolescent (13–18 years): the latency period or introduction, preadolescence, early adolescence, middle adolescence, late adolescence, and postadolescence. Each phase has unique characteristics, and some adolescents may experience these phases more rapidly or differently than others. For example, the developmental task of late adolescence is to consolidate many different skills and abilities developed over time; but some adolescents achieve this milestone earlier and others much later. Adolescence itself is defined in several ways: as a stage in physical development, as an age span, as a specific stage of development, or as a sociocultural phenomenon. It is understood to be a period of transition between childhood and maturity (Rogers, 1981).

During adolescence, the increased activity of the pituitary glands throws the body into rapid change or growth spurt. The onset of adolescence varies from child to child. Along with an increase in height and body weight, marked differences appear at the onset of puberty—appearance of pubic hair, lowering of the voice in males, breast development and menarche in females. Some adolescent girls may have large breasts at 12, while others are only experiencing breast budding at age 15.

The dramatic physical gains of the adolescent are accompanied by cognitive changes as well. Adolescents can think abstractly, engage in complicated problem solving, and project the ramifications of actions and behaviors. They may appear to be more egocentric and self-conscious but also more aware of others. There is a desperate desire to be accepted by peers. The adolescent seeks membership in a select peer group and strives for independence from parents. It is essential to acknowledge that this phenomenon varies from culture to culture. Frequently, parents feel that this newfound independence or the struggles associated with it may result in problems like substance abuse, premature parenthood, or delinquency.

Prone to experimentation and wanting to be independent, adolescents can find themselves engaging in behaviors urged by others. Sometimes there is pressure to conform to peer group expectations (to take drugs, to steal, to engage in sex). Adolescent drug use and pregnancy are alarming social problems in America. With the AIDS epidemic, sexual experimentation without adequate information can be fatal.

Social factors specific to this culture can cause conflict as an adolescent struggles for independence. In the past, sex roles were fairly well defined; today, with the changing roles of women and men, adolescents have many options. For example, androgyny, the combining of traditionally masculine and feminine characteristics, has taken on more importance. The prevalence of unisex clothes, of adolescent males wearing earrings and makeup, and of girls seeking active participation in sports activities historically reserved for adolescent males are all indicators of such options.

Some have noted that the American adolescent has been affected by cultural and societal influences, such as prolonged dependency on parents, protracted educational requirements, the threat of nuclear war, diverse sexual standards, and widespread affluence, to name a few (Allen-Meares & Shapiro, 1989). Middle-class children and youth often have different life experiences that result from the wealth and opportunities afforded them.

By this age, moral development and standards should be fairly well developed. Thus, most adolescents can engage in high-level problem-solving and decision making when presented with a dilemma.

Problems in adjustment, as stated earlier, include alienation, premature pregnancy, school failure, substance abuse, school dropout, suicide, depression, acute anxiety reactions, and eating disorders like anorexia nervosa and bulimia.

CASE ILLUSTRATION: MIKE JACKSON—AGE 11

Mike Jackson lived in several foster homes after the termination of parental rights when reports of repeated abuse were found credible. Mike's infancy was spent in low-stimulating environments with other foster children of various ages. The primary caretakers, who functioned essentially in that capacity, were fearful of forming attachments to the children under their care. In infancy, Mike did not coo, his eyes failed to follow objects, he crawled later than most infants, and he cried excessively.

Now that he is 11, Mike is still living in a foster home; the school reports that he is disruptive in class and has been involved in stealing. His behavior has been deteriorating and becoming strange; he has been placed on probation. In response to this situation, his primary caseworker from the Family Service and Child Welfare Agency requested a complete psychological evaluation.

The psychologist administered a battery of tests, which included Incomplete Sentences, the Bender-Gestalt, and Thematic Apperception Test (TAT), to name a few. Mike was not very cooperative during the testing, but the psychologist persisted. It was clear to the psychologist that Mike sought out fights and blamed others for the consequences. He lacked social skills and had difficulty forming lasting relationships. He had few peers with whom to share his world. He was impulsive and resistant to necessary boundaries imposed upon him by various tasks included in the psychological battery. His drawings were simple, immature, and lacking in effort. In fact, developmentally they were similar to those of a six year old.

The TAT revealed complementary themes. Specifically, Mike wanted someone to help undo all the wrong in his life; he wanted a home, money, and the feeling of being grown-up. On the surface he appeared to be unselfish and sought money to give to others.

He lacked the motivation and cognitive ability to complete a large number of the psychological tests. The diagnostic label assigned was Conduct Disorder, Aggressive Type. From the assessment it was recommended that Mike receive intense counseling in the areas of self-control and self-worth, exposure to appropriate role models, and placement in a specialized and structured foster home.

This case illustrates that the failure to experience closeness with a consistent significant other in the earlier years can have a devastating consequence on later functioning. Mike did not experience closeness in the early years, nor did he have foster parents who desired a close relationship. Of course, it is not too late for Mike, if a relationship develops with a significant person, he can change.

The following list summarizes some of the major developmental characteristics and various *problems* of children at specific years and stages of development. (See the footnote on p. 21.)

Developmental Characteristics and Problems in Development First Years (Newborn to Two Years)

One week to 12 months
Moves head

Will swipe at an object

Develops an attachment relationship

Can sit and hold head erect

Babbles to self and to toys

Sits in high chair

Transfers one object to another hand

Picks up blocks

Crawls and creeps on hands and knees

Stands holding onto furniture

Cooperates when being dressed

Says "baby" and a few other words

Has the capacity for memory

Fails to thrive

One year to two years
Shows fears

Walks alone

Throws a ball

Walks up stairs

Walks down stairs with help

Speaks words "dada, "momma," "ball"

Speaks two-word sentences

Curious about environment

Forms mental images of objects

Imitates the acts of others

Toilet training occurs

May display aggressiveness

Shows separation anxiety

Preschool Years (Three to Five Years)

Three years to five years
Rapid physical growth

Upper part of body becomes more mature

Strength, coordination, and nervous system increase

Psychomotor skills increase

More interest in peers develops

Self-reliance increases

Sentences become more complex (vocabulary increases at a rapid rate)

Capacity for symbolism (the ability to treat objects as symbols) develops

Sex typing (e.g., boys play with footballs; girls with dolls) begins

Observational learning (imitates TV characters—wears a cowboy hat) occurs

Temper tantrums take place

Fear of strange objects or things new in the environment appears

Sleep problems (nightmares) sometimes appear

Middle Childhood (6 to 12 Years)

6 years to 12 years
Rapid physical growth
Increases in physical strength and motor skills
Develops perception and memory (short-term, long-term, and sensory).
Uses strategies to help in remembering
Engages in problem solving (creative solutions)
Becomes reflective
Tells how he or she feels
Understands how to form relationships
Learns that shape does not determine quantity
Learns and understands relative terms (e.g., darker, taller, smaller)
Continues to develop sex typing
May develop phobias
Represses wrongdoing
May experience tics if troubled
May acquire obsessions and compulsive behaviors
Conduct disorder problems may become more apparent
Peers become primary socializers
Learning problems or disabilities may become more pronounced
Uses media in attempts to socialize (imitates dress and behaviors of favorite character)

Adolescence (13 to 18 Years)

13 years
Onset of puberty and sexual maturation (testes and scrotum enlarge, uterus increases in size)
Growth spurts (girls may become taller than boys, but boys later pass girls in height)
Conforms to peer group
Follows complex instructions (though may appear to be forgetful)
Separates reality from possibilities
Predicts ramifications of actions
Engages in more complex and abstract reasoning
Criticizes parents, formulates own opinions and views
Establishes independence from parents
Dresses for peer approval
Seeks sense of identity and self-worth
Fears failure
Develops moral principles

THEORIES OF INDIVIDUAL DEVELOPMENT

In a book like this, it is almost impossible to cover in depth the variety of viewpoints on child and adolescent development theories, including the psychoanalytical, psychosocial, behavioral or learning, cognitive, and moral and humanistic. There is considerable overlap among these theories, and practitioners frequently draw upon several theories simultaneously to understand infant, child, and adolescent development.

Though this book advocates a transactional framework for assessing and intervening on behalf of children and adolescents, a brief summary of different developmental theories traditionally described in the literature is in order. Those most appropriate for grounding the transactional perspective advocated here, however, are the psychosocial, behavioral or learning, and moral and humanistic.

Psychoanalytical Theory

This theory, like learning theory, views human nature as deterministic. It emphasizes innate drives rather than the role of the environment in determining behaviors. Biological drives like sex and aggression are behind most behaviors and are expressed in different ways as the individual personality matures. Freud, the founder of psychoanalysis, was a product of the Victorian era. He probably felt the oppressive sexual attitudes of the time and expressed them in his theory.

Freud's theory of development includes five major stages.

1. The first stage is the *oral*. In infancy and early childhood, the mouth is the major organ of pleasure. For example, infants find pleasure in sucking. If this need is not satisfied, conflict can result; and negative traits such as dependency and depression may occur in adulthood.
2. The *anal* stage, which presents another challenge, is the second layer in this developmental hierarchy. It is similar to the stage called "autonomy versus shame or doubt" in psychosocial theory. During this stage, the anus becomes the target of attention. For example, it is believed that punitive toilet training in early childhood can produce a host of negative outcomes in adulthood (e.g., compulsiveness, overcautiousness, and anxiety). During this stage, which lasts until about age 4, children enjoy controlling the discharge of body wastes.
3. The *phallic* stage is equated with the child's discovery of his or her genitals, or the differentiation of the sexes. Negative manifestations of this stage evidenced in adulthood include possessiveness, exhibitionism, and competitiveness.
4. While in elementary school, children move into the *latency* period, considered one of the less emotional stages of development. This stage is

equivalent to the period of industry of psychosocial theory. Essentially, children learn new skills and develop a greater sense of self-worth.

5. In adolescence, mature genitals are the primary source of pleasure. This is known as the *genital* stage.

In accordance with Freud's view, the child's development may be inhibited as a result of adverse conditions and experiences (those found in the environment—including parents, siblings, and other factors) that block progress toward emotional maturity. In other words the child can become fixated (resist moving into the next stage). The child has received either too much pleasure or too little during a certain stage. For example, if the infant has received insufficient sucking during the oral stage of development, adulthood may be characterized by overeating.

According to Freud's view, the human psyche comprises id, ego, and superego. Babies are born with the id—the drive to satisfy both hunger and sexual needs. The id is the stimulator of drives. The ego, which can discriminate between internal mind and external reality, develops over a period of time. It controls behavior and governs such areas as memory, voluntary movement, and problem solving. The superego, the third component, enables us to discriminate between right and wrong. For example, the id may produce a strong desire to steal, while the superego defines such behavior as immoral. Defense mechanisms are techniques the individual calls upon to lessen tension and cope with negative feelings. These conflict-reducing techniques include denial, repression, regression, rationalization, projection, reaction formation, and displacement.

Psychosocial Theory

Eric Erikson (1968) added psychosocial and crisis concepts to Freud's psychosexual theory of personality and development. He identified eight stages of psychosocial development, each capable of a positive or a negative resolution, known as a crisis. Successful completion of a stage is dependent upon successful completion of the previous stage. The eight stages include the following:

1. Trust versus Mistrust
2. Autonomy versus Shame and Doubt
3. Initiative versus Guilt
4. Industry versus Inferiority
5. Ego Identity versus Role Confusion
6. Intimacy versus Isolation
7. Generativity versus Stagnation
8. Ego Integrity versus Despair

In Erikson's thinking, the child's innate drives are met by parents. He believes an individual has the capacity to influence and control his or her environment. The person is not passive. The environment (parental attitude and social climate) affects the way he or she responds. For example, during infancy (referring to the stage of trust versus mistrust) the child learns to trust the primary caregiver. The infant receives love, warmth, food, and comfort. If these needs are not met, the infant may nevertheless learn to trust; it is not too late for him or her to experience trust during another stage of development. In other words, developmental conflicts or deficiencies of the early stages can be reworked and satisfactorily resolved later in life.

A lack of adjustment at any stage can be altered or reversed later as a child develops. Thus, there is always hope that if needs are not met at one stage but are met later on, the child will continue to grow and no damage will occur.

Another contribution of Erikson (1959) to our knowledge in this area is the notion that "adolescence" is a "normative crisis" involving a number of critical elements that merge to form a consistent ego identity. He sees adolescence as a period of freedom and exploration—an open-ended period in our lives. He also sees two dangers that can occur during this period of development—premature identity formation (the adolescent selects an identity prematurely, without sufficient information and knowledge) and identity confusion (a lack of closure on this stage of development—the adolescent remains unattached and uncommitted).

When discussing adolescent development, it is imperative to acknowledge sexuality. Because patterns of heterosexuality have changed, more teens are experimenting with sex, and many become pregnant each year. An increasing number of adolescents turn from heterosexuality to homosexual relationships or bisexual lifestyles (Mercier & Berger, 1989). A practitioner must be in tune with these different sexual orientations. For some youth, these behaviors reflect the manifestation of deeper problems; for others, such behaviors are manifestations of the youth culture (Mishne, 1986) or forms of self-expression; for many, they are simply normal development.

Behavioral or Learning Theory

Behaviorism emphasizes that learning comes about from the interaction of the person with the environment. Through the interaction with the environment, the child learns various types of behavior. For example, the coping skills of others are emulated by the child, as are ways of making friends and responding to stress. Over years, the child is conditioned to respond to a specific situation; but the response can be appropriate or inappropriate. The child has no way of knowing what is appropriate until he or she has been exposed to other responses, situations, and environments.

Behavioral and learning theories are concerned with the behavioral indicators of growth and development, as well as cognition and personality development. Learning is the process whereby children collect from their environment information that shapes their responses to it. The environment is powerful because it provides models, and it rewards or punishes children for certain behaviors. Over time and through observation, children learn by watching; they are rewarded for behaving in specific ways. Learning begins to occur as soon as a child enters the world. However, the concept of learning also applies to the acquisition of totally new responses and to improvements or changes in the frequency of behavior already learned. Imitation and modeling are a part of the child's behavioral pattern.

Classical conditioning involves the association of an external stimulus with a response. The smell of food and sound of the parent preparing dinner can be stimuli to evoke hunger pains. Operant conditioning involves rewarding appropriate responses whenever certain behaviors occur. The child's behavior brings the reward, and the reward becomes the motivator. Not all learning depends on conditioning; as stated earlier there is observational learning. Often conditioned learning, as previously discussed, and observational learning supplement and complement each other.

Questions the practitioner must ask are these: If a child has maladaptive behaviors, what forces in his or her environment reinforce them? Who are the role models? Do they exhibit these same behaviors? Can I change their behaviors? How can I change the child's behavior without the cooperation of the significant adults who comprise the environment?

Cognitive Theory

Piaget's theoretical framework (1950, 1954) deals primarily with the development of cognition and intelligence. A child goes through a sequence of complex stages. Piaget views the "person," in this case the child, as an active being who attempts to control and learn about his or her immediate environment. Children are not passive recipients; they are continually trying to make sense of their world.

According to Piaget, children experience their environment and then invent ideas and behaviors that address it. Central to his theory is the concept of "operation." Operation is a special kind of mental routine that transforms information for some purpose and is reversible. This process is at the heart of intellectual development. Furthermore, children draw upon assimilation and accommodation to help themselves move on to the next stage of development. Assimilation is the incorporation of new objects or ideas into an existing idea, whereas accommodation is adaptation to a new object, a change in behavior intended to fit new circumstance.

Piaget has divided his theory into four major periods of intellectual development: sensorimotor (birth to two years), preoperational (two to seven years), concrete operation (7 to 11 years), and formal operational (11 years and older). Each stage is the foundation for the next. Every newly learned skill is added to the next stage.

During the sensorimotor stage of development, the infant learns to move arms and hands in a coordinated fashion. Object permanence is also present (in other words, though an object might be out of sight, the child continues to believe that it exists). Temperament also varies from infant to infant as does attention span; these differences may disappear over time.

During the second year of development, according to Piaget, infants become more curious about their environments. By age three to four years, psycho-motor skills increase. Children jump, run, kick, and generally display full vitality. Piaget identifies this period as being egocentric. Children generally want their own ways and often reject the views of others. He draws upon social learning theory to explain language and moral development. Through rewards and modeling children move from being egocentric to behaving in a socially acceptable manner.

According to Piaget, preschool children are in the preoperational stage. Most children at this stage can organize objects, explain rules, and understand how to play games. If spoken to in a manner that does not evoke fear, they can adopt another person's point of view.

From about ages 7 to 12 comes the stage of concrete operations. The child has developed some fairly logical guidelines. During this stage, the child learns that shape does not destroy mass—when a clay ball is transformed into another shape, the mass is the same though the shape is different. This is known as the conservation of mass. A constant question in the practitioner's mind should be, "What terms and words can a child understand, given his or her age and other factors (home, poverty, socioeconomic class) that influence development in general?" Last in terms of this stage and directly related to interviewing, is the fact that the child can recall tasks and information.

The next stage, formal operational thought, involves the ability to examine critically the effects of one variable on another and to think of possible ramifications of actions. The thought processes now include analysis. This stage begins around age 12 and is consolidated during adolescence. During this period, the adolescent's thoughts are flexible, and they can include complex problem solving. Adolescents can also predict and sort out the ramifications of actions given a particular situation or event. Piaget believes that the social environment plays a critical role. Adolescents need opportunities to experiment if they are to move in this direction. They need to test ideas through experimentation and then analyze the results.

In summary, Piaget's theory suggests that at a certain age range or stage of development the child or adolescent is capable of certain forms of thought. Certain things cannot be taught until the child is developmentally ready. Further, the child may not understand certain verbal communications if they are beyond his or her ability to comprehend cognitively. Again, this information is extremely important when interviewing, assessing, and intervening. A child's language and thought patterns are different from those of an adult. Opportunity for experimentation and social interaction are most important in promoting intellectual development (Ginsburg & Opper, 1969). When a practitioner is conducting an assessment, it would seem logical that an analysis of opportunity provided for cognitive development within the environment become a part of the assessment.

Moral Development and Humanistic Psychology

The work of such individuals as Kohlberg (1978) on moral developments and of Maslow (1968) on a humanistic orientation must be acknowledged as fine contributions to our understanding of child and adolescent development. To Kohlberg, there are three levels and types of moral reasoning: (1) the premoral, in which the child is merely obedient but does not fully understand why he or she conforms to wishes of others; (2) morality of conventional rule-conformity, in which the child behaves appropriately because he or she wants to be viewed by others in a certain way (e.g., "good boy")—the desire for approval that occurs around ages five to seven years; and (3) morality of self-accepted moral principles, in which children and adolescents see how morality contributes to a democratically accepted law and is in turn a way of protecting the rights of others (e.g., respect the property of others, return property to the rightful owner). Conscience development requires maturity in terms of cognition; a more sophisticated cognitive process is required. Values and moral beliefs directly influence the child's way of behaving. This becomes extremely important in understanding antisocial behavior. Significant role models in the child's environments (e.g., peers, parents, and relatives) also play a critical role in the development of values and morals.

Humanistic psychologists like Maslow (1968) see the individual as constantly becoming. Maslow's hierarchy of needs includes physiological needs (satisfaction of hunger, thirst), safety (security, order, stability), belongingness and love, esteem (self-respect and feelings of success), and self-actualization. The TIE Framework emphasizes coping to survive and affilitate. These concepts are highly consistent with those advocated by Maslow.

An individual has the opportunity to correct earlier socialization failure in adulthood. The humanistic orientation rejects both the psychoanalytic view that drives determine our behaviors and the environmental view that behavior is solely determined by environment. Instead, the individual is thought to have an innate need for self-actualization. Also, only when lower-level needs are met (e.g., food, shelter, health care) can he or she move to higher levels of potential. Furthermore, a sense of self-esteem and positive feedback from others are required to reach full potential.

RISK FACTORS AND DEVELOPMENT

A discussion of risk factors from a developmental perspective must take into account that the indicators of risk can change with the social context in which children live and must function (Werner, 1986). Risk is defined in epidemiological terms as "the probability of an individual's developing a given disease or experiencing a health status change over a specific period" (Kleinbaum, Kupper, & Morgenstern, 1982, p. 89). Werner offers examples of risk factors classified by major periods of development (1986, p.3). They are as follows:

Prenatal

Genetic:
Chromosomal disorders
Inborn errors of metabolism
Neural tube defects

Environmental:
Harmful drugs
Maternal infections
Metabolic disorders
Nutritional deprivation
Radiation
Toxic chemicals

Delivery:
Congenital malformations
Disorders of labor & delivery
Low birth weight
Preterm birth
Infections
Metabolic disorders

Postnatal

Biological:
Accidents
Chronic disease
Failure to thrive
Infections
Toxic substances

Psychosocial:
Family dysfunction
Illiteracy
Parental psychopathology
Poverty

Individuals who have conducted extensive research and reviews in this area tend to concur that

1. In defining the development at risk associated with any child, the characteristics of the child must be related to the ability of the environment to regulate the development of the child toward social norms (Sameroff & Seifer, 1983, p. 125).
2. The probability of adverse consequences is not fixed or the same across individuals, and tends to vary as a function of interactions between different [risk] factors or different environmental circumstances in which a child is placed (Pollitt, 1984, p. 13.)

It should be mentioned that risk factors change from situation to situation and from country to country. For example, in Third World countries the risk factors might be high illiteracy rates, as well as low birth weights and high mortality rates of infants. As technological and social advances are made to address the various risk factors, these risks decrease.

What emerges from this analysis is an interactional or transitional model of risk associated with development rather than a linear one. This model, though new to some, is rooted in developmental theory, the ecological perspective, and systems concepts. This view forces us to focus on transactions between children and adolescents and the various situations in which they must function (see Table 2.1).

TABLE 2.1   Model of interrelations between risk, stress, source of support, and coping

Chronic proverty
Mother with little education
Moderate-severe perinatal complications
Developmental delays or irregularities
Genetic abnormalities
Parental psychopathology

Major Sources of Stress	**Major Sources of Support**	
In Childhood and Adolescence	*Protective Factors within the Child*	*Caregiving Environment*
Prolonged separation from primary caretaker during first year of life	Birth order (first) CNS integrity	Four or fewer children spaced more than two years apart
Birth of younger sibling within two years after child's birth	High activity level	Much attention paid to infant during first year
Serious or repeated childhood illnesses	Good-natured: affectionate disposition	Positive parent–child relationship in early childhood
Parental illness	Responsive to people	Additional caretakers beside mother
Maternal mental illness	Free of distressing habits	Care by siblings and grandparents
Sibling with handicap or learning or behavior problem	Positive social orientation	Mother has some steady employment outside the household
Chronic family discord	Automony	
Father absent	Advanced self-help skills	Availability of kin and neighbors for emotional support
Loss of job or sporadic employment of parent(s)	Age-appropriate sensorimotor and perceptual skills	Structure and rules in household
Change of residence	Adequate communication skills	Shared values—a sense of coherence
Change of schools	Ability to focus attention and control impulses	Close peer friends
Divorce of parents	Special interests and hobbies	Availability of counsel by teachers or ministers
Remarriage; entry of stepparent into household	Positive self-concept	Access to special services (health, education, social)
Departure or death of older sibling or close friend	Internal locus of control	
Foster home placement (for female, teenage pregnancy)	Desire to improve self	

From "The concept of risk from a developmental perspective" by E. Werner in *Advances in Special Education*, 1986, 5. Reprinted by permission of JAI Press.

Bronfenbrenner's (1979) work has contributed to this thinking. For him, the child is constantly accommodating new situations and environments. For example, as a child moves into middle childhood the need for consistent nurturing that allows self-expression and exploration of the environment takes on more importance. The ways rewards and punishment are rendered can be decisive factors for later functioning. Parents or primary caretakers play a critical role in this very complicated socialization process. Culture and economic opportunity bear on this socialization process.

A multivariate risk model posits that children are likely to develop behavioral problems when they have low coping skills in relation to their net environmental stressors and protectors (Stiffman, Jung, & Feldman, 1985). Logically, children who have high coping skills in relation to environmental expectations and stressors are likely to avoid behavior problems (see Table 2.2). When the net environmental stressors or protectors and child's coping skills are balanced, a

TABLE 2.2 Childhood risk and protective factors identified by research

Risk	Protective Factor
I. Personality Disposition in Infancy and Childhood	
Unresponsive	Responsive, elicits support
Difficult, inflexible	Adaptable, flexible
Aggressive and shy-aggressive (males)	Social competence
Depressed (female)	Sense of humor
Poor health or disabilities	Good health
External locus of control	Self-esteem, self-efficacy autonomy, self-direction
Lack problem-solving, planning, critical-thinking skills	Problem-solving and planning, creative, divergent thinking skills, academic competence
Reading failure	Mastery
Attentional disorder	Ability to concentrate
Sex (male-childhood; female-adolescence)	Sex (female-childhood; male-adolescence)
Intolerant, self-centered	Tolerance, compassion, empathy
Lack of sense of purpose or "compelling future"	Sense of purpose or "compelling future"
II. Family Milieu	
Poverty, low socio-economic status	Higher socio-economic status
Parental alcoholism, criminality, mental illness	Lack of parental alcoholism, criminality, mental illness
Large family size, overcrowded	Children at least two years apart, uncrowded
Mother aloneness (not father absence)	At least one involved caretaker or significant other
Loss of or separation from primary caregiver	At least one involved caretaker, especially during first year

Discord or abuse	Closeness and nurturing warmth; rules and discipline; roles and responsibilities
Mother with serious alcoholism or mental illness	Mother without serious alcoholism or mental illness
Illiteracy	Literate parents value and encourage education
Unemployment	Employment
Maternal abuse	At least one involved caretaker or significant other

III. External Support

Poverty or lack of resources	Access to resources
Lack of perinatal care (pre, neo, post)	Perinatal care
Lack of opportunities or alternatives for meaningful tasks	Scope and range or opportunities for participation and development of responsibilities in meaningful tasks
War	Peace
Ineffective, unnurturing schools	Preschools foster social competence; planning schools foster social academic competence
Lack role models	Role models (teachers, adults, friends)
Lack of social bonds and support (significant others, kinship network)	Existence of social bonds and support
Lack of adequate caregiving environment	Nurturing, caregiving environment

IV. Pattern of Stresses

Greater number (more than 2)	Fewer in number
Greater frequency	Less frequent
Longer duration	Shorter duration
Greater severity	Less severe
Occurs at developmental stage or life transition	Not occurring at critical life transition

From "Bonnie's Research Corner" by Bonnie Bernard in *Protective Factor Research: What We Can Learn from Resilient Children,* Vol. 7, Issue 3, March 1987. Illinois Preventive Forum.

slight change in either one can result in a shift in behavior. This view moves us away from a univariate analysis either that the child is the cause of the problem or that the environment is the source of the difficulty (see Table 2.3).

The concept of risk leads to the notion that if the risk is known for certain children and their families, it may be possible to create and organize buffers to mediate adverse outcomes. These buffers can be identified as factors that act as barriers to prevent or mediate negative outcome. For example, independently of the immediate family, a child may develop coping skills nurtured by others or by an institution such as a school. Because of this unique characteristic, the child may respond to problems and generally cope more effectively with his or her environment. Another child may be raised in an impoverished environment, lacking material goods and opportunities; but his or her family may have strong bonds and an extended family to offset the

TABLE 2.3 Summary of factors contributing to childhood resiliency

Researcher	Situation Environmental Factors	Child Constitutional Factors	
Anthony (1974)	Children of a psychotic or physically ill parent	Tend to be male Intact central nervous system Autonomous capacity for "objective" understanding of parent illness, yet evidencing compassion Self-directed (nonconformist) behavior Ability to elicit adult support Global competence (social ease and intellectual skill) Genetic predisposition for 10%	Child exposed to stress following immunity to its build-up Support, encouragement, candor from an adequately functioning parent Parent promotes child autonomy "Average expectation environment" (people who respond in fairly predictable, stable, and reasonable ways to the child)
Garmezy (1974)	Children with a major physical illness, handicap, or genetic or sociocultural risk	Effectiveness in work, play, and love Positive expectancies and outlook Internal locus of control Positive self-regard Self-discipline Problem-solving skills A sense of humor	Support of at least one parent who nurtures the child's interests and permits child autonomy An external support system that reinforces child's coping efforts and models positive values
Rutter (1979)	Children who experienced several of the following: parental marital discord, low socioeconomic status, large family with overcrowding, paternal criminality, maternal psychiatric disorder, removal from home by local authorities	Easy temperament (adaptable and flexible) No genetic predisposition Tend to be female Experience success, maturity, and self-efficacy Able to plan and implement intentional goals	Fewer life stresses, shorter in duration Positive school climate (opportunities for participation and responsibility, promotion) Warm, personal relationship with an adult
Werner & Smith (1982) Werner (1986)	Several major risk factors, sources of stress	First born High activity level Friendly disposition	Four or fewer siblings spaced more than two years apart

TABLE 2.3   continued

Researcher	Situation Environmental Factors	Child Constitutional Factors	
		Reponsive to peple	Great attention to child in his or her first year
		Free of distressing habits	
		Positive social orientation	Positive parent/child relationship in early childhood
		Autonomous	
		Age-appropriate sensorimotor and perceptual skills	Additional caretaker(s) besides mother
			Care by siblings or grandparents
		Adequate communication skills	Fewer number of stressful life events
		Ability to focus attention and control impulses	Mother has steady employment outside home
		Advanced self-help skills	

From "Primary Prevention and Childhood Resilience: An Emerging Focus for Helping Professionals," unpublished paper, 1987, by Tom Gavac and Paula Allen-Meares.

adversities of poverty. (Another explanation is that the child's constitutional factors act as buffers.) As the number of stressful events in the life of a child increases, more protective factors are required in the child's immediate environment to counteract the stressors. Werner and Smith offer an interesting list of protective factors:

Protective Factors

Developmental Stage: Infancy/childhood
Personality:
  physically robust/active
  elicits positive responses from others
  demonstrates autonomy in toddlerhood
  adequate sensorimotor and language development
  achievement orientation
  self-esteem
  solid communication skills
Family:
  family cohesiveness
  structure and rules
  lots of attention given to children during early years, small family size (less than four (4) children)
  first and second children spaced at least two (2) years apart

Outside Family Environment:
  dependable child care
  presence of multigenerational kinship
  supportive role models (1982, p. 13)

Though most of this discussion has focused on infants and young children, some thought must be given to the adolescent. For example, competence criteria developed by Anthony serve as a protective function for the adolescent:

1. Effectiveness in work, play, and love. Resilient children can make positive relationships.
2. Healthy expectancies and a positive outlook. These children can engage in realistic goal-setting behaviors.
3. Self-esteem and internal locus of control. These children have positive feelings of self-worth and engage in behavior to control their environment.
4. Self-discipline and the ability to delay gratification and to maintain a future orientation all contribute to resiliency.
5. Problem-solving and critical-thinking skills. Children who can identify more than one solution to the problem and think through the ramifications can cope more effectively with stressful events.
6. Humor. There is some research underway concerning the role of humor as a protective factor to minimize stress, not only in childhood and adolescence but also in adulthood. (1974, pp. 134–135)

Garmezy (1974) suggests that protective factors form a categorical triad. For example, the above competencies described by Anthony (1976) can be conceptualized as (1) personality disposition factors, (2) supportive family environment, and (3) external support system.

The following case illustration highlights the interrelationship among major sources of stress, protective factors within the child, and the caregiving environments depicted in Tables 2.1 and 2.2 (pages 35 and 36).

CASE ILLUSTRATION: JOHN—AGE FIVE YEARS

John, age five, is the middle child in a family of five children. The other siblings are two, three and a half, seven, and eight and a half years old. John remained in the hospital for several weeks at birth because of a breathing disorder. When he was finally released, his mother was hospitalized for depression. Thus there was little, if any, physical contact between the mother and baby.

The family resides in one of the poorest rural areas in the United States. Neither the father nor the mother has a high school education. The family has had to endure one major problem after another (e.g., mental health problems, unemployment, death of immediate relatives). The mother's problem-solving capacity had reached its lowest. The father is employed spo-radically, access to quality health care services for the family has been prob-lematic, and none of the children had a preschool educational experience.

Given all this, John is a good-natured, curious child who learns quickly. He plays independently and even at the age of five appears to have a posi-tive social orientation. The older siblings assume a parenting role for the younger children. The family enjoys close relationships with their neighbors and their relatives, who live in a town nearby.

The father is a proud man and exchanges roles with his wife (e.g., nurtur-ing the children, preparing meals) to maintain the family. He is attentive to the children and notices their every accomplishment.

There are many protective factors or strengths in this case illustration. For example, though separated from his mother at birth for an extended period of time, John appears to be responsive to others and curious about his environment. The internal family dynamics appear to be healthy—there is role sharing among the parents and siblings and a sense of pride. The family unit has positive emo-tional and social relationships with external sources (neighbors and kin) to draw upon. Such factors contribute to the positive outcome in this case and perhaps minimize the life stresses described in the case.

Table 2.3 (page 38) contains a review of research on this topic. It highlights the importance of a transactional view that includes the child (constitutional fac-tors), life situation of the child, and environmental factors. It gives direction for preventing emotional and behavioral problems and for development.

SUMMARY

A brief overview of select points of view about child and adolescent develop-ment is offered. Different concepts derived from these points of view often undergird and guide thinking and practice in social work. Development does not exist in a vacuum. Social conditions, family variables, and other potential stres-sors interact with development to cause delays and other difficulties for some children and adolescents. New research and theories suggest that we can reduce, buffer, or modify negative consequences of such stressors and variables.

QUESTIONS FOR DISCUSSION

1. What role does knowledge of infant, child, and adolescent development play in assessment?
2. Of the different theories of child development presented in this chapter, which one or ones would you include in your practice? Why?
3. Identify and describe roles practitioners can play to minimize environmental stressors that operate to increase a child or adolescent's vulnerability.

4. For each of the theories of development, describe the potential implications for interviewing and intervention.
5. A multivariate risk model is discussed. What are the implications for social work practice?
6. Locate other studies on resiliency in childhood and adolescence. Critique these studies in terms of their implications for social work practice.

ADDITIONAL READINGS

Antonovsky, A. (1979). *Health, stress, and coping: New perspectives on mental and physical well-being.* San Francisco: Jossey-Bass.

Bullock, D. (1983). Seeking relations between cognitive and social-interactive transitions. *New Directions for Child Development* 21: 97–108.

Fischer, K., & Silver, L. (1985). Stages and individual differences in cognitive development. *Annual Review of Psychology* 36: 614–642.

Garmezy, N., Masten, A. S., & Tellegen, A. (1984). The study of stress and competence in children: Building blocks for developmental psychopathology. *Child Development* 55: 97–111.

Ginsburg, I. (1982). Jean Piaget and Rudolf Steiner: Stages of child development and implications for pedagogy. *Teachers College Records* 84: 327–337.

Globerson, T. (1983). Mental capacity and cognitive functioning: Development and social class differences. *Developmental Psychology* 19: 225–230.

Ogbu, J. (1981). Origins of human competence: A cultural-ecological perspective. *Child Development* 52: 413–429.

Parkinson, C., Scrivener, R., Graves, L., & Bunton, J. (1986). Behavioral differences of school-age children who were small for babies. *Developmental Medicine and Child Neurology* 28: 498–505.

Prosner, H., Toews, J., & Martin, R. (1981). The life cycle of the family: Parental mid-life crisis and adolescent rebellion. *Adolescent Psychiatry* 9: 170–179.

Thornburg, H., & Jones, R. (1982). Social characteristics of early adolescents: Age versus grade. *Journal of Early Adolescence* 2: 229–239.

Wallerstein, J., & Kelly, J. (1980). *Surviving the breakup: How children and parents cope with divorce.* New York: Basic Books.

REFERENCES

Allen-Meares, P., & Shapiro, C., eds. (1989). Adolescent sexuality: New challenges for social work. *Journal of Social Work and Human Sexuality* 8: 1–178.

Anthony, E. (1974). The syndrome of the psychologically invulnerable child. In E. Anthony et al. *The child in his family: Children at Psychiatric Risk,* 3: 529–544. New York: Wiley.

Blos, P. (1962). *On adolescence.* New York: Free Press.

Bronfenbrenner, V. (1979). *The ecology of human development.* Cambridge: Harvard University Press.

Erikson, E. H. (1959). Identity and the life cycle. *Psychological Issues* 1: 1–71.

Erikson, E. H. (1968). *Identity: Youth and crisis.* New York: Norton.

Garmezy, N. (1974). The study of competence in children at risk for severe psychopathology. In E. Anthony et al. *The child in his family: Children at psychiatric risk*, 3: 77–98. New York: Wiley.

Ginsburg, H., & Opper, S. (1969). *Piaget's theory of intellectual development: An introduction.* Englewood Cliffs, N.J.: Prentice-Hall.

Helms, D., & Turner, J. (1981). *Exploring child behavior.* New York: Holt, Rinehart & Winston.

Kleinbaum, D., Kupper, L., & Morgenstern. (1982). *Epidemiologic research: Principles and quantitative methods.* Belmont, Calif.: Life-time Learning Publications.

Kohlberg, L. (1978). Revisions in the theory and practice of moral development. *New Directions for Child Development* 2: 83–87.

Maslow, A. H. (1968). *Toward a psychology of being,* 2nd ed. Princeton: Van Nostrand Reinhold.

Mercier, L., & Berger, R. (1989). Social service needs of lesbian and gay adolescents: Telling it their way. In P. Allen-Meares & C. Shapiro, eds., special volume of *Journal of Social Work and Human Sexuality* 8: 75–98.

Mishne, J. (1986). Clinical work with adolescents. New York: Macmillan.

Piaget, J. (1950). *The psychology of intelligence.* New York: Harcourt Brace Jovanovich.

Piaget, J. (1954). *The construction of reality in the child.* New York: Basic Books.

Pollitt, E. (1984). *Risk factors in the development of young children,* vol. 1: *Risk factors in the development of young children in the developing world.* Houston: University of Texas Health Science Center.

Rogers, D. (1981). *Adolescent and youth.* Englewood Cliffs, N.J.: Prentice-Hall.

Rutter, M. L. ((979). Protective factors in children's responses to stress and disadvantage. In M. W. Kent & J. E. Rolf, eds., *Primary prevention of psychopathology,* 3: *Social competence in children,* pp. 49–74. Hanover, N. H.: University Press of New England.

Rutter, M. (1984). Resilient children. *Psychology Today* (March): 57–65.

Sameroff, A., & Seifer, R. (1983). Familial risk and child competence. *Child Development* 54: 1254–1268.

Stiffman, A., Jung, K., & Feldman, R. (1986). A multivariate risk model for childhood behavior problems. *American Journal of Orthopsychiatry* 56: 204–211.

Werner, E., & Smith, R. (1982). *Vulnerable but invincible: A study of resilient children.* New York: McGraw Hill.

Werner, E. (1986). The concept of risk from a developmental perspective. *Advances in Special Education* 5: 1–23.

chapter 3

Developmental Considerations—
Assessing and Interviewing

As stated earlier, a comprehensive assessment must include information about growth and development, home and school, and other environmental conditions that affect infant, child, or adolescent. This chapter focuses on two important aspects of the helping process—assessment and interviewing.

THE ASSESSMENT PROCESS

Figure 3.1 represents the major dimensions of an ecosystems assessment framework (Allen-Meares & Lane, 1987). The three dimensions of assessment include critical data variables, significant ecosystems, and relevant data sources. Each cell of the cube represents an area that might require assessment. A practitioner would use this ecosystems assessment framework to guide the collection of data, to produce a comprehensive assessment of children and their environments. For example, data from parents, the school, and even a community-based agency may be needed to understand fully how well children or adolescents function and their degree of responsiveness. Specific information about social skills, behavioral difficulties, learning needs, and family dynamics can be obtained from these sources. In practice it is virtually impossible to assess each of these variables. Constraints, such as agency policies, case load, and client–family resistance, may inhibit completion of a comprehensive assessment.

Meyer defines assessment "as a cognitive process . . . it is a form of logical analysis, where a practitioner comes to know his or her case through acknowledgment of the client's own story, interpreted through the screen of an available knowledge base that is relevant to the case situation" (1993, p. 17).

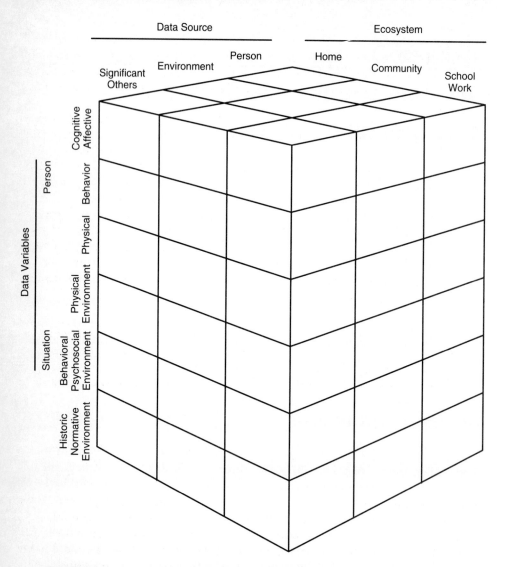

FIGURE 3.1 Ecosystems assessment framework

SOURCE: "Grounding Social Work Practice in Theory: Ecosystems" by Paula Allen-Meares and Bruce A. Lane, *Social Casework,* November 1987. Reprinted by permission of Family Service America.

According to Mishne (1986) the major objective of assessment is to determine in what ways the children or adolescents differ from their peer groups, to assess the chronicity of the presenting concern or problem, and to collect information about the strength of the family. As always, an initial assessment is tentative. An ongoing process, assessment typically includes client contacts, evaluation of family history and present functioning of the child or adolescent, judgment of academic performance, contact with school officials, review of relevant medical reports and history, and so on. Each agency tends to designate what information should be included in the early assessment phase. A practitioner should use professional judgment to adopt or adjust these procedures to individualize the case.

Assessment involves listening, collecting data, observing through structured and nonstructured formats, interviewing the significant others in the child's life, and preparing the child for the interview. Preparing parents for the child's interview may also be necessary because sometimes one or both parents will be present during an initial interview with a young child. An adolescent, however, may not want parents to be present and may oppose their inclusion.

Some advocate empirically based assessment of children or adolescents (Achenbach & McConaughy, 1987). This approach emphasizes assessment techniques that do not depend on a single theory. It does not require a choice between theoretical explanations of certain behaviors. The principles used are derived from psychometrics. Specifically they include the following guidelines:

1. Assessment should employ standardized procedures.
2. Multiple items should be used to sample each aspect of functioning.
3. Items should be such that one can aggregate data to provide for quantitative scores for each aspect of functioning.
4. Scores should be normed, so that an individual can be compared with relevant reference groups.
5. For variables related to development, normative reference groups should be formed according to age levels of development.
6. To be considered psychometrically sound, assessment procedures must be reliable and valid. (Achenbach & McConaughy, 1987, p. 13)

Achenbach and McConaughy claim that these six general principles prescribe standards useful for the construction of sound assessment procedure. They believe that the advantage of standardized assessment procedures is that they reduce variations and subjectivity in data collected on an individual child. Though they may be as time consuming as other approaches, a practitioner using appropriate interpersonal skills can obtain information that confirms and adds insights to informal data by drawing on empirical tools. It has been suggested that empirically based tools, theories, and practice wisdom can thus be artfully combined to enhance our understanding of the client (Meyer, 1993). Essential to implementing empirically based assessment is the collection of different data from multiple sources and situations (see Figure 3.1). By comparing data, the practitioner then formulates dynamics and perceptions of the client and his or her environments.

Kessler (1966) suggests scrutiny of the following factors in assessing a child or adolescent:

1) Difference between the child's chronological age and behavioral age level.
2) Frequency and duration of symptoms.
3) Number of symptoms.
4) Degree of social disadvantage.
5) Intractability of the behavior.
6) Adolescent's personality or general adjustment.
7) Degree of the child's inner self-suffering.

These criteria help determine the child's progression, fixation, or regression in age-appropriate tasks. Here the practitioner is concerned with such matters as locating the difficulty or identifying dimensions such as the history of the problem chronicity and the strengths and coping skills used to respond to the situation.

This information leads to a tentative set of hypotheses about the presenting difficulty. To be consistent with the transactional framework, these hypotheses should also include knowledge and assessment of family and other environmental systems. The bottom line related to this concern is determining the extent to which other environments or persons contribute to or maintain the current difficulty.

When working with children, it is important to know how the family has handled them and learn the nature of early life experiences, in some instances beginning with the postnatal phase (Mishne, 1983). Was this a wanted baby? Were there postnatal difficulties? How did the parents respond to these difficulties? Were the parents prepared to receive the baby in their home? How does this child compare to other children in the home? What are the latent and manifest messages the parents send you, the practitioner, in discussing the child? Are the parents willing to work with you to uncover the sources of difficulty? Assessing the external world of the child is extremely important. As the TIE Framework suggests (see Chapter 1), the interactions and transactions between the person and environments are significant in determining coping patterns. Resources within the environment may be too limited to supply the child with the reinforcement and emotional support needed to develop age-appropriate behaviors.

The assessment of the child's developmental history (when the child sat alone, crawled, walked, spoke first words, used fine-motor skills, identified objects by their correct names) is extremely important. However, equally important are the emotional attitude and practices of the primary caretaker. Did the mother suffer from long periods of depression following the birth of the baby? Was the father involved in nurturing? Was the father present? Were there adequate resources within the family to cope with nurturing? If not, were there resources outside the family (e.g., extended family, church, friends, or social services) that could supplement the family unit? Visits to the home on several occasions and observations of the primary caretaker interacting with the child are valuable in determining diagnostic hypotheses. Observations, which should involve the different family members, can be conducted at different times of day. Also, it is sometimes appropriate to get parental permission to observe the child in the preschool or school setting. The goal of these observations is to determine the feedback the child receives from significant others. When and where is the most difficulty experienced? How does the child respond to daily demands? What role do others play in the maintenance and reinforcement of behaviors?

If he or she is functioning within the normal range of intelligence and physical dexterity, an adolescent can be an active contributor in locating sources of difficulty. On occasion it is important to observe him or her in contact with family and peer group. It is typical of adolescents to resist the practitioner's efforts to engage them in the assessment or helping process. Like the parent, the practitioner is an authority figure; and because adolescents are at the stage of separating self from parents and attempting to form an independent identity, they can project or transfer onto the practitioner the role of parent. Thus, the adolescent may feel uncomfortable about sharing too much of self. Also, contact with the school or other agencies (e.g., probation) may require parental permission. Such contacts are important in that information provided can be useful in formulating a picture of the "adolescent in environment."

Trying to assess children and adolescents is difficult—what constitutes normalcy in adolescence is not always clear because there is considerable variance in functioning. For example, it is typical for adolescents to move away psychologically from the family and gravitate toward peers of their own age. Furthermore, it is typical of adolescents to disagree with authority figures as a part of their efforts to develop self and establish independent opinions. The question for the practitioner then becomes: Which (and how much) of those behaviors are normal and which are abnormal?

Observation

Observation might be one of many strategies used in the assessment process. As mentioned earlier, knowledge of age—appropriate behavior of infants, children, and adolescents—is a requirement. For example, the fine and gross motor coordination of a seven-year-old differs from that of a child of two. A practitioner needs to know specifically how they differ. This same principle holds true of mood swings. Younger children (Greenspan, 1981) may change moods within a few hours (e.g., one moment sad and the next happy), whereas older children may show more stabilization of mood. In addition, the words or sentences of a young child may shift from one topic to another while an older child expresses organized themes and uses words to link them into a whole. According to Greenspan, observational categories include physical functioning (neurological, sensory, motor, integrative); pattern relationships (style of relating—withdrawn, autistic); overall mood or emotional tone; affects (depth of expression, appropriateness, intensity, discriminative capacity); anxiety and fears; and thematic expression (organization of expressions, depth, sequence, relevance to age-appropriate context). Greenspan warns that a practitioner should use multiple perspectives because behaviors are so complicated and determined by so many events in a child's life. A brief observation period can yield many insights about a child. For example, does the child cling excessively to the parent or caretaker? Is the child clumsy, or hyperactive? Does the child appear to be sullen or depressed? Does the child appear to be overly afraid? How does the child interact with toys in the playroom?

Silver (1976) has discussed a playroom diagnostic evaluation of children with neurologically based learning disabilities. Such children frequently suffer from hyperactivity or short attention span; they also develop other secondary problems, such as emotional difficulties. Observing the child in a playroom can reveal inconsistencies in performance or delays in motor development and show whether sensory modality is age appropriate. For example, does the child rely mainly upon auditory inputs? Does he or she prefer tactile stimuli or those of taste or smell? Does the child have difficulty organizing the use of play objects? Or remember the details of games? Does the child respond to questions or control the situation either by ignoring questions or by talking continuously?

The following case illustration underscores the important contribution of observation in a comprehensive assessment.

CASE ILLUSTRATION—JONES FAMILY

Mrs. Jones, a 38-year-old white woman raising her four children as a single parent, was found to be handcuffing her five-year-old son Shawn to the bed. The other two boys, Keith (age seven) and John (age nine), and their sister Paula (age three) were frequently left at home unsupervised. According to reports, Shawn had been sexually assaulted by the mother's live-in boyfriend. This report, along with others, led the local child abuse agency to remove the children from the home. During the period that followed, it was learned not only that Mrs. Jones had a substance abuse problem but also that she suffered from bipolar affective illness.

The children had suffered enormously, so each one's developmental progress had been retarded. They were placed in separate foster homes; and visitations were arranged for the mother. An individual service plan developed for Mrs. Jones outlined changes within the home environment and her functioning and included her input. Specifically, while the children were in foster care, she participated in personal counseling and attended a self-help organization to assist her with substance abuse. However, reports from Mrs. Jones's counselor were not positive. In fact, although the counselor could identify some growth for her client, she found it difficult to develop a professional relationship with her. She expressed concern that Mrs. Jones did not believe in personal therapy.

Of all the children in this family, Shawn experienced the most difficulty in adjusting to the foster home. Though he sometimes appeared to understand the household rules, his behavior fluctuated. In school the teachers reported the same kind of behavior. Finally, when he was placed on Ritalin, there were reports of marked improvement in his behavior. Visits with his mother, however, were followed by aggressive and disruptive behaviors. He seemed to regress after a visit, according to the foster parent. All the other children had some acting-out behaviors; but with medical, dental, and nutritional needs met, there were improvements in all areas.

It appeared that the mother's presence presented a real challenge to Shawn. Thus, after receiving a report from the foster family, the social worker asked to sit in on some of the visits and observe the interactions. Mrs. Jones agreed, and Shawn did not object. The worker discovered that Shawn had a deep attachment to his mother (e.g., he sat very close to her and kept his eyes on her every move), but her interactions were distant and detached from him (e.g., she made poor eye contact, did not touch him). She seemed to blame Shawn for the family's current situation and her forced engagement with a social service agency.

What the practitioner learned from observing the interactions of parent and child was not present in the interview data. This observation lead to some fundamental new insights about the relationship and what was needed in terms of future intervention.

Assessment Tools

Along with informal data collection and intuitive inferences are a wide range of empirical or psychometric tools. Before determining which tools are needed, the practitioner must decide the purpose of the assessment and which areas of a child's life and functioning are to be assessed. What to assess and how to assess it are influenced by the purpose, theoretical orientation, values, and ideology of the practitioner. Traditionally, practitioners have relied upon home and neighborhood visits as approaches to data collection.

Most of the assessment tools target the child or adolescent; too few assess the interaction dynamics between the child and others. There are literally dozens of assessment tools for use with young infants. The Bayley Scales of Infant Development (Bayley, 1969), Gesell Scales of Infant Development (Knoblock & Pasamanick, 1974), Denver Developmental Screening Test (Frankenberg & Dodds, 1968), and the Brazelton Neonatal Behavioral Assessment Scale (Brazelton, 1973) are just a few of the tools used to assess cognitive development. An interesting and new focus of assessment is in the area of temperament (Wilson & Matheny, 1983).

As the infant enters the toddler, preschool, and school-age phase, more assessment tools are available. Some of these instruments measure intellectual development (Horn & Cattell, 1966) and personality.

Many of the techniques used to assess adults cannot be readily adapted for children, especially young children. A child with no or limited verbal skills cannot participate in a structured interview, cannot respond to seminal projective tests such as the TAT, and would find the MMPI unintelligible.

Some of the assessment techniques used with adults have been adapted for use with children. Kanfer, Eyberg, and Krahn (1983) have adapted the psychiatric interview for use with children by taking into account their developmental levels. A children's version of the TAT and the Michigan Picture Test (Hutt, 1980) has been tested with children. Reliability and validity are persistent problems with these projective tests. Attempts have been made to adapt the MMPI for use as a developmental screening tool (Ireton & Thwing, 1974). The Children's Depression Inventory (Kovacs, 1978) is based on the work of Beck (1967).

Assessing Environment

Some researchers have proposed systematic ecological analysis for assessing the natural environment Cantrell and Cantrell (1985) proposed the following steps which essentially are equivalent to problem solving:

A Sequence for Systematic Ecological Problem Solving*

A. Assessment and Analysis

1. Identify critical units and members (home or substitute, school or substitute, peer units, other settings) with relative impact in terms of time and intensity.
2. Identify initial discordances and referral sources.
3. Determine areas of stress or deficiency and of strength or sufficiency (including basic needs in the economic, caretaking, medical, dental, and legal areas).
4. Establish characteristics and behaviors of units and members relevant to the areas of discord and how these interact.
5. Determine expectations of members through their values (implicit or stated, conflictual or consensual) and their incorporated behavioral norms (majority or minority group).
6. Determine critical agents for involvement in change and their approaches to problem solving.
7. Identify required resources (personal and community) and steps needed to interface and mobilize or build resources.

B. Planning

1. List goals to be accomplished.
2. List the steps to be performed, by whom, by what time, at what expense, and from what source.
3. Insert communication or liaison activities required to get steps accomplished.
4. Include evaluation measures, criteria, and checkpoints.

C. Implementation and Evaluation

1. Enact steps or review their accomplishment by others.
2. Check off as accomplished.
3. Collect evaluation data as planned.

SOURCE: "Assessment of the Natural Environment," M. Cantrell & R. Cantrell, 1985.

4. Check data against criteria set.

5. Take appropriate action where steps are not completed as planned (reminders, group communications, or planned revisions).

6. Apprise members of progress or problems.

The process, outlined above, requires actual measurement of environmental characteristics. One recommended approach is to compare the environmental characteristics of the client or client group with those of other groups. Another approach involves predictions based upon patterns evident in the client or client group.

Because children, by definition, are dependent on their families, clinical work with children requires a family perspective; and the family becomes a critical environmental system worthy of assessment. Families experiencing high rates of conflict are likely to have children experiencing high rates of behavior problems (Emery, 1982). Environmental assessment tools that target the family include checklists to be completed by all family members, (Moos & Moos, 1981). Diagrammatic techniques, discussed earlier, can help identify family and individual dynamics that may be contributing to dysfunction (Hartman & Laird, 1983).

Other family-oriented assessment tools require an observer to record the behavior of family members. Caldwell and Bradley (1979) have designed an instrument that measures both cognitive and emotional characteristics in the home to be used primarily with preschool children. Family oriented assessment tools are subject to the same challenges of validity and reliability as most other assessment tools. Efforts to develop measures that can meet tests of reliability and validity continue (Green, 1989).

The HOME Inventory is intended to measure the stimulation potential of a child's early developmental environment (Caldwell & Bradley, 1979). There are two versions of the inventory, one assesses birth to three years, the other three to six years (preschool). The inventory is completed by the practitioner going to the home when the child is awake and the primary caretaker is available, so that interactional patterns can be observed. Each version of the inventory has subscales that include, among others, such areas of assessment as (1) emotional and verbal responsivity of mother, (2) avoidance of restriction and punishment, (3) organization of physical and temporal environment, provision of appropriate play materials, (4) opportunities for variety in daily stimulation, (5) safety and cleanliness of the physical environment and conduciveness to development, (6) modeling and encouragement of social maturity, and (7) stimulation of academic behavior. Summed scores for each subscale and a total score are computed. A practitioner should be aware that one visit may be insufficient to get a representative sampling of the quality of interactions within the home environment.

Another scale that takes the environment into account is the Child Well-Being Scale (Magura & Moses, 1986). It can document changes in the well-being and caretaking environment of children. The scale includes information not only about the child (e.g., physical health care, nutrition and diet, clothing, and personal hygiene) but also about conditions found in the immediate living environment (e.g. household furnishings, overcrowding, household sanitation, security of residence, physical safety in home, supervision of children, substitute child care, quality of parenting and parental cooperation, parental expectations and consistency of discipline, family relations).

There are also ways to measure the responsiveness and expectations of the school. Walker and Rankin (1980) developed an inventory to measure the behavioral expectations and tolerance levels of teachers to whom behavior disordered children were returned after specialized programming. A relatively undeveloped area of assessment for school-age children is sociometric. Peers can have insights that may help the professional identify children at risk. There is some evidence, for example, that ratings by peers of depressed children are more stable than ratings by teachers (Tesiny & Lefkowitz, 1982).

Behaviorists have a unique approach to assessment in that it is not regarded as separate from treatment and is treated as an ongoing process. Behaviorists may engage in direct observations of behavior in the environment. Other assessment techniques include log books and checklists completed by the adults caring for the child (Nay, 1979).

Moos and Moos (1983) describe the development of the Work Environment Scale and the Family Environment Scale, which take into account the person–environment interactions. These scales can be used to describe both work and family settings. They measure the underlying domains of variables that characterize these settings: how people relate to each other (the relationship domain); personal growth goals toward which the setting is oriented (personal growth or goal orientation domain); and the degree of structure and openness to change domain. For example, the Family Environment Scale has been used to assess and compare normal families, distressed families, and ethnic differences in family environments. We learn from an analysis of data yielded by these measures that supportive interpersonal relationships in work and family settings are associated with better individual and family functioning. For example, if Mr. and Mrs. Smith both work in highly stressful situations in which the environment is competitive and policies are unclear there could be detrimental consequences for them, as well as members of their family.

INTERVIEWING

Much attention and discussion have been given to interviewing children and adolescents for court testimony involving alleged child abuse (Bell, 1988). This has always been an area of concern and interest to practitioners. Interviewing for clinical diagnosis is very different. Regardless of the purpose, each child or adolescent is unique, and the process must be individualized.

Greenspan (1981) offers the following schema for approaching the clinical interview: He divides the interview into three phases, (initial, middle, and later). During the initial phase, the practitioner must be warm and patient and allow the client enough space and opportunity to share. Before approaching the interview, the practitioner should take stock of the child's appearance, physical makeup, motor activity, facial expression, and the like. During the middle phase of the interview, the goal of the practitioner is to get to know the child or adolescent by looking for themes, consistency, mood, sequence of affects, and problem-solving capacities (of course, this all depends on developmental stage and age). During the latter phase, the focus of the practitioner turns to preparation for separation and termination. The goal here is to help the client consolidate the therapeutic work and move forward.

The practitioner needs a variety of different communication channels or tools. For example, some younger children may like to play with small toys as they respond to questions; older children may feel more comfortable with a traditional dyad, with no third party present. Good observational skills and solid grounding in child and adolescent development are prerequisite for conducting interviews (see Table 3.1). Those theories of development discussed earlier (Freud, Mahler, Piaget, Erikson, etc.) can serve to delineate the different developmental characteristics.

Parental Interview

Too often in interviews, the child or adolescent is viewed as though separate from his or her environments. Interviewing parents and assessing family function is often essential. As stated earlier, it is important, if at all possible, to make firsthand observation of the family and the client in the natural environment. Parents will often begin the interview by focusing the discussion on the child or adolescent. Parents frequently feel uncomfortable acknowledging that there is a problem and sometimes feel they have failed as parents. On the other hand, some parents are eager to tell all. As stated earlier, the definition of family and parents encompasses a variety of family structures (single head, grandparents raising grandchild, homosexual parent, etc.).

During the initial interview, the practitioner should allow parents to speak freely, sometimes moving from theme to theme. While the parents are engaged in this free association period, the practitioner must observe both the manifest and the latent content of the message, noting the repetition of themes, connections the parents make between discrepancies of the client and themselves, and the emotionality of their speech. For example, John, a 7-year-old boy, was referred for his bullying behavior and frequent fights with classmates. During the initial interview, his father recalled his own childhood inability to defend himself and indicated that he was pleased that John was not like him at that age. He suggested that John needed to temper his behavior but let his classmates know that he was strong. As the father talked, the practitioner learned that he felt powerless in his job and his marriage.

The practitioner should note such critical factors as the number of separations and losses (deaths, divorces) the family has experienced and the internal and external resources it uses to respond to such situations. Issues of bonding and attachment among siblings should also be acknowledged. Babies that were

TABLE 3.1   Developmental considerations for interviewing children and adolescents

Toddler (Ages 2–3)	Preschooler (Ages 4–5)	School Age (Ages 6–11)	Adolescent (Ages 12–18)
• Understanding of language is far superior to the ability to express self verbally • Limited ability to verbalize and generalize • Seeks adult approval • Imitates other's language • Separation is extremely difficult	• Very talkative • Can verbalize but may not understand complex questions • Limited ability to separate fantasy from reality • Beginning to know the difference between right and wrong • Responds well to praise and encouragement • Tends to be protective of the parents	• Can be very independent and self-assured at times • Family is still very important • Has strong likes and dislikes • Forms own opinions and ideas	• Can often be communicated with as an adult • Does not feel understood • Independent yet dependent • Often does not trust adults • Often does not think of consequences of words or acts • Often idealistic—compares life unfavorably with the ideal

From *Investigation: Child Protective Services Inservice Training* (Supervisor's Guide) by K. Drews, M. Salus, and D. Dodge, 1981. Washington, D.C.: Creative Associates, Inc.

difficult to care for, as well as abnormal deliveries, should be noted. It is also important to observe the quality of life (the provision of health care, housing, safety, and income) and the external support systems and strengths of the family (e.g., friendship and family support; good problem-solving skills; positive relationships with societal institutions, such as church, schools, and social services).

It may also be essential to obtain a family history to discover either generational issues or current family functioning. Practitioners can use two techniques to complete these tasks, the genogram and the eco-map, both described in Chapter 1.

Greenspan (1981) highlights several areas important for collecting the developmental history of a particular child or adolescent as it relates to interviewing the family. It should be noted that even though a child may be older, the developmental history can provide insight into present difficulties, including difficulties in communicating. For example, if Sharon, age 15, has a difficult time developing relationships, a social history might indicate that she did not experience closeness with her parents. Because a brother was born only a year after Sharon, her parents, who wanted a boy, essentially ignored her emotional needs throughout her early childhood. Most of their warmth, verbal and nonverbal attention, and communication were directed toward her brother.

Greenspan's developmental history areas include

1. Early homeostatic regulatory patterns (e.g., apathetic, withdrawn, etc.).
2. Early experiences of comfort, care, and protection.
3. Early feeding and weaning (breast and bottle).
4. Early attachment or lack of fit, style, intensity.
5. Birth of siblings, toilet training, initial experiences of separation (e.g., going to school, being placed for temporary foster care), significant separations or losses (death, illness, divorce).
6. Development of affects and impulse control (poor impulse control—aggressive behavior, passivity).
7. Feelings about own body, bodily processes, feelings and thoughts about sex. (Greenspan, 1981, pp. 186–187)

Though it is essential to focus on the here and now in working with children and adolescents, knowledge of their developmental histories and of the characteristics of their immediate environments can contribute useful information. Caseloads and other work demands sometimes prevent practitioners from conducting comprehensive assessments that include both the present and the past.

Interviewing for Court

As stated earlier, much interest has focused on interviewing children and adolescents for testimony in abuse and neglect cases. The goal in this instance is to collect factual information and details. Again, knowledge of development operates both to define the intervening process and to prepare the child or adolescent for court. However, during the process the practitioner must keep in mind that there is considerable variation in development. By being aware of age group traits and pointing them out to a judge, jury, or prosecutor, practitioners can ensure that allowances are made when a child or adolescent must testify (Bell, 1988). The practitioner can also identify such a person as a psychiatrist specializing in infants and young children, who can provide expert testimony and explain infantile psychic trauma.

Though three-year-old children can speak, they may lack the concept of sexuality, and their explanations may not be coherent (Bell, 1988). However, in contrived play situations or through the use of anatomically correct dolls, they can reenact their sexual experiences. Some concern has been expressed whether anatomically correct dolls should be used for expert testimony (see Chapter 7). Children at age seven may be unable to recall specific dates or times and may give inconsistent responses. Nevertheless, these children can explain and describe their sexual encounters in detail and convince a judge and jury that they are telling the truth.

Involving children in decision making, given their developmental readiness, is a part of the process of empowering them. In other words, the goal is to develop age-appropriate autonomy. "Part of children's powerlessness is unavoidable;

their lack of experience, maturity, and resources dictates that many of their needs must be met by adults" (Hegar, 1989, p. 374).

Because children ages 8 through 13 can reason logically and by age 12 or so can think abstractly, they can give detailed accounts of sexual and physical abuse. Some may understand that what has happened is wrong. Some may be impaired by the trauma of the experience and hesitate to "tell all." Practitioners can prepare children to help them withstand the demands of giving testimony and to tell the truth during cross-examination. Clearly, a child's age has a bearing on what can be expected and what he or she can recall regarding a given situation.

SUMMARY

A comprehensive assessment of the child or adolescent requires the practitioner to collect information about and from both the client and the significant others who comprise major environments in which he or she functions. When interviewing, the practitioner must understand the child or adolescent's position on the developmental continuum and adjust techniques accordingly. Interviewing should not be based on the client's appearance or chronological age.

QUESTIONS FOR DISCUSSION

1. Why is it important to assess environmental conditions, as well as clients' functioning?
2. Apply the ecosystem framework shown in Figure 3.1 to the case illustration describing Shawn. What areas would you be most interested in assessing and why? What informal and psychometric tools might you use in this case?
3. This chapter mentions only a few of the many psychometric instruments. Taking into account the developmental stages of infant, child, and adolescent, review the literature to identify scales that might be useful in your practice.
4. How might interviewing be adapted to meet the needs of different groups of children and adolescents (e.g., mentally retarded, learning disabled, economically deprived, ethnic or racial minority, middle class, and others).
5. Conduct a self-analysis. What are some of your characteristics that might facilitate your work with children and adolescents and their families? What is it about you that would hinder relationship development (e.g., you are younger than most parents, you are of a different racial or economic background, you tend to overidentify with the adolescent, or you are coping with these unresolved personal and family issues)?

ADDITIONAL READINGS

Albers, L., Doane, J., & Mintz, J. (1986). Social competence and family environment: 15-year follow-up of disturbed adolescents. *Family Process* 25: 379–389.

Krumboltz, J., & Krumboltz, H. (1972). *Changing children's behavior.* Englewood Cliffs, N.J.: Prentice-Hall.

Matus, A., & Reid, M. (1983). Helping parents deal with children's educational transitions. *Social Work in Education* 5: 89-96.

Mishne, J. (1993). Dilemmas in provision of urban mental health services for latency age children. *Child and Adolescent Social Work Journal* 10(4): 271-287.

Northern, H. (1987). Assessment in direct practice. *Encyclopedia of social work,* 18th ed., pp. 212-222. Silver Spring, Md.: National Association of Social Workers.

Paster, V. (1985). Adapting psychotherapy for the depressed, unacculturated, acting out, black male adolescent. *Psychotherapy* 22: 408-416.

Rich, J. (1968). *Interviewing children and adolescents.* New York: Macmillan.

Wyatt, G. (1982). Sociocultural assessment of home and school visits in psychiatric evaluations of Afro-American children and families. In B. Bass, G. Wyatt, & G. Powell, eds., *The Afro-American family: Assessment/treatment and research issues,* pp. 35-68. New York: Grune & Stratton.

REFERENCES

Achenbach, T., & McConaughy, S. (1987). *Empirically based assessment of child and adolescent psychopathology: Vol. 13. Practical applications.* Beverly Hills, Calif.: Sage Publications.

Allen-Meares, P., & Lane, B. (1987). Grounding social work practice in theory: Ecosystems. *Social Casework* 69: 515-522.

Bayley, N. (1969). *Bayley scales of infant development.* New York: Psychological Corporation.

Beck, A. T. (1967). *Depression: Clinical, experimental, and theoretical aspects.* New York: Harper & Row.

Bell, C. (1988). Working with child witnesses: The caseworker's support of sexually abused child of importance. *Public Welfare,* (Winter): 5-13.

Brazelton, T. (1973). Neonatal behavioral assessment scale. *National Spastics Society Monograph.* Philadelphia: Lippincott.

Broome, M. (1985). The child in pain: A model for assessment and intervention. *Critical Care Quarterly* 8: 47-55.

Caldwell, B. & Bradley, R. (1979). *Home observation for measurement of the environment.* Little Rock: University of Arkansas at Little Rock, Center for Child Development and Education.

Emery, R. (1982). Interparental conflict and the children of discord and divorce. *Psychological Bulletin* 92: 310-330.

Frankenberg, W., & Dodds, J. (1968). *The Denver developmental screening test manual.* Denver: University of Colorado Press.

Green, R. (1989). Choosing family measurement devices for practice and research: SFI and FACES III. *Social Service Review* 63: 304-320.

Greenspan, S. (1981). *The clinical interview of the child.* New York: McGraw-Hill.

Hartman, A., & Laird, J. (1983). *Family-centered social work practice.* New York: Free Press.

Hegar, R. C. (1989). Empowerment-based practice with children. *Social Service Review* (September): 373-383.

Horn, J., & Cattell, R. (1966). Age differences in primary mental ability factors. *Journal of Gerontology* 21: 210-220.

Hutt, M. (1980). Michigan picture test. New York: Grune/Stratton.

Ireton, H., & Thwing, E. (1974). *Minnesota child development inventory.* Minneapolis:

Behavior Science Systems.

Kanfer, R., Eyberg, S., & Krahn, G. (1983). Interviewing strategies in child assessment. In C. E. Walker & M. C. Roberts, eds., *Handbook of clinical child psychology,* pp. 95–108. New York: Wiley.

Kessler, J. (1966). *Psychopathology of childhood.* Englewood Cliffs, N.J.: Prentice-Hall.

Knoblock, H., & Pasamanick, H., eds. (1974). *Gesell and Amatruda's developmental diagnosis: The evaluation and management of normal and abnormal development in infancy and early childhood,* 3rd ed. New York: Harper & Row.

Kovacs, M. (1978). The children's depression inventory: A self-rated depression scale (manuscript). University of Pittsburgh, School of Medicine.

Magura, S., & Moses, B. (1986). *Outcome measures for child welfare services.* Washington, D.C.: Child Welfare League of America.

Meyer, C. (1993). *Assessment in social work practice.* New York: Columbia University Press.

Mishne, J. (1983). *Clinical work with children.* New York: Free Press.

Mishne, J. (1986). *Clinical work with adolescents.* New York: Free Press.

Moos, R., & Moos, B. (1981). *Family environment scale manual.* Palo Alto, Calif.: Consulting Psychologists Press.

Moos, R., & Moos, B. (1983). Adaptation and the quality of life in work and family settings. *Journal of Community Psychology* 17: 153–170.

Nay, W. (1979). *Multimethod clinical assessment.* New York: Gardner.

Orten, J., & Weis, D. (1975). Strategies and techniques for therapeutic change. *Social Service Review* 49: 355–366.

Silver, L. (1976). The playroom diagnostic evaluation of children with neurologically based learning disabilities. *Journal of the American Academy of Child Psychiatry* 15: 240–255.

Tesiny, E., & Lefkowitz, M. (1982). Childhood depression: A six month follow-up study. *Journal of Consulting and Clinical Psychology* 50: 778–780.

Walker, H. M., & Rankin, R. (1980). *The SBS inventory of teacher social behavior standards and expectations.* Eugene: University of Oregon Press.

Wilson, R., & Matheny, A. (1983). Assessment of temperament in twins. *Developmental Psychology* 19: 172–183.

part **II**

Public Policies and Factors Affecting the Mental Health Needs of Children and Adolescents

This section provides an introduction to public policies, programs, and conditions affecting practice that often determine the availability of resources for children and adolescents. Social work practitioners sometimes fail to realize the importance of knowing and understanding social welfare policies and programs, community conditions, and the consequences of poverty, racism, and sexism.

Many readers may question why a book devoted to practice with children and adolescents would include a chapter on public social welfare policies. Nevertheless these factors set the context of practice and often shape the delivery system and programs within which workers operate.

chapter 4

An Overview and Critique of Public Policies and Practices

Elizabeth Segal

Today, children and adolescents represent more than 26 percent of our population and live among 65 million families in this nation. With such significant numbers, the care and well-being of children and their families should be a major policy priority. However, unlike most other Western countries, the United States lacks a comprehensive policy to ensure the social and economic well-being of children and their families. Instead, our social welfare system is a maze of poorly coordinated social programs on the federal, state, and local levels. More than 80 federal programs alone affect children. The result is a patchwork of child and family welfare services which contribute to create a system with both overlap and gaps in service. This system in extremely complicated to understand and to navigate.

The labyrinth of child welfare services and programs presents a challenge to the student of social policy. For the social work practitioner and client of child welfare services, its complexity can discourage use. Nevertheless, all social work practitioners involved with children or adolescents and their families must be familiar with the relevant policies and services. This chapter is their introduction to the welfare service system and the major policies that form the basis and authority for its services. Included is a discussion of the major policy issues and legislation relevant for social work practitioners as well as recommendations for federal action.

HISTORICAL OVERVIEW

The role and the image of children and adolescents have changed over the history of the United States, and childhood has come to be recognized as a unique and important developmental period. Children are no longer considered

63

miniature adults, nor are they regarded as economic assets for their families. With this shift have come changes in social attitudes and policies. Children have ceased to be treated as economically useful and become sentimentally valued (Zelizer, 1985). In addition, adolescence has become a recognized period of human development, with its own body of research and literature. Concurrent with the change in role and value of children and adolescents has been the development of social policies and programs to protect and care for children and adolescents.

The development of social policies for youth has not been a smooth process. Embedded in the public discussion of children's and adolescents' well-being is the struggle between state intervention and family privacy. When should government intercede on behalf of children, and when is the inner sanctum of the family to be protected? For the most part, social welfare policy has been based on the assumption that the family is the primary source of care for children. Only under extreme circumstances of family inability to provide and care for children has the public intervened (Moroney, 1986). The balance between outside intervention and family privacy is still a major component in discussions.

Until the beginning of the twentieth century, policies related to children and their families were the domain of local governments and private charities. The needs of children and adolecents were largely viewed from the perspective of what would best benefit the overall community. Treatment of children, especially those in economic need, varied from town to town. Over the course of this century state and federal involvement in the rights of children and recognizing the unique needs of adolescents has grown apace. Although there have been periods of high and low involvement, state and federal governments entered the child welfare policy arena in the 1900s and have played an increasing important role ever since (Pizzo, 1983).

The key welfare policies and programs that target this group over the past 150 years demonstrate the shift from community control to federal mandate. Early concern for children was championed by private groups, such as the Children's Aid Society founded in 1853. Other organizations followed with new ways to care for orphaned and destitute children (Axinn & Levin, 1992). By the 1900s, care shifted from stressing institutional placement to preserving the family. During the Progressive era, child and family advocates urged greater federal involvement and sponsored legislation restricting child labor, securing juvenile justice, and providing public health care for women and children (Katz, 1986).

The early twentieth century witnessed an increased awareness of the needs of children. The first significant instance of federal involvement was the White House Conference on Children and Youth held in 1909. After that, policy development for children originated with the federal government, which enacted legislation limiting child labor and providing for maternal and child health care and widows' pensions.

Although the role of the federal government in relation to children and their families has been controversial, the initiative for the majority of social services for childern and families lies within federal legislation, which in turn has affected state policies and programs. Whereas the states were the early leaders in developing child welfare policies, the federal government has been the leader for the past eighty years. Today, states are responsible for turning federal legislative requirements into workable services and programs.

It is important to note the residual nature of social welfare policy in this country. Most social welfare policies and programs are developed in response to social problems; they are not part of a preventive approach. Residual programs are targeted to a specific group in need. Residual social policy makes the family and the economic market primary and uses social intervention only as a last resort (Wilensky & Lebeaux, 1958). In contrast, the institutional approach views social welfare policy as an accepted need for the well-being of all society. From an institutional perspective, social programs should be accessible to all, regularly available before problems arise.

Most social welfare programs are residual, including the majority of child and family welfare programs, such as welfare assistance, nutrition programs, housing, and most medical services. In contrast, few social programs are institutional. The closest example of an institutional social program for children is public education. Although there are inequities in quality and delivery, public education is available to all as a part of our social system.

POVERTY AND THE CORRELATES
OF ECONOMIC DEPRIVATION

The greatest social concern facing children and their families today is poverty and the correlated problems. More than one out of every five children lives below the official poverty line, 14.6 million children in 1992 (Bureau of the Census, 1993). These children represent 40 percent of the total poverty population. What does this imply about the condition of children in our society, today and in the future?

A child growing up in poverty begins life at a severe disadvantage. Impoverished children suffer from inadequate nutrition, health care, and housing. Their social environment is often dangerous. Lacking educational opportunities they are likely to remain in poverty into adulthood. Poor children are more likely to be disabled and to live in families without health insurance. They are among the fastest-growing group of homeless; and for each year a child lives in poverty, he or she is more likely to fall behind in school (Select Committee on Children, Youth, & Families, 1988a). While child poverty is not new, it is becoming increasingly more severe and has grown in recent years despite prolonged economic growth.

Ten years ago, fewer than ten million children lived in poverty. Today that number has grown by 25 percent. This increase has occurred despite six years of economic expansion and the lowest unemployment rate in 14 years (Congressional Budget Office, 1988). We are witnessing a distressing phenomenon, that while some groups are prospering economically, children and adolescents as a whole are not.

JUVENILIZATION OF POVERTY

There are many economic and social reasons for the changes in the composition of the poverty population. Nevertheless, one trend stands clear—there is a growing "juvenilization" of poverty (Segal, 1991; Wilson, 1985); more and more children and youth are poor. While much has been written about the "feminization" of poverty (Pearce, 1978)—the increased probability of women living in poverty and the growth in female-headed households in poverty—the significant increase in childhood poverty has not been clearly identified as an urgent problem. However, analysis of Census Bureau data marks the 1980s as the decade of childhood poverty.

With a peak of over 22 percent of all children living in poverty in 1983 (see Table 4.1), the percentage has remained at or greater then 20 percent since 1982 (Bureau of the Census, 1993). This trend represents a national crisis. Children are more likely than any other group in this country to be poor. Childhood poverty is even more pronounced among various racial and ethnic minority children. In 1992, 46.6 percent of all black children lived in poverty, and 40 percent of Hispanic children were poor (Bureau of the Census, 1993). These numbers remain significantly higher than the rates for white children, which stood at 17 percent in 1992. These data highlight the growing economic schism between white families and minority families.

Despite these dismal statistics, public outrage has been confined to child advocacy groups and small citizen groups. Poverty in the United States is not clearly visible. With the help of federal, state, and local programs, many people receive the bare necessities for food, clothing and shelter. The majority of the poor are isolated in urban enclaves or invisible in rural areas. They are not always easy to identify and do not fit commonly held perceptions. Although more than nine million adults worked full or parttime they and their families nevertheless fell below the poverty line (Levitan & Shapiro, 1987). They make up the working poor. This observation contradicts the value base of this country, and the prevailing assumption that those who work are not in poverty. Unfortunately for millions, this is not true.

Children and their families also constitute a significant portion of those homeless families who are often difficult to find and document. In part, this occurs because of the vulnerability of children and women and the hesitancy of families to be identified as homeless by public agencies for fear of losing their children.

In addition to families, thousands of homeless children and adolescents live alone. Most are runaways or "throwaways," children whose families voluntarily or involuntarily no longer keep them. Many of these homeless youth leave abusive homes but eventually turn to drugs, crime, and prostitution. The Federal

TABLE 4.1   Children in poverty

	1977	1980	1983	1986	1989	1992
Total number (in millions)	10.3	11.5	13.9	12.9	12.6	14.6
Percentage in poverty	16.2	18.3	22.3	20.5	19.6	21.9
Percentage of white children in poverty	11.6	13.9	17.5	16.1	14.8	16.9
Percentage of black children in poverty	41.8	42.3	46.7	43.1	43.7	46.6
Percentage of Hispanic children in poverty	28.3	33.2	38.1	37.7	36.2	39.9

SOURCE: Bureau of the Census, 1993.

Office of Juvenile Justice and Delinquency Prevention estimates there are between 1.3 and 1.5 million runaway and homeless youth each year. Other estimates place the number as high as 4 million (Children's Defense Fund, 1988).

FAMILY POVERTY

Changes in family composition, as well as age and race, have an effect on the incidence of children in poverty. Blacks and Hispanics are disproportionately represented among the poor, although two-thirds of the poor are white. The most significant aspect of family poverty is the concentration of poor children among households headed by single women. In 1992, the heads of almost 60 percent of all poor families with children were women with no husbands present, while households headed by single women represented only 23 percent of all families (Bureau of the Census, 1993). The question arises as to why female-headed households are disproportionately poor. Sidel discusses this issue at length. She cites a number of reasons:

> The weakening of the traditional nuclear family; the rapid growth of female-headed families; the continuing existence of a dual-labor market that actively discriminates against female workers; a welfare system that seeks to maintain its recipients below the poverty line; the time-consuming yet unpaid domestic responsibilities of women, particularly child care . . . . unemployment; continuing discrimination on the basis of race, class, and age; and the changing nature of the economy also contribute to the increasing impoverishment of women and children. (1986, p. 15)

Although it is unclear to what extent sex, race, and age increase the incidence of family poverty, there is certainly an overwhelming relationship. The result is a very high incidence of children living in poverty among these families.

SOCIETAL COST OF CHILDHOOD POVERTY

For society as a whole, poverty hurts in two ways. First there is a moral and ideological cost. It is indeed an anomaly that a technologically advanced and wealthy nation like the United States has millions of children living in poverty. That millions of people are without homes, lack enough food, are denied adequate education and health care, and are willing to work yet cannot earn enough to support themselves and their families is contrary to a system that claims to promote the general welfare of all its citizens.

The second cost can be measured in actual dollars. Poverty costs this nation billions of dollars in lost earnings, foregone tax revenues, and outlays for social programs designed to repair the damage caused by poverty. In spite of our residual approach to social welfare, evidence shows that many preventive programs are successful in helping children and adolescents. Lisbeth Schorr presents numerous programs that provide preventive services and benefit poor children. She concludes that if the programs that have proven to be successful were more widespread,

> Fewer children would come into adulthood unschooled and unskilled, committing violent crimes, and bearing children as unmarried teenagers. Fewer of today's vulnerable children would tomorrow swell the welfare rolls and the prisons. Many more would grow into responsible and productive adults, able to form stable families and contributing to, rather than depleting, America's prosperity and sense of community. (1988, p. xxix)

Poverty wastes human potential. It is especially costly in terms of children and their future contributions to society. For moral reasons, as well as economic, it is imperative that solutions be found to the growing problem of children in poverty.

MAJOR POLICY ISSUES, LEGISLATION, AND FEDERAL PROGRAMS

Our response to children and adolescents in need has fluctuated as child welfare policy and responsibility have shifted from the local level to the federal domain. The most significant contributions have been made through federal policy decisions and legislation. The federal government plays a key role by legislating programs and mandating states and localities to provide services designed to address the social needs of children and their families. These services can be divided into two categories: direct cash assistance and in-kind benefits. Cash assistance programs are designed to provide a minimum cash allotment for families to provide for bare necessities. In-kind benefits provide services and resources such as health care, housing, and employment training. Table 4.2 outlines the

TABLE 4.2 Major federal programs to aid children and families in need

Cash Assistance	FY 1992 Funding (in $ millions)
Aid to Families with Dependent Children	14,800
Child Support Enforcement	668
Medical Services	
Medicaid—children under 21	17,000
Maternal and Child Health Services Block Grants	650
Food and Nutrition	
Food Stamps	21,800
WIC	3,500
Housing	
Low-Income Public Housing	7,800
Education	
Head Start	2,200
Education for the Disadvantaged—Chapter 1	6,200
Education Programs for Handicapped Children	2,200
Employment	
Job Corps	926
Summer Youth Employment and Training Program	1
Social Services	
Social Services Block Grant—Title XX	2,700
Child Welfare Services	274
Foster Care and Adoption Assistance	2,500
Child Abuse Grants	39
Runaway Youth Program	36
Juvenile Justice	69
Federal outlays for programs to aid children in need total about 7 percent of the national budget.	

SOURCE: *Budget of the United States Government, FY 1994,* 1993.

majority of federal programs designed to serve children in need. The following highlights some of the major programs and presents an analysis of the effectiveness of these programs in protecting and maintaining the social well-being of children and adolescents and their families.

Cash Assistance Programs

Aid to Families with Dependent Children.   The largest and best-known cash assistance program for poor children is Aid to Families with Dependent Children (AFDC), developed as part of the Social Security Act of 1935. It was originally conceived as Aid to Dependent Children, a temporary, short-term assistance program for widows and their children. Once Social Security had time to develop, all people would be covered under the Old Age Survivors Disability Insurance program (OASDI). Widows and orphans would fall under the categories of survivors or dependents. However, that scenario never developed. Instead, demographic and employment changes, such as the growth in female-headed households, divorce, and women in the workplace, have made AFDC a permanent part of our social welfare system. Thus, AFDC has become the most controversial public welfare program.

Almost 12 million people received assistance through AFDC in 1990 (*Social Security Bulletin: Annual Statistical Supplement 1992*, 1992). Of the total AFDC population, two-thirds, almost eight million recipients, were children. Despite the plans of the founders of the Social Security Act, these children are not eligible to receive survivor benefits through Social Security. The vast majority of them live in single-parent households headed by women. These children were never covered by a parent who worked and paid into the Social Security system for sufficient amounts or periods of time. Consequently, without changes in employment opportunities for single-women heads of households, a significant population of children and their families will never be covered by the Social Security system.

AFDC, like many other programs that serve children in need, is financed by both state and federal monies according to a distribution formula. Federal support of AFDC which ranges from 50 percent to 77 percent (General Accounting Office, 1985) is administered on the state level under overall federal guidelines. Of greatest concern to policy makers over the years has been the struggle to provide cash assistance to needy families while not undermining their efforts to work. This dilemma represents the much-discussed work incentive problem.

In order to ensure the value of work, it must be financially more attractive to be employed than to receive AFDC benefits. This issue has helped keep AFDC payments at a low level. The average monthly payment per family in 1987 was $392 with an average family size of 2.9 persons (*Social Security Bulletin: Annual Statistical Supplement 1992*, 1992). The emphasis on work for welfare has been punitive for poor women and had minimal success. Welfare work programs place women in low-paying, dead-end jobs that do not lift them out of poverty (Miller 1989; Segal, 1989). The choice between employment and welfare becomes a no-win situation and leaves many poor women and their families in poverty.

Social Security—Dependents' Benefits.   While not considered a program for the poor, Social Security benefits many who might otherwise fall into poverty if they did not receive monthly payments. The program is designed to replace lost earnings for family members in the event that a worker dies. Because there is no income test for Social Security, however, it is impossible to determine to what extent children who receive benefits as a result of the death of a parent are in financial need. Furthermore, the prerequisite for Social Security benefits is that the deceased or disabled worker has been employed for a significant period of time to make the family eligible. For these reasons, it is difficult to assess the impact of dependent benefits in keeping children from poverty.

Child Support Enforcement.   In 1975, federal legislation established the Child Support Enforcement Program, which falls under the Social Security Act. The goal of the program has been to assist in establishing support levels and collecting delinquent child support payments. Through such collections, the program requires absent parents to support their children and thereby reduce AFDC expenditures. This program is considered a cash assistance program because the first $50 collected by the state on behalf of the AFDC family is paid directly to the family in addition to the AFDC grant. The rest is kept by the state to offset program expenses and AFDC costs.

The success of the program in aiding poor children is unclear. Legislation in 1984 strengthened the ability of states to collect delinquent support payments, but the overall impact on AFDC collections has been minimal. Abramovitz points out that "child support collection on behalf of AFDC mothers has not provided anywhere near the amount of money spent on the program" (1988, p.365). In 1984 and 1985, about 1 percent of AFDC families were removed from the welfare rolls as a result of child support enforcement efforts (based on calculations from data reported in Subcommittee on Social Security and Family Policy, 1988).

While enforcement definitely aids many women who are due child support but are not receiving it, to what extent AFDC women are lifted from poverty is questionable. It is unclear whether a significant number of the biological fathers of AFDC children are financially able to support their children. If many of them are unemployed and also in poverty, the positive effects of child support enforcement are negligible for children and their mothers living in poverty.

Medical Services

Medicaid.   Passage of the Social Security Act has permanently placed the federal government in the role of providing assistance to the needy. While early supporters hoped for a complete program of assistance, it took 30 more years for the Social Security Act to be amended to include health coverage. In 1965, the Medicaid program was adopted as Title XIX.

Medicaid provides medical assistance for low-income persons through federal matching funds to states. As with AFDC, states administer the program and contribute funds. Recipients obtain medical services, and providers are directly reimbursed by the states for the medical care provided. Consequently, Medicaid is an in-kind benefit.

In order to qualify for federal funds, state Medicaid programs must cover all recipients of AFDC, as well as the aged, blind, and disabled who meet income eligibility standards. States may also offer Medicaid coverage to individuals who are "medically needy"—people who are financially unable to cover their medical expenses. While each state sets its own program, the medical care states offer must include physicians' services; inpatient and outpatient hospital services; laboratory and x-ray services; certain screening, diagnostic, and treatment services for children; and family planning services and supplies.

Medicaid costs have grown considerably over the life of the program. From 1966 to 1986, Medicaid expenditures went from $1.5 billion to $45.8 billion. Even in constant dollars, the cost almost tripled. The increased spending reflects the growth and inflation in medical services for those in need. While financially needy dependent children and their parents have benefited greatly from the Medicaid program and are the majority of recipients, they do not represent the majority of expenditures. Although 70 percent of Medicaid beneficiaries were children and adults from families with dependent children, they accounted for only 24 percent of Medicaid payments in FY 1986 (Congressional Research Service, 1988). Medicaid has become a program of primary importance for low-income elderly and disabled people, as well as the sole source of medical care for poor women and children on AFDC.

Maternal and Child Health Services Block Grants. Another program that falls under the Social Security Act is the Maternal and Child Health Services Block Grant (MCH). Authorized as Title V of the act, the MCH block grants provide health services predominantly to low-income mothers and children. The purposes of the grants are to provide services that help reduce infant mortality and preventable diseases among children and increase the availability of prenatal, delivery, and postpartum care for financially needy mothers. The programs are administered on the state levels with funding shared by the states and the federal government. Part of the federal funding is set aside to facilitate the development of special programs and research projects.

The need for preventive health care for poor women and their children is crucial. Because poor women tend to receive inadequate prenatal care, they experience a greater proportion of complicated births and a higher incidence of infant mortality (McBarnette, 1988).

Food and Nutrition

Food Stamps. One of the largest and best-known welfare programs is Food Stamps. Unlike the majority of programs in our social welfare system, the Food Stamp program does not fall under the Social Security Act. It is administered by the Food and Nutrition Service of the United States Department of Agriculture (USDA). Originally, government food programs were operated to distribute surplus food. When enacted as legislation in 1964, the Food Stamp Act created a program to aid low-income households obtain more nutritious diets. Over the years the method of delivery has developed into a coupon exchange program. Qualifed low-income households receive Food Stamp coupons that can be redeemed for food items at retail stores.

The Food Stamp program is administered by the states but funded entirely by the federal government. State and local welfare agencies determine eligibility, using federal rules, and issue the benefits monthly. The USDA estimates that 68 percent of all participating households have children, and children account for more than 50 percent of all recipients (Congressional Research Service, 1987). In 1992, 22.6 million people received Food Stamps, and the average monthly value per person was $64 (*Social Security Bulletin: Annual Statistical Supplement, 1992*, 1992).

The Food Stamp program has contributed greatly to the well being of poor people in this country. However, it is important to note that in no way does the program provide enough resources for all of a family's nutritional needs. The allotment is based on the USDA's "Thrifty Food Plan," which provides for a nutritionally adequate low-cost diet (Congressional Research Service, 1987). The allotment keeps people from severe starvation and malnutrition, but it is based on a number of assumptions. In order to properly prepare food under the Thrifty Food Plan, one must have nutritional planning skills, proper storage space and equipment, and access to low-cost markets, all largely unavailable to poor families.

Supplemental Food Program for Women, Infants, and Children (WIC). Good nutrition is particularly important for the proper development of children. The WIC program is designed to address the early nutritional needs of infants and thus have a positive impact on children as they grow. Low-income mothers and their infants and children are eligible to receive selected supplemental foods (such as eggs and milk) which are provided either directly or through vouchers.

The WIC program is also administered through the USDA and funded entirely with federal monies. State health departments operate the program and also provide nutrition education services. Pregnant, postpartum, or breast-feeding women, as well as infants and children up to five years old, are eligible to receive benefits. While WIC has provided many women and their children with supplemental foods, less than half the eligible population is served (Select Committee on Children, Youth, and Families, 1989).

Housing

Low-Income Public Housing. Public housing projects are designed to provide standard housing, primarily for families with children, at reduced rent. Eligibility is determined through a means test, and households pay no more than 30 percent of their adjusted income for rent. Most programs are administered by the Department of Housing and Urban Development (HUD). Housing projects are owned and managed by local housing authorities who determine eligibility using federal guidelines.

Because of limited funding for housing programs, only a small portion of the poor actually receive benefits. Less than a third of very low income households receive assistance (Center on Budget and Policy Priorities, 1988). In some urban areas, there are multiyear waiting lists for housing assistance. The lack of affordable housing has been cited as the most critical problem facing today's cities (U.S. Conference of Mayors, 1988). Federal funding for low-income housing was cut by 80 percent during the 1980s (Children's Defense Fund, 1992), thus placing a greater burden on states and localities to house the poor. Inadequate housing leaves children and adolescents in environments that do not promote healthy growth and development, and contribute to other problems, such as poor health and poor performance in school.

Education

Head Start.   The Economic Opportunity Act of 1964 launched the War on Poverty. It created a number of programs specially designed to aid disadvantaged youth and communities. Among its provisions was Title V, which created the Head Start program. Head Start was designed to be a comprehensive service program to help economically disadvantaged preschool children to be better prepared for formal education. The program includes health, educational, nutritional, and social services for children and their families. Although Head Start is administered by the Department of Health and Human Services and offers a variety of social services, it has come to be recognized primarily as an education program. Many children need this program, but it is not widely enough available.

Families at or below the federal poverty line are eligible for the Head Start program. The majority of programs are half-day, although some are for the entire day. Funding is shared by the federal and state governments, with daily administration done at the state level. Research over the past 20 years has found that early childhood education contributes toward improved performance in school, increased employability, decreased criminal activity, and better student self-confidence and self-esteem. In addition, programs such as Head Start are considered cost effective. An investment of $1 in preschool education results in a savings of $6 in money not spent on remedial and special education, as well as lower welfare costs, less crime, and higher worker productivity (Select Committee on Children, Youth, and Families, 1988c).

In spite of the positive results and cost effectiveness of Head Start, the program does not reach all eligible children. In fiscal year 1986, approximately 18 percent of three-to-five-year-old children living in low-income families were served in full-year Head Start programs (General Accounting Office, 1988). Thus, while the benefits of the program are clear, resources have not reached the majority of children in need.

Education for the Disadvantaged—Chapter 1.   Chapter 1 of the Education Consolidation and Improvement Act provides funds for compensatory education services for educationally disadvantaged children. The services include basic and remedial instruction, as well as guidance, transportation, and health services. The program is administered through the U.S. Department of Education and state and local educational agencies. Funding is based on the number of children living in poor communities and must be targeted for children who are the most educationally disadvantaged. Chapter 1 funding also provides services for handicapped, migrant, neglected, and delinquent children. Although Chapter 1 has been shown to help students perform better in school, only about half the students in need receive services (Children's Defense Fund, 1990).

Education for Handicapped Children.   Until passage of the Education for All Handicapped Children Act in 1975, many handicapped children were excluded from attending school. The act authorizes programs to provide quality education for handicapped children. All states participate in the State Grant program which assures every handicapped child aged three to twenty-one years old of receiving an appropriate free public education in the least restrictive educational environment. The act also includes funds for services to preschool handicapped children, deaf or blind children and youth, and related research and demonstration programs. This act was later amended, and the current legislation is the Individuals with Disabilities Education Act of 1990.

Services

Social Services Block Grant—Title XX.   In 1974, the Social Security Act was expanded to include Title XX, which created the Social Services Block Grant and consolidated federal assistance to states for social services into one grant. The overall purpose is to give states flexibility in using social service grants to aid people in achieving economic self-sufficiency and protection from abuse, neglect, and exploitation. Title XX funding covers numerous state programs including child protective services, child day care, home-based and community-based care, family planning services and information, referral, and counseling services. All funding for Title XX comes from the federal government and is administered by the Department of Health and Human Services. Since the early 1980s, Title XX appropriations have declined by 32 percent (Select Committee on Children, Youth, and Families, 1989).

Child Welfare.   As stated in the preface, although this book is not devoted to child welfare per se, many services and programs for children and adolescents funded by the federal government fall under this broad umbrella. Title IV-B of the Social Security Act authorizes a number of child welfare activities. Federal matching grants are available to states for child welfare services. The services are designed to provide for the welfare of children; help prevent neglect, abuse, exploitation, and delinquency of children; prevent the separation of children from their families; and in the cases of those who have been removed, help children to return to their families or find suitable care for those who cannot be returned. In addition, federal funds can be used for child welfare training, research, and program development. Most welfare funds that target children and adolescents are used by the states for foster care services, adoption subsidies, and child protection services.

Foster Care.   The foster care program is permanently authorized under Title IV-E of the Social Security Act. It is required for state participation in the AFDC program. The foster care program provides federal matching funds to states for payments made on behalf of AFDC-eligible children in foster care. The payments are intended to cover all the maintenance needs of these children. The program, linked to the child welfare services provided under Title IV-B, stresses preserving families and keeping children out of the foster care system. Although there are no requirements to report program participation, available data suggest that more than 450,000 children received foster care services in 1984 (General Accounting Office, 1988).

While the number of youth in foster care is increasing, the number of licensed foster homes is decreasing (Select Committee on Children, Youth, and Families, 1989). The purpose of foster care is to provide safe alternative environments for abused, neglected, or abandoned children. Although this has been accomplished to varying degrees, the foster care system has also been plagued with large numbers of youths and insufficient funding and resources. Unfortunately, while removing many children and adolescents from dangerous environments, the system has neglected the growth and self-sufficiency needs of the young people in its care (Sims, 1988). Permanency planning services mandated by Public Law 96-272 (42 USC 625, Sect. 425 (a) 1) include essentially three kinds of services: (1) home-based services, which include preventive, remedial, and reunification services (restoring children to their families, after they have been removed for a period of time); (2) adoption services—placing children in suitable homes; and (3) foster-care or institutional services, assuring that each child has some form of care (Kadushin & Martin, 1988). Permanency planning came about because large numbers of children and youths became lost in the child welfare system. For example, many would be moved from foster home to foster home without attention to the consequence of such disruptions for their well-being. Today, many child welfare agencies are working toward finding permanent living arrangements for such children.

Adoption Assistance.   The adoption assistance program of Public Law 96-272 is also permanently authorized under Title IV-E. Like foster care, it is a required part of the AFDC program. The program provides adoption assistance payments to parents who adopt AFDC-eligible children with special needs, including those who would not be placed without assistance payments because of specific situations or conditions, such as ethnic background, age, or mental or physical handicap. Before a child is placed, all efforts are made to return a child to his or her family or make a placement without assistance payments. The Department of Health and Human Services administers the adoption assistance program. As is true of the foster care system, the number of suitable adoptive homes, particularly for special needs and minority children, is less than the need.

Runaway Youth Program.   The runaway youth program provides federal funds for temporary residential care for runaway and homeless youth. The funding is allocated according to the population under 18 of each state and paid directly to the shelters. Grants may be used for providing shelter, general operating costs, counseling, and staff training. The program also sponsors a national toll-free hotline that provides crisis counseling and links youths to community resources. Although the transient nature of runaway and homeless youth makes it difficult to assess program participation, estimates for 1985 suggest that more than half a million young people used centers funded by the runaway youth program and the national hotline. The National Network of Runaway and Youth Services estimates that there are one to one and a half million runaways and that shelters and programs to serve them are insufficient (Subcommittee on Human Resources, 1988).

Juvenile Justice.   The Juvenile Justice and Delinquency Prevention Act, originally passed in 1974, stresses the prevention and treatment of juvenile delinquency. The act authorizes funding for state grants to develop programs to strengthen families, serve delinquent youth, and provide both alternatives to incarceration and special education. The general goal of the act is to improve the juvenile justice system, enhance state capability to prevent juvenile delinquency, and provide research and training in the prevention of juvenile delinquency. Although there have been increases in cases of juvenile delinquency and gang activity, funds for the Juvenile Justice and Delinquency Prevention Act were reduced by one-third between 1980 and 1988 (Select Committee on Children, Youth, and Families, 1989).

PROGRAM EFFECTIVENESS—IS THE SAFETY NET SECURE?

The list of programs that involve children and youth appears to be quite comprehensive. All basic needs are met, childern with special needs are addressed, and some programs take a preventive approach. However, the existence of these programs does not necessarily guarantee that the needs of children and their families are adequately being met. The 1980s witnessed a period of retrenchment in resources and federal involvement in caring for children. This posture had severe effects on the well being of children. For those who work in child welfare and related social services, the shrinkage of programs and resources had serious implications.

Unique Concerns of Youth—Inadequate Response

A number of social problems are unique to young people. Education is a major guarantee of economic self-sufficiency in our society. The overall school drop-out rate in this country is almost 14 percent, while in some inner-city schools the rate is as high as 50 percent (General Accounting Office, 1987). Without a high school diploma, a young person is unlikely to find a job that pays enough to keep him or her out of poverty. Unemployment is particularly severe for youth. According to Bureau of Labor Statistics, the overall unemployment rate for youth aged 16 to 19 was 16.9 percent in 1987, compared with 6.2 percent for adults. For minority youth the rate was even higher—more than 34 percent. These statistics suggest that programs that aid in education and employment training are extremely valuable for youth. However, programs such as Job Corps and Summer Youth Employment have not fared well. Job Corps serves about 3 percent of those officially unemployed, and Summer Youth Employment serves even fewer youths (Children's Defense Fund, 1988).

A Changing Society

Although life for youth and their families today is very different than it was 15 or 20 years ago, many of our social programs and policies are products of that time. In order to meet the social welfare needs of children in the 1990s, we must examine current trends and consider the changing nature of our society.

The Economic Policy Institute reports that "in 1987, after five years of [economic] recovery, the average working American appears to be worse off economically than he or she was at the peak of the last business cycle" (Mishel & Simon, 1988, p. iii). The reasons are numerous.

The composition and distribution of jobs in the economy have shifted. While new jobs have been created, the rate is slower than it was during other growth periods, and the vast majority of new jobs, 85 percent, have been in the lowest-paying service industries (Mishel & Simon, 1988). So, while it is true that there are more new jobs, they do not pay enough, nor do they provide adequate benefits such as health coverage.

Income inequality, the difference between the earnings of the wealthiest and those of the poorest, is at its widest point in 40 years (Select Committee of Children, Youth, & Families, 1988b). In 1987, the wealthiest 20 percent received almost 44 percent of national family income, while the lowest 20 percent received only 4.6 percent (Bureau of the Census, 1989).

The relationship between economic decline and social disorder has helped create what has been called the rapidly growing "underclass"—concentrated areas of poverty where there are high proportions of high school dropouts, unemployed working-age young men, welfare households, and households headed by single women. Estimates in 1980 placed the underclass population at 2.5 million, most of them livng in urban areas (Urban Institute, 1987). The growing underclass and the changing inner city have grave consequences for all of society.

RESPONSIBILITIES AND RECOMMENDATIONS

Understanding the System

Social welfare practitioners, especially those working with children and their families, must have a thorough understanding of the welfare system and its policies and programs. In addition to limited resources, ineffective programs, and the barriers to education and employment, being poor and being on welfare imposes a terrible psychological weight. For those who work with low-income people, it is necessary to see the social welfare system through their eyes. The social welfare practitioner can learn a great deal from spending part of a day sitting in the waiting room of a public aid office or joining a required workfare "class," or staying overnight in a shelter for the homeless. While this is not the same as being *dependent* on these services, it can help the practitioner to begin to understand what it is like to be a part of the welfare system.

For children growing up in this system, it becomes their frame of reference. It affects their outlook on life, their response to those in authority, and their expectations of the system. Insights into the system are crucial in being able to best serve poor children and youth. Without understanding the environment and system in which poor children live, the social service practitioner cannot provide the most appropriate services. Social workers must also be aware of the barriers that prevent vulnerable populations from participating in the social and economic aspects of society. With an ecological and transactional perspective, it is possible to think in terms of programs that are preventive in nature and respond to the causes of problems, not only to symptoms. This perspective requires becoming familiar with the specifics of programs and taking opportunities to witness the programs firsthand from the recipient's perspective. It also requires mapping out problems from a macroperspective—what are all the systems, groups, and individuals that are involved and how are they related?

Developing a Proactive and Preventive Approach to the Social Needs of Children and Adolescents

To meet the challenge of developing a successful policy program for serving children and youth in need, an agenda for action must be established. It should include

1. Support and expansion of programs that work, particularly those that use a preventive approach.
2. Emphasis on programs that provide parents with sufficient resources and supports to care for their own children adequately.
3. Adequate support to plan for permanent placement of children as a policy priority on each level of government, using the media and other ways to increase public awareness;
4. Lobbying of policy makers and advocacy for needed services through the legislative arena.
5. Encouragement of self-advocacy by nurturing community organization and political involvement on the part of disenfranchised and vulnerable groups.

In addition to building an individual and professional awareness of youth service needs, programs, and policies, social service practitioners must stay alert to the changes in social structure and the activities in government that affect the social well-being of children and their families.

Social work practitioners must play a role in the formulation of policies and programs. They must inform decision makers of gaps in services, share their observations about interventions and programs that appear to be most effective, become advocates in state and national legislative discussions through professional associations and other relevant groups, and provide testimony at hearings on public policy that have impact on groups at risk. Practitioners can affect policies, but this requires them to develop skills in effective communication (e.g., how to write letters and memos), organization, mobilization (e.g., bringing forces together), and comprehension of the legislative process. Before one can have any impact on policy making, one must learn how to analyze both policies themselves and the process whereby they are formulated.

SUMMARY

This chapter provides a brief overview of important child and adolescent welfare policies and programs. In social work practice, both clients and practitioners are affected by such policies and programs. In Chapter 1 a transactional framework is suggested for assessing and intervening on behalf of children and adolescents that takes into account such policies and places them on the environmental side of the interface. Social workers have the challenge of implementing policies, as well as evaluating their degree of successfulness in meeting the clients needs. Policies and programs shape not only what practitioners do but also the nature of the services they provide.

QUESTIONS FOR DISCUSSION

1. What is the difference between a residual approach to work with children and families and an institutional approach? Which is preferable?
2. When is it appropriate for the state or federal government to intervene into the affairs of families?
3. What should be the role of social work in the intervention process?
4. In what areas of child welfare is the policy arena lacking in services? What service priorities should there be?
5. On the basis of changing social and demographic variables, where should social policy for children and adolescents be directed in the future?
6. How can the political and policy position of children be changed?
7. What can social workers do to contribute to the improvement of social policy for children and adolescents?
8. What are the strengths and weaknesses of current programs for children, adolescents, and families? How might they be improved to better serve the needs of the young and their families?

ADDITIONAL READINGS

Brieland, D., Costin, L. B., & Atherton, C. R. (1985). *Contemporary social work,* 3rd ed., Chapter 10. New York: McGraw-Hill.

Costin, L. B., Bell, C. J., & Downs, S. W. (1991). *Child welfare: Policies and practice.* White Plains, N.Y.: Longman.

Edelman, M. W. (1992). *The measure of our success.* Boston: Beacon Press.

Edleman, M. W. (1987). *Families in peril.* Boston: Harvard University Press.

Hayes, C. D., ed. (1982). *Making policies for children: A study of the federal process.* Washington, D.C.: National Academy Press.

Johnson, L. C., & Schwartz, C. L. (1988). *Social welfare: A response to human need,* Chapter 8. Boston: Allyn and Bacon, Inc.

Kadushin, A. (1987). Child welfare services. *Encyclopedia of Social Work,* pp. 265–275. Silver Spring, MD: National Association of Social Workers.

Kimmich, M. H. (1985). *America's children, who cares?* Washington, D.C.: Urban Institute Press.

Pecora, P. J., Whitaker, J. R., & MaLuccio, A. N. (1992). *The child welfare challenge.* New York: Aldine De Gruyter.

Richan, W. C. (1988). *Beyond altruism,* Chapter 10. New York: Haworth Press.

Zigler, E., Kagan, S. L., & Klugman, E., eds. (1983). *Children, families, and government: Perspectives on American social policy.* Cambridge: Cambridge University Press.

REFERENCES

Abramovitz, M. (1988). *Regulating the lives of women.* Boston: South End Press.

Axinn, J. & Levin, H. (1992). *Social welfare: A history of the American response to need* (3rd ed.). White Plains, N.Y.: Longman Publishing Group.

Budget of the United States Government, FY 1994. (1993). Washington, D.C.: U.S. Government Printing Office.

Bureau of the Census. (1989). *Money income and poverty status in the U.S.: 1988.* Current Population Reports, P-60, Number 166. Washington, D.C.: Department of Commerce.

Bureau of the Census. (1993). *Poverty in the U.S.: 1992.* Current Population Reports, P-60, Number 185. Washington, D.C.: Department of Commerce.

Center on Budget & Policy Priorities. (1988). *Holes in the safety net.* Washington, D.C.: The Center.

Children's Defense Fund. (1992). *The state of America's children.* Washington, D.C.: The Fund.

Children's Defense Fund. (1990). *The nation's investment in children.* Washington, D.C.: The Fund.

Children's Defense Fund. (1988). *A children's defense budget: FY 1989.* Washington, D.C.: The Fund.

Congressional Budget Office. (1988). *The economic and budget outlook: An update.* Washington, D.C.: Congress of the United States.

Congressional Research Service. (1988). *Medicaid source book: Background data and analysis.* Committee print 100-AA. Washington, D.C.: U.S. Government Printing Office.

Congressional Research Service. (1987). *Federal programs affecting children.* Washington, D.C.: Library of Congress.

General Accounting Office. (1988). *Children's programs*. Washington, D.C.: U.S. Government Printing Office.

General Accounting Office. (1987). *School dropouts*. Washington, D.C.: U.S. Government Printing Office.

General Accounting Office. (1985). *Federal benefit programs: A profile*. Washington, D.C.: U.S. Government Printing Office.

Kadushin, A., & Martin, J. (1988). *Child welfare services*. New York: Macmillan.

Katz, M. B. (1986). *In the shadow of the poorhouse*. New York: Basic Books.

Levitan, S. A., & Shapiro, I. (1987). *Working but poor*. Baltimore: Johns Hopkins University Press.

McBarnette, L. (1988). Women and poverty: A demographic overview. In C.A. Perales & L.S. Young, eds., *Too little, too late*, pp. 55–82. New York: Harrington Park Press.

Miller, D. C. (1989). Poor women and work programs: Back to the future. *Affilia* 4 (1): 9–22.

Mishel, L., and Simon, J. (1988). *The state of working America*. Washington, D.C.: Economic Policy Institute.

Moroney, R. M. (1986). *Shared responsibility: Families and social policy*. New York: Aldine De Gruyter.

Pearce, D. (1978). The feminization of poverty: Women, work and welfare. *Urban and Social Change Review* 11 (1–2): 28–36.

Pizzo, P. (1983). Slouching toward Bethlehem: American federal policy perspectives on children and their families. In E. F. Zigler, S. L. Kagan, & E. Klugman, eds., *Children, families, and government*, pp. 10–32. Cambridge: Cambridge University Press.

Schorr, L. B. (1988). *Within our reach*. New York: Doubleday Anchor Press.

Segal, E.A. (1991), The juvenlization of poverty in the 1980s. *Social Work* 36 (5): 454–457.

Segal, E. A. (1989). Welfare reform: help for poor women and children? *Affilia* 4 (3): 42–50.

Select Committee on Children, Youth, & Families. (1989). *Children and families: Key trends in the 1980s*. Washington, D.C.: U.S. Government Printing Office.

Select Committee on Children, Youth, & Families. (1988a). *Children and families in poverty: The struggle to survive*. Washington, D.C.: U.S. Government Printing Office.

Select Committee on Children, Youth, & Families. (1988b). *A domestic priority: Overcoming family poverty in America*. Washington, D.C.: U.S. Government Printing Office.

Select Committee on Children, Youth, & Families. (1988c). *Opportunities for success: Cost effective programs for children*. Washington, D.C.: U.S. Government Printing Office.

Sidel, R. (1986). *Women and children last*. New York: Penguin Books.

Sims, A. R. (1988). Independent living services for youths in foster care. *Social Work* 33 (6): 539–542.

Social Security bulletin: Annual statistical supplement, 1992. (1992). Washington, D.C.: Social Security Administration.

Subcommittee on Human Resources. (1988). *Reauthorization of the Juvenile Justice and Delinquency Prevention Act: Runaway and homeless youth*. No. 100-72. Washington, D.C.: U.S. Government Printing Office.

Subcommittee on Social Security & Family Policy. (1988). *Welfare: reform or replacement?* S. Hrg. 100-395. Washington, D.C.: U.S. Government Printing Office.

Urban Institute. (1987). *Poverty and the underclass*. Reprinted in Task Force on Income Security. *Budgetary review of income security programs*. Washington, D.C.: U.S. Government Printing Office.

U.S. Conference of Mayors. (1988). *A status report on children in America's cities*. Washington, D.C.: The Conference.

Wilensky, H. and Lebeaux, C. (1958). *Industrial society and social welfare*. New York: Russell Sage Foundation.

Wilson, G. (1985). The juvenilization of poverty. *Public Administration Review* 45 (6): 880–884.

Zelizer, V. A. (1985). *Pricing the priceless child*. New York: Basic Books.

chapter 5

Family and Cultural Contributors to Emotional and Behavioral Problems

In 1979 the U.S. Department of Health and Human Services issued a report on the status of children, youth, and families (Calhoun, Grotberg, & Rackley 1979), which documented that the structure of the family in America was changing, mainly because of soaring divorce rates, alternative lifestyles, and economic upheaval. Since this report was published, new knowledge and terms that characterize the American family have crept into the discussion—the feminization and juvenilization of poverty (U.S. Department of Health and Human Services, 1993)—indicating that more women and children are poorer today than they were two decades ago. Unfortunately, social services have simultaneously undergone major reduction at a time when families are so vulnerable and needy. Almost all data support the observation that a child's future and success depend heavily on the educational attainments economic status of his or her family (Banchi, 1984). Furthermore, the economic situation of a child is a reflection of family income. Children and adolescents who live in households headed by women and those who are black or of Hispanic origin, disproportionately live in poverty.

This chapter is devoted to family and cultural factors (attributed to institutional racism) that serve as barriers to healthy social functioning and all too often produce psychological problems and maladaptive behaviors in children and adolescents. Identifying characteristics of children and youth born into life situations that offer them little if any opportunity for success and healthy social functioning become readily apparent, as do the ways the larger society discriminates against these families.

Critical terms, essential for understanding the developmental difficulties associated with these factors include—stress, coping, risk, vulnerability, and protective factors. Consistent with the transactional framework, stressors can be considered as environmental inadequacies (e.g., the lack of food, shelter, medical care) that produce a child or adolescent at risk or vulnerable to failure or poor social or psychological functioning. This is discussed more fully in Chapter 1. Coping refers to those skills and behaviors a child or adolescent calls upon to influence and control his or her environment. Risk is defined as the probability that a child or adolescent will develop a specific problem or disorder. Protective factors are conditions that act to prevent or serve to minimize the consequences of the risk factors.

THE ROLE OF FAMILY IN DEVELOPMENT OF CHILDREN

Family can be either the context in which growth and positive social functioning develops or a context in which a child encounters little or no emotional and physical support and no opportunity to develop in a meaningful way. Secure attachment to a parental figure is fundamental for the development of future relationships.

Although one of the many tasks of the family is to produce autonomous children, culture and circumstance (e.g., poverty, mental illness, divorce, failure to marry, racism, pressures of unemployment) influence both family structure and family functioning (Parker, 1983). With the increasing number of female-headed households, it is necessary to ask how the absence of a male figure affects the development and social functioning of children. Data suggest that the problems faced by single women and their children may be a reflection of poverty and stress, not of psychiatric disorder or poor functioning on their part (Weissman, Leaf, & Bruce, 1987). One study reported that the bond between father and daughter, for example, adds a dimension of nurturing, representing the outside world and assisting in the socialization of the daughter (Dickman, 1986). The question then becomes, How does a social work practitioner intervene after a divorce to maximize contact between a father (or a similar figure) and daughter or a mother (or a similar figure) and son? Although divorce is indeed stressful and contact between children and noncustodial parents is important for the child's development, stressors can be minimized through the use of planful and appropriate intervention. However, to select an appropriate intervention from the wealth of options, a practitioner must be familiar with the literature and research on the topic and the client or group he or she is serving.

Postdivorce family functioning rather than family structure influences children's adjustment. It is suggested that a child's adjustment to divorce should be viewed as a developmental process rather than a single event (Rassmussen, 1987). Research is needed to focus on the ways in which the single-parent family—its structure and psychological functioning—can be affected to mediate the negative consequences of divorce.

Parental disturbance or mental illness can also set children and adolescents up for a variety of developmental risks and maladaptive behaviors. Substance abuse (e.g., cocaine and the attendant problem of AIDS babies), depression, and other psychological disturbances found in the parent or parenting system can have devastating consequences. Kashani et al. (1982) found that many delinquent adolescent boys had depressed parents. Recent estimates indicate that each year over one million children experience some form of maltreatment, an estimated 6.6 million children under age 18 have an alcoholic parent, adolescent girls between 15 and 19 bear more than three million babies a year, and girls under age 14 bear an additional 10,800 children.

In terms of the internal family dynamics, Daniels, Dunn, Furstenberg, and Plomin (1984) found that though siblings may live within the same family environment, each has a different experience within that environment. Within the family, environmental differences are related to differences in development between siblings. The sibling who is psychologically better adjusted (as reported by parent, peers, siblings, and teachers) also experiences more maternal closeness, more peer friendliness, more family decision making, and more parental chore expectations than other siblings in the same family. Thus the family environment is not homogeneous when we explore correlations between maternal affection and developmental outcome of a child in a family.

The emotional climate of the family has been shown to play an important role in the mental health and well-being of infants, children, and adolescents. For example, in the development of schizophrenia and other psychiatric disorders, the expression of high levels of parental emotion, such as hostility and critical comments directed at those within a family diagnosed as schizophrenic or depressed (in this case children or adolescents recovering from an emotional problem) caused relapses within both groups (Vaughn & Leff, 1976).

Another study (Garbarino, Sebes, & Schellenbach, 1984) investigated families at risk for destructive parent–child relations in adolescence. It was found that high-risk families were characterized by a formidable set of contributors to problems for adolescents (e.g., chronic internalized development problems, positive values and attitudes concerning coercion, and chronically enmeshed interpersonal system). Low-risk families in the same study were characterized by a flexible connected family system, a disavowal of coercion, and a less punishing style of parenting. These researchers concluded that the development of psychopathology in adolescence depends in a large measure on the context established by the family systems.

Frequently, because of the lack of economic resources, some families find it difficult to secure resources (e.g., child care, health services, mental health services) to assist them in nurturing and coping. The availability of social services based on a sliding fee for this particular group is frequently limited.

Socio-Cultural Factors

As stated earlier, race and ethnic identity often interact with poverty. Also, society reacts differently to members of some racial or ethnic minorities, (e.g., African Americans and Hispanics). A disappropriate number of these minority families and children are poor. Children born to these racial and ethnic families are frequently both impoverished and constrained socially and psychologically by the limited resources in their environments. Institutional racism and sexism restrict the available opportunities.

The United States continues to become more and more diverse in ethnic and racial composition. In the past, a cultural-deficit model was advocated to "fix" and help some minorities "fit" into the prevailing societal norms. Today, a bicultural view is advocated (de Anda, 1984). These children and their families are encouraged to function in two environments—their own cultures and that of the mainstream society. It is consistent with a transactional framework that the interactions between individuals (in this case the child and family) and the environment may be dysfunctional. Furthermore, many families want to retain their unique cultural distinctions while they function in the mainstream society. These individuals could be considered bicultural. According to de Anda, at least six factors affect the degree to which a member of an ethnic or racial group can or is likely to become bicultural:

1. The degree of overlap or commonality between the two cultures (e.g., norms, values, and beliefs).
2. The availability of cultural translators, mediators, and models.
3. The availability and type of corrective feedback to clarify what is appropriate behavior and in which context.
4. The conceptual style and problem-solving approach of the racial/ ethnic group, the more consistent it is with the majority's style, the more likely it is that the person will become bicultural. For example, in one study it was found that native American children understand their environment through intuitive, visual, and pictorial means, while success and achievement in the school is dependent on auditory processing, abstract reasoning, and language skills. Also, these children are severely disadvantaged due to racism and poverty and show higher rates of suicide, alcoholism, and alienation.
5. The degree of bilingualism. In other words the minority person who becomes proficient in the language of the majority is more likely to become a bicultural individual.
6. The dissimilarity of physical appearance between individuals in the majority and minority groups. This can be an obstacle to the process of bicultural socialization. (1984, p. 102)

The cultural and ethnic backgrounds of children have much to do with how they view their futures and the opportunities that appear to be available to them. If children see the adult members of their racial or ethnic group entrapped by poverty, isolated by racism, lacking adequate education, and holding few (if any) dreams for the future, their goals and aspirations will be adversely affected. When they compare themselves with a peer reference group of the majority, they are likely to internalize the differences and develop poor self-esteem and negative outlooks on life. Logan (1981) argues present theories of child development give little attention to the role of culture on development. In fact, they tend to minimize this dimension. For example, blacks experience a variety of restrictions, frustrations, and conflicting messages that can affect the quality of their emotional and psychological functioning from birth to death. In practice, the adaptations and behavior accommodations of minorities are often labeled deviant and pathological.

Children develop ethnic awareness, self-identification, and attitudes early in life; as they grow and their world widens, cultural factors play a more important role in their socialization. This is especially true for those minority children who become aware that they occupy lower status, have less power, and enjoy fewer economic resources than their nonminority peers (Phinney & Roternman, 1987). For example, black children are at risk because of structural factors in society that hinder their optimal development. They face racial prejudice in the schools, and their parents face it in their employment. Discrimination in the workplace leads to economic dependency for many black families. Because of their color, blacks stand out more vividly within white society—it is more difficult for them to blend in. Changing their name, customs, or religious affiliation will not affect their assimilation.

The critical developmental task of all minority children seems to be the acquisition and internalization of positive identity formation in a society that frequently rejects their characteristics (color, physical features, etc.). Because of these factors, these children are particularly at risk. Identity is formed through a series of exchanges between children and the various environments in which they function. Thus identity is intimately related to the responses individuals elicit from the socializing agents within their immediate environments. If the white majority rejects a black minority, it is bound to experience devastating consequences. Moreover, the white majority frequently engages in behavior that throws all blacks into one large group, the assumption being that all blacks are alike—the assumption of cultural homogeneity founded on racist beliefs.

Social workers assessing children must take into account their families' racial and cultural variations, how society responds to them, and how these variations affect functioning and development. Variations should not be equated with deviant or different behavior—such terms have negative implications. A part of this assessment must take into account the strengths of these families and children and their interactions with larger systems. This suggestion fits into current research trends as listed by Lask & Lask (1981):

Characteristics of Vulnerable Children and Adolescents*

Environmental Factors
1. The family
   Emotional bonds and relations
   Maternal deprivation and employment

---

* From *Child Psychiatry and Social Work* by Judith Lask and Bryan Lask, Copyright © 1981. Reprinted with the permission of Tavistock Publications, New York.

    Child-rearing practices
    Provision of life experiences
    Communication patterns
    Family composition
    Parental disturbance
    Parental family history
    One-parent family
    Adoption
    Deprivation

2. Sociocultural
    Poverty
    Racial and ethnic background
    Urban versus rural
    Housing
    Peer groups
    Effects of schooling

3. Biological factors
    Genetics
    Prenatal and postnatal care
    Child's physical condition
    Sex difference
    Temperament characteristics

Three trends that are receiving considerable attention by researchers include the increasing emphasis on the concept of interaction within families, concern with the larger context within which families must function (societal), and the biological and genetic determinants of development (e.g., human social attachments, sex-role identity, alcoholism).

    The following case illustration depicts a Hispanic boy who lives in poverty. It accentuates some of the major points raised in both this chapter and Chapter 4. Though there is a grave lack of health care services, informal supports to draw upon in a time of crisis, and preschool programming, the strengths within this family are very evident. There is an exchange of roles and jobs to maintain the family unit. The family draws upon the church, and there is the desire for self-sufficiency.

CASE ILLUSTRATION—JUAN

Juan is a 12-year-old Hispanic boy who lives in one of the poorest communities in the United States. His father and mother have moved the family of six children several times in search of farm work. The father has an eleventh-grade education; and the mother, several years younger than the father, has been hospitalized several times for physical and emotional fatigue. The children have not had consistent schooling or peer relationships. Spanish is almost always spoken within the home. There are few family members or friends to call upon when the mother has been hospitalized. Juan has frequently acted as the primary spokesperson and caretaker for the younger children.

The family lives in a small trailer, surrounded by other Hispanic families who live in an essentially poverty-stricken environment. The children have had little if any consistent health care services, and one of them appears to be suffering from a speech delay. One child clings to the mother and becomes very tearful when separated from her. The children have had no preschool experience, and they tend to isolate themselves from other children.

When visiting the family, one finds a number of strengths: each family member has a specific job to perform that maintains the family unit; each freely shares with the others; periodically they pray together and attend church when one is available; and the family is proud of its independence: "We are not on welfare."

However, Juan's teacher recently reported that he had few friends in school and appeared to be more concerned about other matters. His homework was consistently late, and he was somewhat inattentive in class. Juan's parents immediately expressed displeasure with the report and reprimanded him. Juan felt very hurt and resented his teacher for invading his privacy. He felt that she did not understand. He was insulted that she had implied that he was irresponsible.

SUMMARY

His or her family, the resources available to it, and its unique characteristics, such as being persons of color or belonging to a particular ethnic minority, can limit opportunity and prevent optimal growth and development for the child or adolescent. Sometimes practitioners inadvertently blame victims for their situations. This chapter is intended to elevate awareness of cultural and family conditions over which clients have little, if any, control.

QUESTIONS FOR DISCUSSION

1. Give some examples of ways race and ethnic identity variables affect child and adolescent development.
2. What challenges does the bicultural orientation hold for our work with racially different children and adolescents? Are these challenges realistic?
3. Identify and study an ethnic or racial minority group and discuss its strengths. How might these strengths be misunderstood and taken as weaknesses when viewed by the majority?
4. If you were the practitioner in the case of Juan, what would your course of action be and why? If the situation continues, how might Juan be affected?
5. How can a practitioner maximize the life options for vulnerable populations such as children born into poverty and female-headed households?

6. What roles can and should social workers play in terms of working toward the elimination of institutional racism and sexism to enhance the quality of life for vulnerable groups of children or adolescents and their families?

ADDITIONAL READINGS

Clark, J. (1983). *Family life and school achievement: Why poor black children succeed or fail.* Chicago: University of Chicago Press.

Comer, J., & Hill, H. (1985). Social policy and the mental health of black children. *Journal of the American Academy of Child Psychiatry* 24: 175–181.

Derezotes, D., & Snowden, L. (1990). Cultural factors in the intervention of child maltreatment. *Child and Adolescent Social Work Journal* 7: 161–175.

Devore, W., & Schlesinger, E. (1981). *Ethnic-sensitive social work practice.* St. Louis: Mosby.

Dunn, B. (1993). Growing up with a psychotic mother: A retrospective study. *American Journal of Orthopsychiatry* 63(2): 177–189.

Gardner, R. (1991). *Psychotherapy with children of divorce.* Northvale, N.J.: Jaronson.

Kim, B. (1973). Asian-Americas: No model minority. *Social Work* 18 (March) 44–54.

Masten, A., Miliotis, D., Graham-Berman, S, & Ramirez, M. (1993). Children in homeless families: Risks to mental health and development. *Journal of Consulting and Clinical Psychology* 61(2): 335–343.

McLeod, J., & Shanahan, M. (1993). Poverty, parenting, and children's mental health. *American Sociological Review* 58(3): 351–366.

Pinderhughes, E. (1989). *Understanding race, ethnicity, and power: The key to efficacy in clinical practice.* New York: Free Press.

Sotomayer, M. (1977). Language, culture and ethnicity in the developing self-concept. *Social Casework* 58: 316–322.

Mendes, H. (1977). Counter-transference and counter-culture clients. *Social Casework* 58: (March): 159–163.

Padilla, A. (1981). Pluralistic counseling and psychotherapy for Hispanic Americans. In Marsella A., & P. Pedersen, eds., *Cross-cultural counseling and psychotherapy.* New York: Pergamon Press.

Zuniga-Martinez, M. (1988). Chicano self-concept: A practice stance. In Jacobs, C., & D. Boules, eds., *Ethnicity and race: Critical concepts in social work.* Washington, D.C.: National Association of Social Workers.

REFERENCES

Banchi, S. (1984). Children's progress through school: A research note. *Sociology of Education* 57: 184–192.

Calhoun, J., Grotberg, E., & Rackley, W. (1979). *The status of children, youth and families—1979.* Washington, D.C.: U.S. Dept. of Health and Human Services.

Daniels, D., Dunn, J., Furstenberg, F., & Plomin, R. (1984). Environmental differences with the family and adjustment differences within pairs of adolescent siblings. *Child Development* 56: 764–774.

de Anda, D. (1984). Bicultural socialization: Factors affecting the minority experience. *Social Work* 29: 101–107.

Dickman, D. (1986). The father/daughter bond. *Medical Aspects of Human Sexuality* 20: 80-84.

Garbarino, J., Sebes, J., & Schellenbach, C. (1984). Families at risk for destructive parent-child relations in adolescence. *Child Development* 55: 174-183.

Kashani, J., et al. (1982). Depression in diagnostic subtypes of delinquent boys. *Adolescence* 17: 943-949.

Lask, J., & Lask, B. (1981). *Child psychiatry and social work.* London: Tavistock.

Logan, S. L. (1981). Race, identity, and black children: A developmental perspective. *Social Casework* 62: 47-65.

Meyers, C. (1970). *Social work practice.* New York: Free Press.

Parker, G. (1983). Fathers, peers and other family influences on the socialization of the child. *Australian Journal of Sex, Marriage, and Family* 4: 5-13.

Phinney, J., & Rotherman, M. (1987). *Children's ethnic socialization.* Newbury Park, Calif.: Sage.

Rasmussen, J. (1987). The custodial parent-child relationship as a mediating factor in the effects of divorce on children, pp. 1-53. Dissertation, Biola University, City California.

U.S. Department of Health & Human Services (1993). *Child mental health in the 1990s: Curricula for graduate and undergraduate professional education.* Rockville, Md.: The Department of Health and Human Services.

Vaughn, C., & Leff, J. (1976). The measurement of expressed emotion in the families of psychiatric patients. *British Journal of Social & Clinical Psychology* 15: 157-165.

part III

Groups of Children and Adolescents at Risk

This part is devoted to emotional disturbance, abuse and neglect, school failure, sexuality, and substance abuse within childhood and adolescence. Although many at-risk groups could be addressed here (e.g., gang behavior, cocaine babies, and the like), a thorough discussion of each would be beyond the scope of any book.

What should become clear is that problems in social and emotional functioning among children and adolescents can often be attributed to adverse environmental conditions in society, the community, and their families (broadly defined).

Interventions found to be effective in development are presented here. The authors have culled these from the literature on remedial and preventive interventions. Furthermore, interventions that target the individual, the family, groups, and the community are also highlighted. Implicit in this part is the notion that multiinterventions are frequently required to achieve goals and that success often requires targeting the different environments and significant others who impinge on the child or adolescent.

chapter 6

Emotional Problems of Children and Adolescents

Nora Gustavsson

Some of the difficulty in designing and implementing effective interventions with children and adolescents is due, in part, to the confusing concept of childhood. The term encompasses a large group with diverse abilities. A child is legally defined as anyone under the age of majority, usually 18 years. The needs and potential problems of the infant differ from those of the preschool-age child and the adolescent. A four-month-old who does not play well with peers, a 14-month-old who is not toilet trained, a five-year-old with nightmares, and a sixteen-year-old who cannot do division or multiplication, are not suffering from pathological conditions. In order to determine the existence of a problem, it is necessary to know what is normal. Deviations from what is considered normal provide a basis for concern and justify further investigation. Clinical work with children and adolescents requires a knowledge base that includes, but is not limited to, a developmental understanding of their emotional, social, biological, and cognitive characteristics and capacities.

A substantial minority of America's young people suffer from emotional disturbances. A recent survey of the mental health needs of those under 18 years of age indicated that 12 to 15 percent of this population need mental health treatment but fewer than 30 percent of that number are receiving treatment. In raw numbers, at least four million children who need treatment are not receiving it (Office of Technology Assessment, 1986). Some studies indicate that although fewer than 4 percent of the child population is psychotic or severely disturbed, another 15 to 20 percent suffer emotional disturbances, usually of a transitory nature (Wood & Zabel, 1978).

CLASSIFYING CHILDHOOD DISTURBANCES

Many of the terms used to describe children with emotional and behavioral problems are ambiguous, focusing on internal processes and ignoring the role of environmental factors. The lack of exact and universally accepted definitions of constructs, such as schizophrenia, mental illness, conduct disorder, and emotional disturbance, adds to the challenge of developing nosology. In spite of the difficulties of definition, children and adolescents are perceived by the adults in their environments to suffer from emotional and behavioral problems. As stated in Chapter 1, those individuals who comprise the significant environment in which a child functions can also cause and reinforce problematic behaviors and emotional illness. Infants and young children do not refer themselves to mental health facilities. Therefore, part of the definition of emotional disturbance in children involves an environmental dimension. If the adults caring for a child do not recognize that the child's behaviors are troublesome, the child is not referred for evaluation. Many factors influence the definition of emotional disturbance. The age, sex, socioeconomic status (SES), race, and attitudes of family, friends, and teachers play a vital role in the definition process. Behaviors that are annoying or upsetting, such as fire setting, encopresis, chemical dependency, or cruelty to younger children and animals, which are likely to attract adult interest, are classified as externalized behaviors. Behaviors that do not annoy, such as passivity, shyness, or withdrawal, however, which can be ignored, are classified as internalized behaviors. Many children who experience considerable internal emotional distress are not referred for evaluation.

Criteria for Evaluation

Some of the criteria used to define adult disorders have been applied to children and adolescents, including frequency, duration, and intensity of the distressing behavior. For example, although crying is a common behavior for children, long periods of intense sobbing or cases of children who appear to be sad for extended periods of time should alert the adults in the young person's life to the possible need for evaluation. Practitioners should be cautious when applying criteria used to define adult disorders to children and adolescents. In Chapter 2 it is stated that children and adolescents progress through specific stages of development. They are not adults, and they must be viewed accordingly.

The nature of childhood adds additional criteria to the evaluation process. Since childhood is a time of rapid, occasionally nonlinear development, some problems experienced by children may be transitory. On occasion, even "normal" children display behaviors, such as fighting with siblings and peers, that are troublesome to adults (Weiner, 1982). These behaviors do not necessarily predict later adjustment problems. The transitory nature of some childhood problem behaviors, such as pica or specific fears, is well known. There are other sets of problem behaviors, however, that do appear to be predictable. Mental retardation, psychotic disorders, long periods of sadness, and antisocial behavior tend to be long-lasting disorders requiring interventions (Gelfand, Jenson, & Drew, 1982; Robins & Price, 1991; White, Moffitt, Earls, Robins & Silva, 1990). Classifying and defining these more serious behavioral and emotional problems have been fraught with difficulty.

Multiaxial Classification Schemes

Intensive efforts to define disorders in young people and develop classification schemes appropriate for them are a relatively new development. In 1975 the World Health Organization developed a multiaxial taxonomy for disorders in children. Four axes were identified in an attempt to deal with the confusion that results when a child is psychiatrically disturbed, mentally retarded, or suffering from a physically disabling condition such as epilepsy. The four axes are psychiatric syndromes, intellectual level, biological factors, and psychosocial influences. The last two axes are similar to axes III and IV of the 1987 *Diagnostic and Statistical Manual of Mental Disorders,* Third Edition Revised (American Psychiatric Association, 1987). Three years later, a fifth axis was added for developmental delays (World Health Organization, 1978). There are a number of advantages to this multiaxial classification scheme. Children are evaluated across five important dimensions. By including a "no abnormality" code, professionals are not forced to assign labels in instances where there is little evidence of an abnormality. The most widely used taxonomic paradigm is the Diagnostic and Statistical Manual (DSM) of the American Psychiatric Association. The first edition of the DSM was published in 1952. Only two categories were reserved exclusively for children. The second edition added six behavior disorders for children and adolescents (American Psychiatric Association, 1968). The third edition (DSM III), a dramatic departure from earlier editions, included more disorders of children and adolescents and introduced the use of axes (American Psychiatric Association, 1980). The third edition revised (DSM III-R) included some minor changes in categories affecting children (American Psychiatric Association, 1987).

The clarity of diagnostic categories and their suitability to distinguish among clusters of problem behaviors remains problematic. One study reported that many children who met the criteria for oppositional disorder also met the criteria for conduct disorder and attention deficit disorder (Costello, Edelbrock, Dulcan, Kalas, & Kloric, 1984). In another study, children meeting the criteria for depressive disorders (another area of controversy discussed later in this chapter) also met the criteria for attention deficit disorder, anorexia nervosa, and conduct disorders (Carlson & Cantwell, 1980). The apparent inability of DSM III-R to discriminate among some disorders raises serious challenges to the validity of the categories.

One of the major obstacles to the competent use of DSM III-R is a direct result of the medical model upon which the taxonomy is based. For example, axis III is concerned with physical or biological conditions. Nonmedical users of DSM III-R are unable to make competent diagnoses of physical conditions. This can be remedied, in part, by requiring a physical examination of the child to identify or rule out physical conditions or deferring diagnosis on this axis. In spite of the grave questions about the validity of DSM III-R for use with children, it remains a major taxonomic paradigm, used in a variety of settings, especially mental health settings. Thus social workers need to be familiar with DSM III-R and keep in mind its limitations. Practitioners who bring a transactional view of the child and the environment are in an excellent position to help the child.

Ecological Classification Schemes

Educational definitions of emotional and behavioral disturbance contained in Public Law 94-142, combined with discontent with the deficiencies of a medical model for assessing childhood disorders, have contributed to the development of ecologically and developmentally oriented models. These models attempt to take into account the roles of the environment and of institutions that influence and are influenced by the child. It is consistent with the transactional perspective that problems are not said to belong only to the child (Salzinger, Antrobus, & Glick, 1980); the environment is also a unit of intervention. The unit of assessment and intervention is expanded in these models to include the institutions and systems that interact with the child—family, neighborhood, and school.

One of the better known ecologically oriented classification systems was developed by Hobbs (1980) for use with handicapped children. This system focuses on the transactions between the child and the environment and the services needed by the child. The first step in this model is to conduct an assessment to identify both assets and deficits in the ecosystem of the child. The second step is to identify the services and resources needed to enable the child to proceed toward agreed-upon developmental goals. Hobbs's interdisciplinary system helps ensure that children get the services they need and are entitled to. Although the impediments to service delivery that can result from unintended bureaucratic barriers may be minimized with this model, this approach has limitations. The goals selected for the child may be representative of the bias of the professionals involved in the process (Sarason & Klaber, 1985). In addition, there are problems with reliability and validity. Hobbs has acknowledged that his scheme is not amenable to research or epidemiological and demographic studies.

In spite of recent attention to an ecological perspective, it is not surprising that there are no DSM III-R codes for racism, sexism, or poverty. Case records rarely contain descriptive information about the physical environment and how supportive or hostile it may be (Proctor, Vosler, & Sirles, 1993). It is doubtful that third party reimbursement will be made available to fund interventions designed to redistribute wealth, power, or status. Nonetheless, such environmental interventions offer as much promise as individual or family intervention, although interventions designed to change the environment can be difficult for individual professionals to accomplish. There is little doubt, for example, that many of the factors that place children at emotional and educational risk could be reduced if health care, safe housing, adequate nutrition, and financial support were made available to all children and their families (see Chapter 4).

Perhaps the most ominous aspect of the psychologically oriented classification schemes is their focus on deficits. Human beings are reduced to a listing of problems, negatives, or defects. Richness, diversity, and uniqueness are sacrificed in deficit-oriented models. Children and adolescents are more than a collection of symptoms, even when their symptoms annoy or upset adults. Children and adolescents possess capacities, talents, interests, areas of competence, and strengths that are easily overlooked in classification schemes focused on pathology (Poertner & Ronnau, 1992).

Failing to recognize the positives and capacities of young people increases the likelihood of harm. Many psychiatric labels carry a life sentence, for they imply little prospect for recovery. By focusing on defects, interventions become directed at eliminating or minimizing the defects. The inherent strengths are bypassed; they are not used to help the young person improve her or his life. Young people are not actively engaged in enriching the environment; and they may eventually view themselves as collections of deficits. This is indeed a great injustice.

Professionals working with children and adolescents must be alert to the insidious nature of the defect-oriented models and learn to focus on the strengths and capacity for change that characterize young people. This can be difficult to accomplish since most helping professions incorporate a medical model of diagnosis and treatment. Policies, regulations, and third-party insurers can also require the use of the medical model.

Much of the research on these children and adolescents examines what is wrong with them, how many problems they have, and why they have these problems. An alternate perspective suggests that these are exceptionally capable children or adolescents to have survived such difficult circumstances. Many were removed from their biological parents because of maltreatment. They have been placed in a state-run substitute care system that is plagued by serious problems. They may spend protracted periods of time in the homes of strangers, moving from placement to placement; changing schools, friends, and caseworkers. In spite of this, and because of the inherent capacity of human beings, they do surprisingly well on measures of success. The overwhelming majority of youngsters reared in foster care grow up to be productive adults. About 90 percent of adoptive placements are stable, and young people are able to grow up in one home (Barth & Berry, 1990).

Nevertheless, these young people do have special needs, and they may often benefit from intervention. Helping the children to understand what is happening to them and why and fostering their coping capacities can help reduce the stress of placement. Actively working for policies and services to help families care for their members would either reduce the number of children entering substitute care or enable children to return to their biological families.

ETIOLOGY AND INTERVENTION

To explore the implications of conflicting notions about the etiology of emotional disturbances in children and adolescents, two categories of disturbances will be discussed.

Depression, the most common and one of the more disabling psychiatric symptoms, appears to be a pervasive and persistent problem for some children. Its persistence is clear from follow-up studies indicating that a majority of depressed children still suffer from symptoms of depression years after their initial diagnosis (Eastgate & Gilmour, 1984). There is little consensus on the etiology of depression. While much early work was based on the medical model, an ecological perspective and developmental point of view have also been used.

Eating disorders, which generally have an onset during adolescence, also represent grave threats. They produce high morbidity and mortality among young people. There is more consensus about the etiology of eating disorders, and most of the research is based on the medical model. An ecological perspective is rarely brought to eating disorders.

DEPRESSION IN CHILDREN

The discovery, or rather the recognition, of childhood depression is a recent development (Clarizio, 1989). Although most professionals acknowledge its existence, there is disagreement about the nature of childhood depression. Standards used to assess depression (as well as other affective and thought disorders) have been developed primarily by observations of adults. DSM III-R assumes that the major features of depression are essentially the same for children, adolescents, and adults. Adult depressives articulate feelings of sadness, worthlessness, and hopelessness. Children, particularly young children, rarely admit to long-lasting feelings of sadness (Glasberg & Aboud, 1982). Adolescents do admit to feelings of depression (Albert & Beck, 1975). Other adult symptoms of depression, such as eating and sleep disturbances, as well as crying, are not infrequent occurrences in children.

In an attempt to broaden the concept of depression in children and adolescents, other types of behaviors have been assumed to be indicative of a depressive condition. Somatic complaints such as headaches and abdominal pain could be symptoms of depression (Frommer, 1967). Other disturbing behaviors, such as conduct disorders, aggression, and hyperactivity in young children, could be attempts on the part of children to "mask" their depression and defend against feelings of despair (Chiles, Miller, & Cox, 1980; Puig-Antich, 1982; Cytryn & McKnew, 1972). Suicide, which is related to depression, is a serious threat to adolescents (Cole, Protinsky, & Cross, 1992). Adolescent abuse of alcohol and other mood altering chemicals may also be a symptom of depression (Grueling & DeBlassie, 1980). Learning disabilities have been reported as a mask of depression (Colbert, Newman, Ney, & Young, 1982). However, it is not clear whether depression incapacitates young people to such a marked degree that they have little energy available to concentrate on school work or if the consequences of being labeled disabled add to a negative self-image and contribute to depression.

Parents, teachers, peers, and children themselves have established that depressive syndromes do exist. It is still not clear when depression is a cause of other problems and when it is a result of other problems. For instance, there seems to be a relationship between depression and anxiety making it difficult to determine the primary disorder (Kovacs, Feinberg, Crouse-Novack, Paulauskas, & Finkelstein, 1984; Hershberg, Carlson, Cantwell, & Strober, 1982). Depressive affect may even be the result of interventions, such as referral to a mental health facility, which can be interpreted by children and adolescents as punitive. Depression seems to have become a catchall term that can include most internalized externalized behaviors. Depression has little specificity; the term seems to refer to four broad categories of behaviors. It can be a response to loss or stress; a disorder; or a cluster of symptoms, such as change in appetite, sad affect, thoughts of death, change in school performance, somatic complaints, and change in weight.

While the arguments over the nature of childhood depression continue, scales have been developed that purportedly measure depression in children and adolescents. Three of the better known and researched scales are the Beck Depression Inventory (1962), Schedule for Affective Disorders and Schizophrenia for School-Age Children (Puig-Antich et al., 1981), and the Multiscore Depression Inventory (Berndit & Petzel, 1980).

Correlates of Depression

The nature of childhood depression is controversial and so are theories of its etiology (Kasanin, Husain, Shekim, Hodges, Cytryn, & McKnew, 1981). Three major correlates of depression—biological, cognitive, and familial dysfunction, are briefly reviewed here. These correlates assume added significance because many interventions are based upon assumptions about the etiology of depression. For example, if depression is the result of chemical imbalances in the brain, intervention may focus on the introduction of chemicals into the brain (i.e., the use of medication) to correct these imbalances.

Research on the biological correlates in childhood depression is still in its infancy. There appears to be some difference in the urinary metabolites and cortisol secretion (as measured by the dexamethasone suppression test) of depressed versus nondepressed children (Cytryn, McKnew, & Logue, 1974; Klee & Garfinkel, 1984). Because of the rapid growth and change in children, the clear biological correlates of adulthood have not yet been established.

Other ideas based on work with adults focus on the roles of negative cognitions, stress (especially loss), and family dynamics. While each of these is correlated with depression, there is no evidence to support a causal relationship between depression and any factor or set of factors. The lack of empirical research and prospective studies has hampered both the identification and the treatment of depression in children and adolescents.

During the last twenty years, the role of negative self-perception in depression has been explored (Beck, 1967; Beck & Rush, 1978). It is not surprising that many children and adolescents who suffer from depression also suffer from low self-esteem (Kaslow, Rehm, & Siegel, 1984; Battle, 1980). Cognitive skills are required to assess situations and select actions. Young people with limited problem-solving abilities, who are unable either to correctly identify problems or to develop alternative solutions to problems, appear to be at greater risk for depression than young people with more adequate problem-solving skills (Mullins, Siegel, & Hodges, 1985).

Some believe that depression is in fact a learned behavior developed by the child or adolescent as he or she observes significant adults who are depressed (Allen-Meares, 1991). The social learning model discussed in an earlier chapter lends support to this point of view. Cognitive and behavioral intervention are sometimes combined to assist these children.

The role of the family in depression has been receiving increased attention (Dadds, Sanders, Morrison, & Rebgetz, 1992). The intergenerational transmission of both thought and affective disorders has been debated for years (Welner, Welner, McCrary, & Leonard, 1977). Whether there is a genetic or an environmental transmission of thought and mood disorders has yet to be determined. The child of a parent with a psychiatric diagnosis has been assumed to be a child at risk (Cohler & Musick, 1983; Baldwin, Cole, & Baldwin, 1982). Other research suggests that the multiple problems of isolation and lack of social support, child abuse, and depression place the child at greater risk than a parental psychiatric diagnosis (Sameroff, Seifer, & Barocas, 1983). Families are facing increasing levels of stress. Economic pressures, lack of consistent, good-quality child care, increasing rates of child abuse and neglect, high rates of marriage dissolution and absent or uninvolved fathers are all taking a toll on children (Emery, 1982). Researchers have found conflict between parents associated with children's psychological adjustment (Shaw & Emery, 1987; Wolfe, Jaffe, Zak, & Wilson, 1986).

Which intervention to use when working with the depressed young person is determined, in part, by the theoretical orientation of the professional. There is a dearth of literature on the effectiveness of interventions with children and adolescents, especially in comparison with the number of outcome studies focusing on adults. Although most models of intervention used with young people are adaptations of strategies used with adults, such strategies should not be unilaterally applied to children and adolescents. Part of the difficulty in evaluating effectiveness is a lack of consensus on what constitutes depression in children and adolescents, what is meant by the term *effective,* and how and when effectiveness should be measured (Allen-Meares, 1987). Since children are rarely self-referred, questions arise as to which person is in a position to offer comments on the effectiveness of intervention. Parents, teachers, peers, and the child may have markedly different views on the outcome of intervention.

Behavioral Intervention with the Depressed Child or Adolescent

Behavioral and cognitive based treatments claim high rates of effectiveness (Sayger et al., 1988; Abikoff, 1979). In this approach, specific, measurable, problem behaviors are targeted for change. Techniques are adjusted for the developmental level of the child. For example, depressed children with externalized (aggressive or disruptive) behaviors would be subject to rewards when they remain seated. The depressed adolescent with internalized (withdrawn, quiet) behaviors would be rewarded for talking to others or participating in activities and punished for avoiding contact with others. Questions have arisen about the generalizability of treatment gains (Weissberg, et al., 1981). Gains made in the school setting or in a therapeutic setting have limited value if they are not carried over and maintained in other areas of a child's life.

Cognitive Intervention

Similar to the behaviorist approach are cognitive-behavioral interventions. Techniques used in this approach include cognitive restructuring, role modeling, problem solving, and behavioral rehearsal (Goldfried & Davison, 1976). Cognitive restructuring involves changing how the young person thinks. Depression is assumed to be the result of erroneous thoughts and thought processes. Distortions in thinking, such as not learning from experience, reaching inaccurate conclusions from inadequate evidence, and assigning inflated importance to single events, add to depression. By changing thought patterns, practicing new methods of thinking, understanding consequences, and exploring alternative solutions to problems, the negative view of self will reportedly be eliminated (Beck, 1976).

Serving the Family

A necessary and sufficient condition for successful intervention with children and adolescents is the involvement of families. Children are dependent upon their families for emotional and physical survival. Parents bring their children to mental health facilities usually because of concerns about troublesome behaviors. Since the parents' tolerance for behaviors influences the definition of a problem, their involvement in the therapeutic process is essential. Research suggests that parents can feel excluded from the treatment process and blamed for the mental health problems of their children (Collins & Collins, 1990; Wahl, 1989). This is countertherapeutic.

Ideally, the family provides the supportive environment necessary for the developing child. With older children, cooperation from the family is essential if they are to continue in treatment (Fleischman, 1981). Behavioral therapy requires the active involvement of the family if changes observed in the therapeutic setting are to be generalized to the other areas of the child's life. Families that are disorganized, enmeshed in conflict, or chaotic may prevent the child from incorporating positive changes. Therefore, the family must be involved in both the assessment and intervention (Green, 1989).

CASE ILLUSTRATION—JAIME V., EIGHT YEARS OLD

Jaime V. was a Latino boy referred to a mental health agency by his school early in the academic year. Jaime was in the third grade and functioning at grade level. He had been referred for corporal punishment four times in a two-week period. The principal thought Jaime was depressed. His teacher described him as obdurate. Upon receiving the referral, the intake worker contacted Jaime's mother and set up a home visit.

Jaime lived with his mother and two older sisters, ages 13 and 16. Jaime's father had recently moved out of the home because of marital problems. Mrs. V. indicated that she felt depressed and had been unable to give her usual amount of energy to Jaime. She had asked her daughters to help, but they were leading active social lives and had little time for their baby brother. Mrs. V. could not understand why Jaime was getting into trouble at school since he was a good student and used to like to go to school. Jaime was reluctant to speak with the worker.

The worker offered Mrs. V. couple, individual, and group counseling. Mrs. V. accepted a referral to a support group and individual counseling. Jaime was referred to after-school programs that emphasized social and sports activities. Two months later, Jaime was still in trouble in his classroom. The worker established contact with Jaime's teacher. The teacher indicated that corporal punishment was the "only thing those kind of boys understand." The worker contacted the principal, who indicated he knew that the teacher had difficulty with minority male children. She had been sent to training programs on cultural sensitivity, but the training did not seem to help. The worker requested Jaime be removed from her classroom. The principal was opposed to the request because it could be interpreted as an affront to the teacher. The worker persisted, and eventually Jaime was moved to another classroom. By the winter recess, Jaime was doing well in school, and his mother reported she was less depressed.

The worker could have used a number of interventions with Jaime. In the medical deficit model, he could have been medicated for aggressive behavior, subject to behaviorism with rewards for good behavior and punishments for bad behavior (although he was receiving corporal punishment), or provided with individual counseling to help him resolve issues about the departure of his father. Instead, the worker expanded the unit of assessment and viewed Jaime as a child with resources, capacities, talents, strengths, and abilities. Jaime did not want to talk with a mental health professional. He was a talented soccer and chess player. The worker built upon those competencies. The worker noted in the closing summary that while Jaime and his mother were feeling better, the worker remained concerned about other male minority children in Jaime's old classroom.

EATING DISORDERS

Eating disorders have been discussed in the psychoanalytic literature for decades (Waller, Kaufman, & Deutsch, 1940). The last 20 years, however, have witnessed a dramatic increase in research into these disorders. This change may reflect an actual increase in their incidence, especially in wealthy nations. Poor countries, faced with both the reality and the threat of unintentional starvation, do not seem to suffer from these disorders. There is a lack of consensus on the definition, etiology, and treatment of eating disorders. It is suggested here that transactions between the client and significant others or environments are the cause of the problem. The client attempts to exercise control over some aspect of his or her life even though the consequences can be deadly. Eating disorders are generally manifested in one of three ways—obesity, anorexia, or bulimia. These are not mutually exclusive categories, and there are subtypes within them. This discussion here focuses on the latter two disorders.

Defining Anorexia and Bulimia

The distinguishing features of anorexia include intentional starvation, distorted body image, morbid fear of obesity, adolescent onset, and overrepresentation of middle-class females. DSM III-R describes anorexia as a disorder of females with a mortality rate between 5 percent and 18 percent. A number of other psychological and behavioral traits are associated with anorexia, although there is disagreement among theorists about the importance of specific behaviors in both the etiology and maintenance of anorexia. The Eating Disorders Instrument (EDI) is the most recognized tool for assessing behavioral and psychological factors associated with anorexia and bulimia (Garner, Olmstead, & Polivy, 1983). The EDI is a self-report, forced-choice instrument with eight subscales. Two of the subscales, perfectionism and maturity fears, are highly correlated with anorexia.

Bulimia can be both a characteristic of anorexia and a separate disorder. DSM III-R recognizes bulimia as a separate disorder with the following characteristics: episodic binge eating, depressed mood following eating, awareness that the bingeing is abnormal, purgative behaviors following the binge, and the proviso that bulimia is not due to anorexia or a physical disorder. Weight fluctuations are common in bulimia but rarely reach the life threatening proportions that can occur in anorexia. Bulimics may be of normal weight while most anorexics are morbidly underweight.

Bulumics may differ from anorexics on some general personality and psychological characteristics. One study has reported that bulimics are less psychiatrically impaired than anorexics (Johnson, Stuckey, Lewis, & Schwartz, 1983). Many bulimics suffer from depression and have family histories of depression (Pyle, Mitchell, & Eckert, 1981). A fear of becoming fat, accompanied by an intense desire for thinness, can characterize bulimics (Boskind-Lodahl, 1976), but anorexics also have a morbid fear of fat.

Etiology

Eating disorders are the result of multiple factors, but family characteristics and individual psychopathology are the variables most frequently researched (Gremillion, 1992). This approach has the disadvantage of reducing the young person who is bulimic or anorexic to an eating disorder, disregarding his or her abilities and strengths—the competencies that might be building blocks for intervention. Viewing an eating disorder as a series of symptoms to be treated unfortunately also minimizes the role of environmental factors. The role of cultural factors may help to explain the overrepresentation of females. Sex-role stereotyping contributes, since women are encouraged to be thin, submissive, conforming, and passive and to base their self-worth on the evaluation of males (Orbach, 1978; Nagel & Jones, 1992). The news media are saturated with the "be thin" message.

Some researchers view eating disorders as a type of affective disorder (Cantwell, Sturzenberger, Burroughs, Salkin, & Green, 1977). Mood swings from depression to mania have been observed in anorexics. Winokur, March, and Mendels (1980) reported a higher incidence of affective disorders in the relatives of anorexics than in normal controls. Relatives of bulimics are more likely to have histories of affective disorders than are relatives of anorexics (Strober, 1981; Strober, Salkin, Burroughs, & Morrell, 1982). There are limitations to the few genetic studies of eating disturbances. Additional studies that use twins (monozygotic and dizygotic), as well as adoption studies of siblings reared apart, should add to this knowledge base.

Psychoanalytic theory has been used to explain two of the unique characteristics of eating disturbances—adolescent onset and the overrepresentation of middle-class females. Because females are more likely to suffer from eating disorders, attention has been directed to features unique to the psychosexual development of girls. The major proponent of a psychodynamic interpretation of anorexia is Bruch (1973, 1978). From this theoretical perspective, the anorexic feels powerless and ineffective, fails to experience her body as belonging to her, suffers disturbed perception of body experiences, acts in response to the demands of others, is arrested in the concrete operations phase of cognitive development, and defends herself against the feeling of not having a core personality. Adolescent onset is to be expected since this is the time when young people begin to move beyond their families and actively engage in relationships with peers. Prognosis may be related to age at onset. Early onset, ages 11–15, may indicate a poorer prognosis than later onset, although the research does not provide consistent evidence to support this notion (Swift, 1982).

The families of those with eating disorders have been studied in an attempt to identify the role of disturbed family relations in the development and maintenance of these disorders (Yager, 1982). Minuchin, Rosman, and Baker (1978) characterize the families of anorexics as enmeshed, rigid, overprotective, and conflict-avoidant. The anorexic helps the family avoid other conflict areas, and stabilizes the family system by focusing attention on a single problem behavior.

Humphrey (1986) describes eating-disordered families as chaotic, detached, and isolated.

Intervention with Eating Disorders

Ideas about the causes of eating disturbances influence the choice of intervention. Hospitalization involving forced feeding (hyperalimentation), combined with behavior modification and psychotropic medications, is a well-described regime (Bemis, 1978; Maloney & Farrell, 1980; Halmi, 1974). Hospitalization can be used for a few weeks or a few months, depending on a number of factors, such as the severity of the condition. Hyperalimentation results in weight gain; and behavior-modification programs reward eating and punish noneating. Those who subscribe to the view that eating disorders are affective disorders favor the use of antidepressants or tranquilizers. Cognitive therapy has also been suggested (Wilson & Fairburn, 1993). Since anorexia can be life threatening, hospitalization may be an appropriate intervention; but there is disagreement over its effectiveness.

The initial goal of treatment, weight gain, is not difficult to achieve (Hsu, 1980). The challenge arises when these patients are released and must maintain their weight. Readmission rates are high (Piazza, Piazza, & Rollins, 1980). Hospitalization intensifies feelings of inadequacy experienced by the eating disordered and does little to increase their sense of autonomy. A hospital requires compliance, has a staff to supervise and care for the individual, and encourages regression. There is little opportunity in a hospital setting for individuals to exercise autonomy, an essential task for the eating disordered.

There is no evidence to support the superiority of any specific treatment. The research indicates that eating disorders, like depression, are multidetermined. Reliance on the deficit model results in guarded optimism about the success of recovering from serious emotional problems such as depression and eating disorders. Treatment or intervention after a difficulty has developed is more costly, time consuming, and problematic than preventing the development of the difficulty. Although prevention could reduce both the number of young people suffering with emotional problems and the costs associated with dealing with these problems, there is little research on how to prevent them.

PREVENTION OF EMOTIONAL PROBLEMS

Rather than waiting for the first signs of an emotional problem to appear, efforts can be directed toward establishing conditions that promote physical and mental health. Vulnerability and risk are two variables that determine whether an emotional disturbance will develop. Emotional disorders result from the interaction of biological, familial, and sociological or environmental factors. Risk is defined as the degree of probability of a negative outcome (Tarter, 1983).

Prevention efforts could be directed toward ameliorating the correlates of emotional disturbance. For example, the physical health of children is a neglected area, and physical problems can play a role in emotional disturbance. A substantial number of children suffer from medical neglect, low hemoglobin levels, lack of immunization, and inadequate or nonexistent health insurance. Black children are more likely to be poor, live in substandard housing, die before their first birthdays, or be victims of violent crime than are white children (Children's Defense Fund, 1985). These factors place such children at grave risk.

Components of Prevention

The implementation of prevention programs and services requires resources. Adequate funding is a major resource but by no means the most important. People and their skills are resources that are often ignored. Resource allocation is both a result and a reflection of the political process. Prevention programs for children must compete with other programs both for funding and for service providers. This competition is likely to intensify in the next decades.

Since there is a lack of consensus on the definition, nature, and criteria for identifying childhood emotional disturbances, designing specific prevention programs is problematic. Rather than trying to prevent the development and maintenance of specific maladaptive behaviors, some prevention strategies focus on promoting normal development and increasing the social skills of children and adolescents. Social skills enable young people to interact successfully with peers and adults. A deficit in social skills can lead to conflict and isolation, which exacerbate emotional and academic problems (Silverman, 1991). (Social skills are discussed more fully in Chapter 8.)

Adolescents seem to benefit from programs designed to increase their competency and communication skills (Henry, Stephenson, Janson & Hargett, 1993). Preventive programs have focused on specific issues such as anxiety about public speaking on the part of adolescents (Cradock, Cotler, & Jason, 1978). The intervention consisted of helping the adolescent clarify distortions in thinking and role playing. Another model based on promoting competence focused on helping the adolescent resist peer pressure; develop empathy; and use techniques like role playing, modeling, and feedback (LeCroy & Rose, 1986).

Affective education promotes normal development and improves social skills (Baskin & Hess, 1980). This kind of program is designed for elementary school age children and helps them to understand their feelings and the feelings of their peers. For this age child, self-control is an important skill. Programs focused on helping such children identify problems clearly and develop a variety of problem-solving strategies indicate that gains can be maintained as long as a year after termination of the program (Kendall & Zupan, 1981).

Research in Prevention

Prevention efforts are similar to intervention efforts in that both require a knowledge base and theories about etiology. In order to understand the long-term effects of both intervention and prevention efforts, longitudinal studies are needed; but this type of research is costly. Much of the information used to develop prevention programs and evaluate the role of correlates in emotional disturbance is retrospective. To understand the role of the correlates of emotional disturbance in children, prospective studies are needed.

Assessing effectiveness of prevention efforts requires the use of multiple measures of outcome. For example, if programs such as Head Start and the Perry Preschool Program are judged solely on the basis of IQ scores, both programs were a failure since the initial gains in IQ were lost as children advanced through grade school (Ziegler & Valentine, 1979). Multiple, longitudinal measures have been used to assess early intervention programs. A benefit–cost analysis of the Perry Preschool Program, for example, used a number of measures unrelated to IQ level (Barnet, 1985). As adults, youngsters who participated in the program were less likely to have been arrested, more likely to be employed, less likely to receive AFDC, and more likely to be older at the time of birth of their first children than youngsters in the control group.

SUMMARY

The goal of developing linear causal models of emotional disturbance in children and adolescents is unrealistic and leads to false assumptions that result in blaming the victim. Research supports the notion that disturbances are multi-determined. Factors have been identified that increase the vulnerability of children. Efforts could be directed toward reducing or preventing these correlates, thus diminishing the risk of emotional disturbance.

There is a lack of consensus on the definitions and causes of emotional disturbance and on effective interventions. It is clear, however, that certain variables that increase vulnerability and risk in children are preventable. For example, longitudinal studies that examine the effects of homelessness on the cognitive and emotional well-being of children have yet to be reported. However, there is no basis for believing that living on the streets, in tents, or in a series of shelters is conducive to good physical, mental, or emotional health in children. In spite of this knowledge, there are homeless families. Advocacy efforts are an essential component of working with children and adolescents.

QUESTIONS FOR DISCUSSION

1. A dilemma of any classification or diagnostic scheme is trying to distinguish the normal from the abnormal. When classifying children's problems, this dilemma is attenuated. Change, temporary regression, and variability characterize childhood. How can diagnostic schemes take these normal conditions into account in an attempt to develop parameters of pathology?

2. The role of gender has been explored to some degree in the distribution of emotional disturbance. The role of race and class is beginning to receive attention. Preliminary

research indicates that minority youth may be at a greater risk of depression and suicide than nonminorities. What do you think is the role of race in depression?

3. How is depression in children manifested, what are the correlates, and how is it similar or dissimilar to depression in adults?

4. There is a pressing need for a prospective and longitudinal research. Retrospective studies may be able to suggest correlates of emotional disturbance, but they cannot determine the relative contributions of the correlates. Design a research project that could account for the variance of any three correlates of emotional disturbance in children.

ADDITIONAL READINGS

Allen-Meares, P. (1991). A study of depressive characteristics in behaviorally disordered children and adolescents. *Children and Youth Services* 13: 271–286.

Early, T. J., & Poertner, J. (1993). Families with children with emotional disorders: A review of the literature. *Social Work* 38(6): 743–751.

Goodyer, I. M. (1990). *Life experiences, development and childhood psychopathology.* New York: Wiley.

Hains, A., & Szyjakowski, M. (1990). A cognitive stress-reduction intervention program for adolescents. *Journal of Counseling Psychology* 37: 79–84.

Leone, P. F., Ed. (1990). *Understanding troubled and troubling youth.* Newbury Park, Calif: Sage.

Stiffman, A. R., & Davis, L., eds. (1990). *Ethnic issues in adolescent mental health.* Newbury Park, Calif: Sage.

REFERENCES

Abikoff, H. (1979). Cognitive training interventions in children: Review of a new approach. *Journal of Learning Disabilities* 12: 65–76.

Albert, N., & Beck, A. (1975). Incidence of depression in early adolescence: A preliminary study. *Journal of Youth and Adolescence* 4: 301–307.

Allen-Meares, P. (1987). Depression in childhood and adolescence. *Social Work* 32: 512–516.

Allen-Meares, P. (1991). A study of depressive characteristics in behaviorally disordered children and adolescents. *Children and Youth Services* 13: 271–286.

American Psychiatric Association. (1952). *Diagnostic and statistical manual of mental disorders,* 1st ed. Washington, D.C.: The Association.

American Psychiatric Association. (1968). *Diagnostic and statistical manual of mental disorders,* 2nd ed. Washington, D.C.: The Association.

American Psychiatric Association. (1980). *Diagnostic and statistical manual of mental disorders,* 3rd ed. Washington, D.C.: The Association.

American Psychiatric Association. (1987). *Diagnostic and statistical manual of mental disorders,* 3rd ed. rev. Washington, D.C.: The Association.

Baldwin, A., Cole, R., & Baldwin, C., eds. (1982). Parental psychopathology, family interaction, and the competence of the child in school. *Monographs of the Society for Research in Child Development* 47 (5) Serial No. 197.

Baskin, E., & Hess, R. (1980). Does affective education work? A review of seven programs. *Journal of School Psychology* 18: 40-50.

Barnett, W. (1985). Benefit-cost analysis of the Perry Preschool Program and its policy implications. *Education Evaluation and Policy Analysis* 7: 333-342.

Barth, R. P., & Berry, M. (1990). A decade later: Outcomes of permanency planning. In North American Council on Adoptable Children, *The first ten years,* pp. 7-40. St. Paul, Minn.: The Council.

Battle, J. (1980). Relationship between self-esteem and depression among high school students. *Perceptual and Motor Skills* 51: 157-158.

Beck, A. (1967). *Depression: Clinical, experimental and theoretical aspects.* New York: Harper & Row.

Beck, A. (1976). *Cognitive therapy and the emotional disorders.* New York: International Universities Press.

Beck, A., et al. (1962). An inventory for measuring depression. *Archives of General Psychology* 4: 561-571.

Beck, A., & Rush, A. (1978). Cognitive approaches to depression and suicide. In G. Serban, ed., *Cognition deficits in the development of mental illness,* pp. 235-257. New York: Brunner Mazel.

Berndit, D., & Pretzel, T. (1980). Development and initial evaluation of a multiscore depression inventory. *Journal of Personality Assessment* 44: 396-403.

Bemis, K. (1978). Current approaches to the etiology and treatment of anorexia nervosa. *Psychological Bulletin* 85: 593-617.

Boskind-Lodahl, M. (1976). Cinderella's stepsisters: A feminist perspective on anorexia nervosa and bulimia. *Journal of Women in Culture and Society* 2: 342-356.

Bruch, H. (1973). *Eating disorders: Obesity, anorexia nervosa and the person within.* New York: Basic Books.

Bruch, H. (1978). *The golden cage.* Cambridge: Harvard University Press.

Bruch, H. (1982). Anorexia nervosa: Therapy and theory. *American Journal of Psychiatry* 139: 1531-1538.

Cantwell, D., Sturzenberger, S., Burroughs, J., Salkin, B., & Green, J. (1977). Anorexia nervosa: An affective disorder? *Archives of General Psychiatry* 34: 1087-1093.

Carlson, G., & Cantwell, D. (1980). Diagnosis of childhood depression: A comparison of the Weinberg and DSM-III criteria. *Journal of the American Academy of Child Psychiatry* 21: 247-250.

Children's Defense Fund. (1985). *Black and white children in America.* Washington: The Fund.

Chiles, J., Miller, M., & Cox, G. (1980). Depression in an adolescent delinquent population. *Archives of General Psychiatry* 37: 1179-1184.

Clarizio, H., (1989). Continuity in childhood depression. *Adolescence* 24: 261-267.

Cohler, B., & Musick, J. (1983). Psychopathology of parenthood: Implications for mental health of children. *Infant Mental Health Journal* 4: 140-164.

Colbert, P., Newman, B., Ney, P., & Young, J. (1982). Learning disabilities as a symptom of depression in children. *Learning Disabilities* 15: 333-336.

Cole, D. E., Protinsky, H. O., & Cross, L. H. (1992). An empirical investigation of adolescent suicidal ideation. *Adolescence* 27 (108): 813-817.

Collins, B., & Collins, T. (1990). Parent-professional relationships in the treatment of seriously disturbed children and adolescents. *Social Work* 35: 522-527.

Costello, A., Edelbrock, C., Dulcan, M., Kalas, R., & Kloric, S. (1984). *Report on the diagnostic interview for children.* Pittsburgh: University of Pittsburgh Press.

Cradock, C., Cotler, S., & Jason, L. (1978). Primary prevention: Immunization of children for speech anxiety. *Cognitive Therapy and Research* 2: 389-396.

Cytryn, L., & McKnew, D. (1972). Proposed classification of childhood depression. *American Journal of Psychiatry* 129: 149-155.

Cytryn, L., McKnew, D., & Logue, M. (1974). Biochemical correlates of affective disorders in children. *Archives of General Psychiatry* 31: 659-661.

Dadds, M. R., Sanders, M., Morrison, M., & Rebgetz, M. (1992). Childhood depression and conduct disorder: II. An analysis of family interaction in the home. *Journal of Abnormal Psychology* 101(2): 505-513.

Eastgate, J., & Gilmore, L. (1984). Long-term outcome of depressed children: A follow-up study. *Developmental Medicine and Child Neurology* 26(1): 68-72.

Emery, R. (1982). Interparental conflict and the children of discord and divorce. *Psychological Bulletin* 92: 310-330.

Fleischman, M. (1981). A replication of Patterson's "intervention for boys with conduct problems." *Journal of Consulting Clinical Psychology* 49: 342-351.

Frommer, E. (1967). Treatment of childhood depression with antidepressant drugs. *British Medical Journal* 1: 729-732.

Garner, D., Olmstead, M., & Polivy, J. (1983). Development and validation of a multidimensional eating disorder inventory for anorexia nervosa and bulimia. *International Journal of Eating Disorders* 2: 15-34.

Gelfand, D., Jenson, W., & Drew, C. (1982). *Understanding children's behavior disorders.* New York: Holt, Rinehart and Winston.

Glasberg, R., & Aboud, F. (1982). Keeping one's distance from sadness: children's self-reports of emotional experience. *Developmental Psychology* 18: 287-293.

Goldfried, M., & Davison, G. (1976). *Clinical behavior therapy.* New York: Holt, Rinehart & Winston.

Green, R. (1989). Choosing family measurement devices for practice and research: SFI and FACES III. *Social Service Review* 63: 304-320.

Gremillion, H. (1992). Psychiatry as social ordering: Anorexia nervosa, a paradigm. *Social Science & Medicine* 35(1): 57-71.

Grueling, J., & DeBlassie, R. (1980). Adolescent suicide. *Adolescence* 15: 589-601.

Halmi, K. (1974). Anorexia nervosa: Demographic and clinical features in 94 cases. *Psychosomatic Medicine* 36: 54-55.

Henry, C. S., Stephenson, A. L., Hanson, M. F., & Hargett, W. (1993). Adolescent suicide and families: An ecological perspective. *Adolescence* 28(110): 291-305.

Hershberg, S., Carlson, G., Cantwell, D., & Strober, M. (1982). Anxiety and depressive disorders in psychiatrically disturbed children. *Journal of Clinical Psychiatry* 43: 358-361.

Hobbs, N. (1980). An ecologically oriented service-based system for the classification of handicapped children. In S. Salinger, J. Antrobus, & J. Glick, eds., *The ecosystem of the "sick" child*, pp. 271-290. New York: Academic Press.

Hsu, L. (1980). Outcome of anorexia nervosa. *Archives of General Psychiatry* 37: 1041-1046.

Humphrey, L. (1986). Family relations in bulimic-anorexic and nondistressed families. *International Journal of Eating Disorders* 5: 223-232.

Johnson, C., Stuckey, M., Lewis, L., & Schwartz, D. (1983). Bulimia: A descriptive study of 316 cases. *International Journal of Eating Disorders* 2: 3-16.

Kasanin, J., Husain, A., Shekim, W., Hodges, K., Cytryn, L., & McKnew, D. (1981). Current perspectives on childhood depression: An overview. *American Journal of Psychiatry* 138: 143-153.

Kaslow, N., Rehm, L., & Siegel, A. (1984). Social-cognitive and cognitive correlates of depression in children. *Journal of Abnormal Child Psychology* 12: 605-620.

Kendall, P., & Zupan, B. (1981). Individual versus group application of cognitive behavioral self-control procedures with children. *Behavior Therapy* 21: 344-359.

Klee, S., & Garfinkel, B. (1984). Identification of depression in children and adolescents: The role of the dexamethasone suppression test. *Journal of the American Academy of Child Psychiatry* 23: 410-415.

Kovacs, M., Feinberg, T., & Crouse-Novack, M., Paulauskas, S., & Finkelstein, R. (1984). Depressive disorders in childhood. I: A longitudinal prospective study of characteristics and recovery. *Archives of General Psychiatry* 41: 229-237.

LeCroy, C., & Rose, S. (1986). Evaluation of preventive interventions for enhancing social competence in adolescents. *Social Work* 31: 8-16.

Maloney, M., & Farrell, M. (1980). Treatment of severe weight loss in anorexia nervosa with hyperalimentation and psychotherapy. *American Journal of Psychiatry* 137: 310-314.

Minuchin, S., Rosman, B., & Baker, L. (1978). *Psychosomatic families: Anorexia nervosa in context.* Cambridge: Harvard University Press.

Mullins, L. L., Siegel, L. J., & Hodges, K. (1985). Cognitive problem solving and life event correlates of depressive symptoms in children. *Journal of Abnormal Child Psychology* 13: 305-314.

Nagel, K. L., & Jones, K. H. (1992). Sociological factors in the development of eating disorders. *Adolescence* 27(105): 107-113.

Office of Technology Assessment. (1986). *Children's mental health: Problems and services—a background paper.* Washington, D.C.: U.S. Government Printing Office.

Orbach, S. (1978). Social dimensions in compulsive eating in women. *Psychotherapy: Theory, Research, and Practice* 15: 180-189.

Piazza, E., Piazza, N., & Rollins, N. (1980). Anorexia nervosa: Controversial aspects of therapy. *Comprehensive Psychiatry* 21: 177-189.

Poertner, J., & Ronnau, J., (1992). A strengths approach to children with emotional disabilities. In D. Saleebey, ed., *The strengths perspective in social work practice.* White Plains, N.Y.: Longman.

Proctor, E., Vosler, N., & Sirles, E. (1993). The social-environmental context of child clients. *Social Work* 38: 256-262.

Puig-Antich, J. (1982). Major depression and conduct disorder in prepuberty. *Journal of the American Academy of Child and Adolescent Psychiatry* 21: 118-128.

Puig-Antich, J., Orvaschel, H., Tabrixi, M. A., & Chamberg, W. T. (1981). *Adoption of the schedule for affective disorders and schizophrenia for school age children.* Albany: Department of Child and Adolescent Psychiatry, New York State Psychiatric Institute.

Pyle, R. L., Mitchell, J. E., & Eckert, E. (1981). Bulimia: A report of 34 cases. *Journal of Clinical Psychiatry* 42(2): 60-64.

Robins, L. N., & Price, R. K. (1991). Adult disorders predicted by childhood conduct problems: Results from the NIMH Epidemiologic Catchment Area Project. *Psychiatry* 54: 116-132.

Salzinger, S., Antrobus, J., & Glick, J., eds. (1980). *The ecosystem of the "sick" child.* New York: Academic Press.

Sameroff, A., Seifer, R., & Barocas, R. (1983). Impact of parental psychopathology: Diagnosis, severity, and social status effect? *Infant Mental Health Journal* 4: 236-249.

Sarason, S., & Klaber, M. (1985). The school as a social situation. *Annual Review of Psychology* 36: 115-140.

Sayger, T. V., Horne, A. M., Walker, J. M., & Passmore, J. L. (1988). Social learning family therapy with aggressive children: Treatment outcome and maintenance. *Journal of Family Psychology* 1(3): 261–285.

Shaw, D., & Emery, R. (1987). Parental conflict and other correlates of the adjustment of school-age children whose parents have separated. *Journal of Abnormal Psychology* 15: 269–281.

Silverman, W. (1991). Intervention strategies for prevention of adolescent substance abuse. *Journal of Adolescent Chemical Dependency* 1: 25–34.

Strober, M. (1981). The significance of bulimia in juvenile anorexia nervosa: An explanation of possible etiologic factors. *International Journal of Eating Disorders* 1: 28–43.

Strober, M., Salkin, B., Burroughs, M., & Morrell, W. (1982). Validity of the bulimia-restricter distinction in anorexia morbidity. *Journal of Mental and Nervous Disease* 170: 345–351.

Swift, W. (1982). Long-term outcome of early onset anorexia nervosa. *Journal of the American Academy of Child Psychiatry* 21: 38–46.

Tarter, R. (Ed.) (1983). *The child at psychiatric risk.* New York: Oxford University Press.

Wahl, O. F. (1989). Schizophrenogenic parenting in abnormal psychology textbooks. *Teaching of Psychology* 16: 3–33.

Waller, J., Kaufman, R., & Deutsch, F. (1940). Anorexia nervosa: A psychosomatic entity. *Psychosomatic Medicine* 2: 3–16.

Weiner, I. (1982). *Child and adolescent psychopathology.* New York: Wiley.

Weissberg, R., Gesten, E., Rupkin, D., Cowen, E., Davidson, E., de Apodaca, R., & McKim, B. (1981). Evaluation of a social problem solving training program for suburban and inner-city third grade children. *Journal of Consulting & Clinical Psychology* 49: 251–261.

Welner, Z., Welner, A., McCrary, M., & Leonard, M. (1977). Psychopathology in children of inpatients with depression—a controlled study. *Journal of Nervous and Mental Disorders* 164: 408–413.

White, J. L., Moffitt, T. E., Earls, F., Robins, L., & Silva, P. A. (1990). How early can we tell? Predictors of childhood conduct disorder and adolescent delinquency. *Criminology* 28(4): 507–525.

Wilson, G. T., & Fairburn, C. G. (1993). Cognitive treatments for eating disorders. *Journal of Consulting & Clinical Psychology* 61: 261–269.

Winokur, A., March, V., & Mendels, J. (1980). Primary affective disorders in relatives of patients with anorexia nervosa. *American Journal of Psychiatry* 137: 695–698.

Wolfe, D., Jaffe, P., Zak, L., & Wilson, S. (1986). Child witnesses to violence between parents: Critical issues in behavioral and social adjustment. *Journal of Abnormal Child Psychology* 14: 95–104.

Wood, F., & Zabel, R. (1978). Making sense of reports on the incidence of behavior disorders/emotional disturbance in school-aged populations. *Psychology in the Schools* 15: 45–51.

World Health Organization. (1978). *Mental disorders: Glossary and guide to their classification in accordance with the ninth revision of the international classification of diseases.* Geneva: The Organization.

Yager, J. (1982). Family issues in the pathogenesis of anorexia nervosa. *Psychosomatic Medicine* 44: 46–60.

Ziegler, E., & Valentine, J. (1979). *Project Head Start: A legacy of the war on poverty.* New York: Free Press.

chapter 7

Abused, Neglected, and Sexually Victimized Children and Adolescents

The variation in family socialization practices is well known. Many cultural and situational variables determine the level of conflict and harmony in the family and parent–child relationship. This chapter essentially reflects the situation in the United States. Some believe that rather than viewing an abusive parent as someone different from a nonabusive parent, a dichotomous view, child abuse can be viewed in terms of the degree to which a parent uses negative, inappropriate control strategies with the child (Wolfe, 1987). Thus, child abuse is not a disorder; instead it is an extreme to which a parent goes in disciplining a child. Here, the focus is on parenting style.

The ultimate cause of the alarming abuse of children and adolescents is the violent strain in American society. "In Idaho, children were placed in straight jackets [sic] and hung upside down by their ankles as punishment. In Mississippi, children were beaten for bedwetting and fed watermelon and cookies for lunch. In Kentucky, a child was so deprived of food that at age 9, he weighed only 17 pounds" (Gratteau & Dold, 1986, p. 8). Social workers see abused and neglected children and adolescents in a variety of settings; and reporting abuse and neglect is mandatory in all states.

The news and entertainment media reinforce the use of physical force to achieve an end. Gelles sets forth the following assumptions that serve as the basis for a national program of prevention.

1. Family violence typically moves from the mild form to the more severe and lethal.
2. The private nature of the family and the hesitation on the part of society to become agents of social control to intervene in family violence allow milder forms of family violence to escalate.

3. There is a lack of places for victims to go for help; thus they remain in the situation and experience more violence.
4. Interventions that prevent milder violence also prevent severe violence.
5. Ninety percent of instances of family violence are caused by social factors; 10% are attributed to mental illness or some other problem.
6. Primary interventions that aim at altering the social structure and cultural attitudes about violence could reduce it by 60%.
7. Secondary interventions implemented after an initial recognized incident could reduce further incidence by 70% (1984, pp. 7–10).

PHYSICAL ABUSE AND NEGLECT

Garbarino (1984) argues that adolescents are virtually ignored in the discussion of child abuse and neglect. Perhaps because of their physical development, adolescents are thought to be less vulnerable and more capable of self-protection—in fact, many adolescents pose physical threats to adults. Nevertheless, the national incident study indicates that despite public and professional information about child abuse and neglect, maltreatment of adolescents accounts for some 47 percent of the known cases of maltreatment. Such maltreatment, moreover, is less likely to be reported than the maltreatment of younger children. For example, when the author of this book reported suspected abuse of an eleventh grader (her father had beaten her with a belt until her legs were bloody and blue), the intake worker responded, "We have other priority cases." What can we do with an adolescent? Foster homes just are not available. Garbarino (1984) reports that girls are more likely to be abused as they pass through adolescence. Sometimes abuse of adolescents is merely a continuation of abuse and neglect begun in childhood. It appears that step-parent families are at a higher risk of maltreatment. It also appears that abused adolescents are less socially competent and more likely to exhibit developmental problems than their peers.

Others who have sought to examine abused adolescents through an analysis of developmental histories have found adolescents who came from home circumstances where violence was pervasive and who had become scapegoats in marital disputes (Mouzakitis, 1984).

The Child Abuse Prevention and Treatment Act (PL 93-247) of 1974 mandated reporting of child maltreatment in all states receiving certain federal funds. The Abused and Neglected Child Reporting Act (P.A. 81-1077) of Illinois, effective July 1, 1980, defines abuse and neglect as follows:

1. "Child" means any person under the age of 18 years.
2. "Abused child" means a child whose parent or immediate family member, or any person responsible for the child's welfare, or any individual residing in the same home as the child, or a paramour of the child's parent:

    a. inflicts, causes to be inflicted, or allows to be inflicted upon such child by other than accidental means any of the following: a serious physical injury; death; disfigurement; impairment of physical or emotional health; or loss or impairment of any bodily function

    b. creates a substantial risk of physical injury to such child by other than accidental means which would be likely to cause death or serious disfigurement or impairment of any bodily function

    c. commits or allows to be committed a sex offense against such child

    d. commits or allows to be committed an act or acts of torture upon each child or

    e. inflicts excessive corporal punishment.

3. "Neglected child" means any child whose parent or other person responsible for the child's welfare does not provide the proper or necessary support, education as required by law, or medical or other remedial care recognized under State law as necessary for his or her well-being; or who is abandoned by his or her parents or other person responsible for the child's welfare (Illinois Department of Children and Family Services, 1980, pp. 1–20).

Some suggest that to prevent abuse and neglect, statewide programs must enhance parent–child bonding, emotional ties, and communication; increase parenting skills; provide appropriate social support services, such as social welfare and health services; and increase parental knowledge of child management (Paisley, 1987).

Family Characteristics, Risk Factors, and Indicators

Two types of parenting styles have been discussed in the literature: accepting-responsible (child centered) or rejecting-unresponsive (parent centered) (Wolfe, 1987). Rejecting parents are frequently called authoritarian. This style of parenting is believed to be related to child abuse. Authoritarian parents lack the sensitivity to relate to their children's level of ability, emotional needs, interests, and self-esteem needs. They rely upon power, threats, and punishment to control their children. Such parents affect their children in other ways. The children tend to be socially withdrawn; to avoid taking initiative; and to lack the spontaneity, affection, and curiosity of their peers.

    Abusive families are frequently characterized by violence between family members, including patterns of intergenerational abuse. Thus parenting can be viewed as an adaptional challenge influenced by a previous generation. No institution within society prepares anyone for parenting—a family passes its style from one generation to the rest. If the family has sufficient supports, abusive patterns may remain dormant. If it is confronted by stress or repeated crises, such patterns may reappear (Wolfe, 1987).

Some authors maintain that a seesaw model of child abuse is most appropriate, particularly because it illustrates the abusive family in relation to the "normal functional" nonabusive family:

> Children quickly learn the concept of equal quantities balancing one another on the lever-fulcrum playground device known as the seesaw. In the present model, stresses are at the right end of the seesaw lever and resources are at the left. The "normal" or functional (nonabusive) family can be pictured as being in balance with sufficient resources to equalize stresses. The lever of the seesaw is in a balanced horizontal position (Ostbloom & Crase, 1980, p. 166).

The model relates to several family dynamics. First, the family unit is in itself a dynamic resource—the whole is more than the sum of its parts. In many instances the family has sufficient internal strength to cope with crisis. Second, families must all deal with stress. Some are more resourceful than others and have sufficient external resources; thus they respond in such a way that their functioning is not impaired. When a family is functioning successfully, it has the resources to overcome stresses. A balance has been reached and is maintained.

These concepts imply that abuse occurs when families are functioning poorly and stresses overwhelm their resources. Abuse is unlikely when things are going well. Some families live under overwhelming stress; one stress leads to another. For example, illness can lead to chronic unemployment and poverty. Some families respond to stress by striking out or adopting aggressive behavior. This model or conceptualization directs practitioners' efforts toward decreasing stress and increasing resources in order to restore balance. Two services are provided: crisis intervention to relieve stress and enrichment of resources to strengthen the family. For this conceptualization to result in effective intervention, a broad array of services must be readily available—telephone counseling, emergency daycare and caretakers, emergency foster and shelter care, 24-hour on-call child protection services, and long-term services such as mental health and environmental manipulation services.

Prenatal Risk Factors.   Factors associated with high-risk parent–child relationships can be identified as early as the prenatal stage and include the following (Wolfe, 1987): *quality of intrauterine care*—substance abuse, lack of medical care and a sound diet, and low birth weight may affect the mother and child's future relationship and their ability to form strong ties; *maternal adjustment and parental preparation*—the nature of maternal and parental feelings around the pregnancy is determined by several questions. Was the baby planned? Was the baby wanted? What role did the father play in the pregnancy? Did the mother feel supported by friends and others?

Some parents are isolated from family and friends and thus lack external support in a time of crisis (Seagull, 1987). These parents sometimes feel ashamed to indicate that they are having difficulty or need external assistance to function as parents. Some also, lack the social skills to ask for help. As Mrs. Roberts once stated, "We keep our problems to ourselves. We do not bother grandparents with them and we do not have friends." Resources available to help parents with their nurturing role are very important. For example, social support appears to enhance parental competence by facilitating problem solving, increasing access to accurate information about children and parenting practices, fostering opportunities for positive reinforcement, and offering worth in the parenting role (Wolfe, 1987).

Psychiatric Diagnoses. When abusive parents are compared with nonabusive parents, a greater incidence of affective disorders is found (Famularo, Barnum, & Stone, 1986). Bipolar disorders, major depressive episodes, and alcoholism were found to be prevalent within the abusive group.

Environmental Variables. Inadequate income and poor living conditions have been associated with high incidence of abuse. Household crowding, at 1.51 persons per room, was frequently associated with incidents of abuse and neglect (Zuravin, 1986).

Stress has been recognized as a contributor to subsequent abuse. Stressful events both within a family and externally imposed on it contributed to abuse and neglect (Browne, 1986).

Indicators of Physical Abuse

Practitioners should be familiar with a number of indicators of physical abuse. However, caution should be used because children can also obtain bruises and other wounds from play.

1. *Bruises*
   a. Bruises and welts
   b. Bruises in various stages of healing
   c. Clustered bruises, indicating repeated contact with an object
2. *Burns*
   a. Cigarette burns
   b. Rope burns
3. *Lacerations*
   a. Tears in tissue (especially the lip, an indication of forced feeding)
4. *Skeletal Injuries*
   a. Fractures of long bones and splintering at the ends of the bones (these are caused by twisting or pulling)
5. *Head Injuries*
   a. Absence of hair, bald spots on the scalp
   b. Jaw and nasal fractures
   c. Subdural hematomas
6. *Internal Injuries*
   a. Inflammation of the lining of the abdominal cavity

    b. Blood clots in the small intestine (from being kicked in the abdomen

    c. Ruptured organs

7. *Other Indicators*

    a. Serious developmental delays

    b. Inconsistent medical history

    c. Inconsistent explanations why and how a child has obtained injuries

Indicators of Sexual Abuse

Medical practitioners in pediatrics should be aware of and able to respond to the sexual abuse of children in a quick and efficient manner. In one report covering a four-month period, 40 pediatric patients were treated for gonorrhea (Terrel, 1977). The mean age of these children was 4.5 years, and most were girls. The author concluded that prepubertal children who contract a venereal disease may have been sexually abused and perhaps need protection; thus medical personnel need to be trained properly to intervene in a responsible manner. Such training must address the types of abuse, methods of treatment relevant to type of abuse, legal mandates for reporting abuse, and recording results of medical examinations for use in court.

    Lack of knowledge about the many forms of abuse and neglect is not limited to the medical setting. Teachers have reported that they received little, if any, information about identifying abuse and neglect as a part of their educational preparation and postgraduate inservice (McIntyre, 1987).

    Physical indicators of sexual abuse might include:

1. The presence of venereal disease in young children

2. Physical trauma to the genital areas (red, swollen, torn tissue)

3. Offensive odors

4. Pregnancy

5. Seductive behavior

6. Preoccupation with genitals

7. Explicit information about sex atypical of a child's knowledge

INTERVIEWING VICTIMS OF SEXUAL ABUSE

Though interviewing is discussed in Chapter 5, some unique aspects of interviewing a sexually abused child or adolescent warrant further discussion. Child sexual abuse interview protocol is child or adolescent victim, siblings, nonoffending parents, and the alleged perpetrator (who may be a parent). Some things to remember include the following:

1. Do not ask leading questions; ask open-ended questions. What happened? When did it happen? Where did it happen?

2. Use language the child or adolescent uses and try to relax the interviewee.
3. Remember that children (depending on their ages and cognitive abilities) have short attention spans and that most adolescents can give accurate accounts.
4. Interview the child or adolescent in a relaxed environment, away from home and family members in the case of intrafamilial sexual abuse.
5. Be prepared to believe the child; though he or she may not have an accurate perception of time, the practitioner can help establish time by giving the child reference points. For example, was it hot or cold outside? What house did you live in?
6. Anatomically correct dolls may be introduced in the following manner: ask the child to identify the body parts (mouth, eyes, hands, fingers, legs, feet, etc.) to test his or her competency. The child can touch the dolls and tell his or her experiences.

Are dolls useful for expert testimony? There is some concern as to whether anatomically correct dolls should be the basis for this purpose (Yates, 1988). In two decisions by the California Supreme Court of Appeals, the court concluded that use of dolls constitutes a new scientific method of proof admissible in court only if it has been accepted as generally valid and reliable in the scientific community. Though limited, there is some empirical evidence that children who have been sexually abused are more likely to engage in sexual play than nonabused children (Yates, 1988). Perhaps what should be recommended here is that this testimony must be considered along with other evidence.

CASE ILLUSTRATION—MAGGIE, AGE SEVEN

Maggie reported that her stepfather was putting his "thing" into her mouth. Maggie's mother denies this and feels that Maggie and her sister were set up by the babysitter to tell these stories. Mother also states that Maggie and her sister have been exposed to "dirty movies" while in the care of the babysitter. Mother believes the child is saying this for attention. Mother complains that there has been a change in Maggie's behavior since the first of March when she started to blatantly disobey her. Last week Maggie was caught shoplifting, and lately there has been an increase in fighting between Maggie and her sisters. Mother also states that Maggie acts very babyish when she is around her stepfather. A couple of weeks ago Maggie tried to choke her sister.

Maggie's four-year-old sister supports Maggie's story. She denies being abused but says she watched through the bedroom door. Children and Family Services believes the allegations and has proceeded with prosecution. Maggie's stepfather denies the allegations. Because of the denial Maggie continues to live with her mother, stepfather, and two sisters, ages four and two. She has no contact with her birth father.

The names in this case are fictitious.
Gail Folaran, faculty member, Indiana University, Indianapolis, prepared this case.

This brief summary illustrates the contradictory information a practitioner may receive when investigating or counseling a child who claims to have been sexually abused. Given Maggie's age and her mother's report that she and her sister have been watching pornographic movies, one could conclude that her story is merely a figment of her imagination. In that case, why would the babysitter encourage the children to report such a story? Why is the mother such a key figure in explaining the story from so many different perspectives?

How you would go about interviewing Maggie? What developmental considerations are important? Would you use anatomically correct dolls? If so, how would you introduce them? What would you ask Maggie about the dolls? Would you ask her to illustrate what her stepfather had done to her? If so, how would you comfort Maggie as she tells her story?

CASE ILLUSTRATION—TAMMY, AGE FOUR

Presenting Problem

Mrs. Green (mother) brought Tammy in because "somebody was messing with her." Mother stated that approximately one month ago Tammy reported that her "butt hurt," and upon investigation it was noted that her vagina was very red. Mother wondered whether sexual abuse had occurred because in December 1991 a family friend had been reported for sexually abusing Tammy. Mother stated the man left for Kentucky, so she is sure he is not the abuser. She wonders if someone else has been "messing with" Tammy.

Mother stated that the child has been upset all the time and appears depressed. She is always frowning. The parents have been letting her have her way because they felt so bad about her abuse.

Tammy's family has been involved with Children and Family Services since 1991 when the mother applied for food stamps. At that time, the father was in jail for physically abusing his nephew. Since that time, there have been several reports of physical abuse and neglect of Tammy and her two younger siblings; and in December 1991 the children were removed from the home. The children were returned the following February, and the family was required to attend counseling.

Current Living Situation

Tammy prefers her father and has had a hard adjustment to her father's working. Mother stated that she used to work while her husband stayed at home with the kids, but he has recently found a job. Tammy also had to adjust to a new babysitter. Mother states that additional stresses include the Children and Family Services, which is always "in their business," and classes required by the Welfare Department. She says she is criticized because her children are not clean although they have a bath every night. Father wonders if his reaction to the fact that Chester was sexually abusing his daughter has affected Tammy. He said that he would like to see the "son of a bitch hung up." He was also concerned that Tammy is becoming more sexually active. He stated that during the week of June 24 he caught Tammy and her younger brother behind the grapevine with their underwear down. According to Tammy, Mike (a 15-year-old neighbor boy) told them he would give them one dollar if they would pull down their underwear. Mr. Green reported this to the police and the Welfare Department. Father also stated that Tammy has explored sex with her brother and they have been separated. On several occasions, he has caught them riding each other.

Parent and Family Relationships

Tammy has been acting very angry and "bitchy." Mother stated that she has even been hard to get along with at the babysitter's. She has been destructive with her dolls and ripped off their heads, stating that they are "family members." The members change, however. Sometimes it is mother, sometimes it is father, and sometimes it is brother and sister. She used to be more responsible than the other children. Tammy is the oldest of the three siblings.

The parents have been married six years. Father states that there is no love life, and mother states that father talks too much for her. Parents would like to work on their marital relationship and may be doing so with another counseling center although mother was quick to state "that's my hour; that's my therapist."

The names in this case are fictitious.
Gail Folaran, faculty member, Indiana University, Indianapolis, prepared this case.

The Tammy story illustrates not only the sexual abuse of Tammy but the environmental stresses present (father jailed, insufficient money for food, poor parenting skills). Tammy's behavior (e.g., she is destructive with her dolls and ripped their heads off, is always frowning and depressed) might be considered typical of a child who has been sexually abused. She has regressed and is angry, the manifestations of abuse.

CASE ILLUSTRATION—ANNIE, AGE TEN

Annie is a winsome, frail-looking, pretty ten-year-old girl. For the last six weeks, she has been living with a foster mother, Mrs. Jefferson, a 64-year-old widow. This is Annie's sixth foster home. She was left with a babysitter by her mother at about one month of age and retrieved by her father, who had not seen her before that date. She then lived with her father until she was six, when her father remarried. According to him and his second wife, right after they married, Annie started lying, stealing, not "minding," and hurting her younger half-sister. Talking to her and whipping her did not have any effect, so they asked her if she wanted to live with her mother, and she said yes. She then lived with her mother (and two different husbands and an older stepbrother, Douglas) for about two years before she was taken into protective custody by Children and Family Services. This occurred after several indicated incidences of abuse (beating, being tied to a chair, and one report by Annie that her father "touched her down there," during a weekend visit). Between the ages of six and eight, Annie missed a great deal of school.

Her IQ scores on two occasions have been low normal; her achievement test scores generally indicate that she is performing below grade level by at least one year in reading and social studies and about three years in math and science. Annie is in a regular fourth grade classroom but receives tutoring in math and reading. Her teachers believe she can do C work, but her grades are typically Ds and Fs.

Annie's foster mother reports that she has had two major blowups with Annie about not doing her schoolwork. These resulted in Annie going "totally out of control," screaming and hurling furniture and objects around her home till the foster mother finally was able to restrain her physically by lying down on top of her. The foster mother also described a series of other "unusual" behaviors, including rummaging through every drawer, closet, and cabinet and having to place her hand on every piece of paper in the house. She voiced the concern that on three occasions when Mrs. R's grown sons came for a visit Annie rushed to them and insisted on sitting on their laps and kissing them on the face. Mrs. Jefferson, the foster mother, talked to Annie about this behavior and told her it was not appropriate.

Annie's biological mother has relinquished rights to her. Children and Family Services is now pursuing relinquishment of parental rights by Annie's father. Annie last saw her father eight months ago when meetings with him and her stepmother at the mental health center ended in August. The mental health worker recorded that Annie's father had unrealistic expectations for a 10-year-old girl. He is described as extremely angry and rigid (he and three siblings were placed in an orphanage by his mother when he was ten). The end of these counseling sessions occurred when Annie's father issued an ultimatum about strict obedience to his rules. Annie then said she wanted to be adopted by the foster mother with whom she was currently living and did not want to live with her father.

The names in this case are fictitious.
Katharin Moroz, Assistant Professor, University of Vermont, Burlington, prepared this case.

Annie's behaviors are the result of many years of unstable living situations; lack of attachment and bonding to a significant adult figure, required for social and psychological maturity and closeness; physical and sexual abuse; rejection by those who should typically love her; and a rigid parental figure whose expectations exceed the capacity of a ten-year-old girl.

In this case, returning the child to her home would probably be more destructive than constructive. It is important to remember that each case must be assessed individually, and practitioners should be careful to avoid making broad generalizations and thus developing inappropriate service plans. In this case, a permanent adult figure is also needed for this child. Permanency planning was required of states with the passage of the 1980 Child Welfare and Adoption Assistance Act, PL 96-272. This legislation stresses the importance of and the need for permanent child–adult relationships, an adult who can act as the child's psychological parent. More discussion of the practice implications of this act is presented elsewhere in this chapter.

Returning children to their homes, the new thrust toward family reunification and preservation, is the current federal and state goal. There is nevertheless no clear formula about when a child should be returned, and there are no guarantees that once the child is returned he or she will be safe. This is a difficult aspect of work with this population. About one-fourth of the 82 Illinois children who died from abuse or neglect in 1985–1986 lived in families previously cleared of alleged abuse in earlier state investigations (Champaign-Urbana *News Gazette,* 1986). For the fiscal year ending June 30, 1986, records indicated that the state-wide death toll from child abuse and neglect rose 49 percent over the 55 deaths recorded in 1985.

It appears that the federal government has been reluctant to provide families with the basic support systems that could help reduce abuse and neglect (Gratteau & Dold, 1986). It also appears that the government would rather spend thousands of dollars to remove a child from the home than give the family $1,000 a month to stabilize it and provide counseling and other services.

CASE ILLUSTRATION—KATHY, AGE 15

The following letters were written to Kathy, a sexually abused youth, after her father was sentenced and jailed for sexual assault. They highlight the conflicts within the family and the role blurring that is more implicit than explicit in such families. In the first letter, the father comes across as a man wanting to protect his child and please "his little girl." In the second, he begs for forgiveness and vows love forever. In the third, he essentially denies guilt and begs Kathy to tell her mother that he did not rape her. He also indicates to Kathy that her mother will forgive her—as though Kathy is the guilty person rather than the victim. Imagine the internal conflicts and pain these letters create for Kathy.

September 18, 1991

Kathy,

I just thought I would drop you a line and to tell you hi and I am sorry for the way I acted in the visiting room. I will never say another word to hurt you.

I just worry an awful lot about you so please understand what I am about to write.

I haven't forgotten my promise to you. The very day I get out I will sign that check that your mother is holding for me and I will give [you] enough to buy a bike after that you and I will be even. You don't even have to worry about me or any promises that you made me! I hope that you will understand that I was uptight being locked up in here and I was worried sick about you because I missed not being there for you when you needed me! You were to me my little girl and it meant a lot to me but I will just have to remember that in your letter that you aren't my little girl anymore. I am sorry and

I still love you. I guess I was just over protective of you. I guess you have grown up and don't need me like you said you did. I will always have a special place in my heart for you, Kathy.

If when I get out I guess I better just forget everything and not wrestle with you or anything like that because you will be sixteen and too grown up for that. I am sorry that I made you feel bad the last time you came to me.

Tell your brother I love him and I will see him about January sometime.

> Bye for now.
>
> I really do miss you.
>
> Please don't hate me.
>
> I got the picture of you. Thanks.

October 7, 1991

Kathy,

In writing you this letter on this time it really comes from my heart. So here goes everything.

I want you to realize that I love you very much and I haven't forgotten you. I have had a lot of time to think it over. I know that in the past I was too strict with you and I am sorrier now than you will ever know. I promise you I won't be that way ever again. I just don't want to lose your love because believe me that is very important. Please give me one more chance to make it up to you. I promise you I will never hurt you again. I miss you very much and I worry all the time that I am in here. I know that you will be 16 when I get out and you will be all grown up but I'll get used to it if you give me that chance. I promise you that I will be there if you need me even if it is only to talk I'll be there.

Can I still think of you as my little girl but I will treat you like a young lady cause that is what you are. You can forget everything else just don't forget that I love you very much, more than anything else in the world. I promise that I will do my best to be there only if you want me to.

Please take care and do good in school. I will send you a birthday card. I won't forget.

Tell everyone I said hello and to take care.

> I love you
> Lost and lonely
> Sam

Will you please write to me, Kathy, please.

October 8, 1992

Please Kathy,

Please tell your mom that it wasn't me. I beg you to tell her that. I didn't rape you. We both know that is the truth. I don't want to go to jail for something that we both know better. It is bad enough that I am going to lose the only family that ever meant anything to me, honest. Just tell her that it wasn't that way at all. Please Kathy, I can't stand to be in jail much longer than what time I have left. You don't know what this place can do to a person. Please tell her that you lied about us and you know that you have always had a problem with your period if that is the deal. Tell her that she scared you by threatening to send you away forever that you said all them things about me. I wouldn't hurt you for anything in the world like you have me. I am not mad at you and I told you I was sorry that I was so strict with you so please help me Kathy. I already told you that I would help you out not what your mother had thought. She took that letter all wrong. Just because of that now I can't even come back. That was just like someone had reached in and ripped my heart out so now I got to suffer because of what you said. I was always there when you needed me when you were sick or when you hurt so I am asking you to please help me just this once. I will never ask anything of you again, you know that. I am sorry that it has come to this. Please help me. Your mom will forgive you if you tell her you lied on me but she won't believe me at all.

I still love all of you very much.

Sam

The names in this case are fictitious.
Gail Folaran, faculty member, Indiana University, Indianapolis, prepared this case.

THE IMPACT OF ABUSE ON THE VICTIM

One study examined the records of 125 children six years of age who had been sexually abused (Mian et al., 1986). Intrafamilial abuse accounted for 60 percent of the children and extrafamilial abuse for 36 percent. In 4 percent of the cases, the perpetrator could not be identified and was listed as unknown. In 87 percent of the cases, the children were acquainted with their offenders; but 9 percent were abused by strangers. Of the named abusers, 14 percent were members of the extended family and 56 percent were members of the nuclear family. Biological fathers were the offenders most commonly named. They constituted 37.5 percent of all identified abusers and 79 percent of abusers within the nuclear family. Others were brothers, stepbrothers, and biological mothers (4 percent). Preschoolers were 1.7 times more likely to be abused by family members. The type of sexual activity included fondling, vulvar "dry" intercourse, oral–genital contact, and exhibitionism. Symptoms of the children at the time of disclosure included: emotional problems, such as nightmares, disruptive behavior, clinginess, and fearfulness, and physical symptoms such as vaginal discharge, bleeding, sexually transmitted diseases, bruises in the genital area, and abdominal pain. These children also showed sexual behaviors. Effects of maltreatment of children include delinquency, prostitution, intellectual disabilities, runaway behavior, and higher situational anxiety. Suicide is three to six times more likely in the sexually abused during adolescence (Ney, 1987).

The effects of abuse on children are numerous. For example, abused children may not interact well with others. They may be less verbal, they give uninvolved gazes, and they avoid both social engagement and engagement with the environment to a greater extent than nonabused children of the same age (Hecht et al., 1986).

The kind of abuse affects children differently. Interview data have been collected on different groups of children: those who were physically abused, verbally abused, physically neglected, emotionally neglected, or sexually abused. Those children who had endured mild physical abuse felt that they were to blame for such treatment, whereas verbally and sexually abused children did not believe they were to blame. However, verbally abused children were more angry and pessimistic about their futures (Ney et al., 1986).

Sexually abused children also suffer considerable psychological damage. In a study that compared sexually abused children with other groups, it was found that both male and female sexually abused children demonstrated higher levels of sexualized behaviors (such as masturbating in inappropriate settings) and higher rates of somatic complaints (National Conference on the Sexual Victimization of Children, 1986).

According to Lamphear (1985), the research on the psychosocial adjustment of maltreated children is flawed with a number of methodological problems. The definition of maltreatment varies from study to study, more adequate verification of the absence of maltreatment in the control groups is needed, and studies have contained a wide age range (two to twelve years). Knowledge of the lifetime impact of child abuse is still very limited. It is known that children who grow up in environments that include multiple child abuse threats and actions are vulnerable to a range of outcomes. Being the victim of child abuse, however, does not doom a person to any particular future.

Those Who Survive Abuse

One study conducted in Israel examined the extent to which children's patterns of coping with extreme situations, such as abuse, can help us understand the personal and situational factors crucial for survival (Zimrin, 1986). This longitudinal study, which began when the children were about four years old and included a 14-year follow-up, found that abused children tended to be fatalistic, aggressive, and self-destructive. They had poor self-esteem, difficulty expressing emotions, an incapacity to establish personal relationships, and inadequate cognitive development. Survivors of abuse, however, were in control of their destinies, showed good self-esteem, good cognitive performance, and absence of self-destructive behavior. They also had supporting adults in their lives. Both groups were found to be similar in terms of high aggression, difficulty expressing emotions, and difficulty developing relationships. It appears that children who survived abuse had adults in their lives to whom they could attribute good content and positive interaction. The practice implications that can be generalized from these findings include the possibility of increasing external support by encouraging the presence of a nurturing adult figure, strengthening the child's inner confidence, and developing coping behavior within the child.

Twenty-seven incest victims aged 12 to 18 responded to their ordeal with self-destructive behavior (Lindberg & Distad, 1985). According to these authors, many mental health professionals have acknowledged the positive correlation between runaway behavior, promiscuity, substance abuse, and other self-destructive behaviors among sexually abused adolescents. Lindberg and Distad examined these behaviors as logical survival responses of the adolescent. In other words, although these behaviors are negative and damaging, they serve the purpose of reducing stress or overcoming feelings of helplessness. These so-called survival behaviors become generalized to other settings where they are not needed. The implication for practice is that adolescents may not understand the reasons for these behaviors; they may have little insight, and distortion or a desire on their part to forget may result in further denial. As stated earlier, they may believe that they are "bad." It appears that a strong therapeutic alliance to redefine the child's role in the incest experience, recognize behaviors as survival responses, and manage self-destructive behaviors is the aim of therapeutic intervention.

INTERVENTION

Individual and Family

There are essentially ten ways children respond to abuse and neglect:

1. *Identification with aggression*
2. *Neurotic adaptation*—for example, obsessive, compulsive, or phobic behaviors
3. *Quiet*—they believe they are responsible for the events that caused their turmoil
4. *Folie à deux*—they accept their parents' psychotic view of the world and live in a semipsychotic confused state
5. *Depression*—they place blame on themselves
6. *Apathy*—they shut off aspects of their existence
7. *Revenge*—they nurture their wounds while plotting reprisal
8. *Rebellion*
9. *Searching*—they find security elsewhere
10. *Precocious development*—they become pseudoadults

The literature suggests that neglected and abused children, as well as parents who were abused themselves, tend to follow a seven-phase progression while undergoing treatment (Ney, 1987).

1. *Realization*—that they are indeed victims and that they have been afraid to acknowledge their true feelings

2. *Protest*—once they realize that they are victims, they can begin to experience their pain and true feelings; and they should be allowed to rehearse their feelings in treatment sessions
3. *Quiet*—as they gain new awareness and insight, these children begin to feel that they are partially responsible, in either a passive or an active way; for some reason or other, they feel that "they have asked for it"
4. *Despair*—as therapy progresses, children become aware that their childhoods were not normal; they typically move into mourning this loss. This stage is especially evident in those who do not enter therapy until they are adults
5. *Reevaluation of relationships*—these children and adults who were abused as children are looking for completeness, for relationships to gratify their interpersonal needs
6. *Reconciliation*—once these children and adults have faced their emotions, they are then ready to face the perpetrators
7. *Reconstruction*—children are encouraged to reach out to others.

Groupwork with Abusive Parents.   The author was assigned the task of directing and organizing parent training groups for abusive parents who no longer had custody of their children. The local Child and Family Services and the courts had removed their children from their care. As a part of the effort of the court system and of the child welfare agency to improve their functioning, these parents were required to participate in parent training classes. Some social work practitioners, like the author, might ask themselves whether these parents were truly invested in learning other ways of behaving or were attending these classes because it was the socially accepted reaction to their situation.

This group met weekly, with 10 to 12 members aged 18 to 48, most of them considered low income. The content of each session was prescribed by a training program developed by the Child and Family Welfare agency. The author found that she had to modify some of the material to meet the needs of the group participants. Topics included communication skills, behavior management, how to respond to stressful situations, knowledge of human development, and community resources. Homework assignments were given for each unit of material, and time was made before each session to hear from group members about their experiences implementing their new skills. Some had considerable success, while others questioned whether "doing something different" would help. "They had tried everything."

From this experience, the author made several observations. First, some of the abusive parents had been abused themselves, were poorly educated, and did not understand the developmental needs of their children. One young woman reported, "My toddler goes into the kitchen and removes all of the plasticwear, pots, and pans from the cabinet. The kitchen is always messy! He is a bad boy! When he does this I place him in a corner and demand that he stay there! He never does. You would think that he could understand me." Second, some parents claimed they had tried new approaches to behavior management, but all that seemed to work was physical force. These attempts, however, were not consistent or used long enough to change a child's way of responding. Third, parents felt alone. Most were without the support of family or friends, and many were ignorant of child care and crisis services they could draw upon. In fact, one woman stated, "If I only had a few minutes to myself, I could be a better parent. I care for my children seven days a week. I am tired!" Fourth, some of the parents had given up on their children. One woman reported, "I beat her because I care about her," describing her 13-year-old daughter. "She'll be pregnant before you know it! She'll live a miserable life, like myself. I want something better for her. My parents beat me, and I'm better because they cared so much."

The development of empirically based assessment tools is discussed briefly in Chapter 3. A multidimensional inventory for assessment of parental functioning used to evaluate a family support program intended to reduce child abuse and neglect has been developed (Reis et al., 1987). Components of the inventory assess key aspects of parenting behavior as defined by ecological theories of human development (social support, childrearing attitudes, depression, and developmental expectations).

Development of stress management skills for parents is one of many approaches that can easily be integrated into a group setting. Schinke and colleagues (1986) have evaluated the effects of stress management skills intervention with mothers and fathers of developmentally disabled children. Parents received training to increase their self-centered, interpersonal communication, and child discipline skills and to expand their social support networks. This group, at posttest stage, improved in areas of coping and self-control.

Family Preservation and Homebuilders.   In some cases, it is not in the best interest of a family to preserve it. If the family is dysfunctional and the lives of its children are at risk, the children need to be relocated to a safe environment. As stated in Chapter 4, the foster care system has been known to hold children in placement or custody for extended periods of time while providing too few services to rehabilitate their families. This situation stimulated Congress to pass the Child Welfare Act (PL. 96-272) in 1980. The primary intent of the law is to redirect funds to services that keep children with their families. This intent has been labeled family-based preventive and restorative service.

The Child Welfare League of America has conceptualized three levels of services designed to preserve the family (1989, p. 13). They are (1) *community-based* services that assist and support adults in their roles as parents; (2) *family-centered* services given to stabilize the family (e.g., case management, counseling or therapy, educational skills, advocacy, and the provision of concrete services); and (3) *intensive family-centered crisis* services, which are provided when there is a situation that requires removal of the child.

Homebuilders is "an intensive, in-home family crisis counseling and life-skills education program designed to prevent unnecessary dissolutions of troubled families and reduce placements of children into publicly-funded care. . . . Homebuilders is based on the belief that it is usually best for children to grow up in their own homes" (Homebuilders, 1990, p. 1).

Consistent with the perspectives advocated here, Homebuilders draws upon the ecological perspective and developmental concepts and the development of competence. Some of the skills required to implement this orientation are assessing the family's strengths, changing the environment, planning goals, setting time limits, contracting with families, teaching specific life or social skills, intervening during crises, working with families in their homes, and individualizing services to meet the needs of a family (Maluccio, 1991). Other assumptions that undergird the Homebuilders movement are that it is not always possible to determine which families are hopeless and which can benefit from intervention, that families are often doing the best they can, that Homebuilders can offer families hope and present new possibilities.

Providing treatment in the homes has a number of advantages. The worker gets a firsthand point of view of the family and its interaction in its natural environment; going into the home conveys concern for the family's well-being; the worker can construct more personalized interventions to meet the needs of the family. Some disadvantages should also be noted. This intervention requires very skilled professionals; the work is very intense; and to some degree the presence of the worker can hamper normal interactions among family members.

Techniques for Children.   The "lifebook" is a concrete therapeutic tool that can be used to help children in placement and those who have had a number of changes in their lifebooks (Backhaus, 1984). A lifebook is an individualized book covering a child's life from birth to the present, written in the child's own words. It generally includes a narrative describing the child's life events—what has happened, when, and why—as well as the child's feelings about these events. Of course, the book does not solve the child's emotional or behavioral problems, but it does offer the child a sense of history and belonging by helping the child to integrate the past, present, and future. It helps children avoid fantasy and denial. In terms of clinical work, a lifebook can decrease anxiety and enable the practitioner to identify unfinished business for a particular child.

Dance and movement therapy in the context of multidisciplinary treatment of abused and neglected children has also been suggested for some children (Goodwill, 1987). Such intervention strengthens the child's image of body and self, allowing for self-expression.

Environmental Interventions and the Use of Natural Helpers

The use of natural helpers in preventing child abuse and neglect has also been empirically explored (Ballew, 1985). The assumption underlying this research is that natural helpers in the family's immediate environment (friends, relatives, neighbors) are available and are often in more contact with a family than the practitioner. Of 430 at-risk families identified for this study 130 were randomly selected. Natural helpers existed for most families, though it is widely believed that such families are socially isolated. These were friends, neighbors, or relatives whose relationships with the family were not based on family needs or on particular problems. It was found that the practitioners often dismissed extended family, friends, or neighbors because they were thought to be too confused to draw into the clinical picture. The transactional perspective advocated in this book draws upon the use of natural helpers and institutions within the client's immediate environment as resources for the promotion of positive change. In this study, natural helpers were found to be very effective. When appropriate, the worker should consider natural helpers as members of the interventive team. Of course, their involvement in the helping process should be sanctioned by the client. Another advantage of natural helpers over professionals and volunteers is that they often remain involved with a family long after other relationships have been terminated.

In one study, an early-intervention program that targeted parents at risk of child abuse and neglect was explored (Wolfe et al., 1988). Its premise was that a healthy relationship with his or her parents provides a child with a critical foundation for development, but among maltreating families the quality of this relationship was poor. Several criteria were employed to identify the experimental group, including scores obtained on the Child Abuse Potential Inventory, as well as home observations. The goals of the intervention included (1) early development of positive habits of child rearing through rewarding parent–child interactions, (2) improvement of parents' abilities to cope with stress, and (3) promotion of children's adaptive behaviors that contribute to healthy psychological development. Thus, agency-based family support services and training in child management, relying upon behavioral concepts, comprised the intervention. Instruction included modeling and rehearsal procedures, and instruction in how to give concise demands. A control group received information about health and family-related topics. The experimental group reported fewer and less intense child behavior problems associated with the risk of maltreatment than the control group. At a one-year follow-up, the experimental group still showed greater improvement.

Medical Intervention

As stated earlier, medical practitioners have reported that they feel unprepared to offer the psychological and protective service assessments that child abuse cases require in addition to medical evaluation and treatment (Sink, 1986). An interdisciplinary model for sexual abuse assessment has been offered. The philosophical underpinning of the program is that sexual abuse cases present complex psychosocial and legal problems that require the skills of medical, legal, and psychological professionals. In this model a sex abuse treatment team posited in a pediatric setting included an emergency response (walk-in clinic) with psychological assessment of the sexually abused child and his or her family (conducted by a social worker, a psychologist, a psychiatrist, and others). Consultative services were made available to physicians to help them in managing children and their families and to help their staffs address the anxiety typically associated with these cases. A specialty clinic was available where practitioners not only assessed the quality of a child's ability to cope with stress, trauma, and the impact of disclosure but also worked with the child-protective agency. A case-finding system was also introduced into a pediatric emergency room to remind the medical staff of the possibility of maltreatment (Pless et al., 1987).

University and Community-Based Intervention

A university program developed in cooperation with a social service department was found to be cost-effective in keeping abused children out of the foster care system (Meter, 1986). Participants in the project were either at risk of being placed out of the home or scheduled to return from placement in one to six months. Parents in the project had to be in a treatment program if involved in substance abuse. Parents did not have chronic psychosis, they had functional intellectual abilities, and they wanted their children. Practitioners assigned to work with the families functioned as advocates and educators; they tried to motivate these families to develop better home environments for individual growth. The program was based on an ecological systems perspective. In-home counseling techniques, issues of child rearing, approaches to studying the family, and topics on abuse and neglect, drug abuse, and burnout in human services were included in the training. Practitioners spent considerable time in the home and community. Evaluation of the project found that clients continued to use their newly acquired parenting attitudes and skills.

Educating School Personnel and Children in Awareness of Sex Abuse

Suggestions for prevention of physical and sexual abuse and for intervention must include the education of school personnel and children. Much attention has been devoted to remediation. A proactive strategy could include the education of large numbers of school personnel, children and adolescents, and community groups. A school-based program integrated into various curriculum areas is the ideal. Sex education, family life education, and health education are areas in which this content could be infused. In one such effort with fourth and fifth graders, presentation of information (e.g., it is ok to report someone, get help right away, you may feel embarrassed and fearful), skits, films, and discussions were found to be effective both in increasing the children's knowledge and in changing behavior when compared with an experimental group (Wolfe et al., 1986).

PREVENTION AND LONG-RANGE PLANNING

Garbarino (1986) outlined a strategy for assessing the success of efforts to reduce the incidence and severity of child abuse in the United States. What is obvious about this strategy is that prevention does not come cheaply. It takes person power and systematic efforts at a variety of levels. What we attempt to do should rest on the available empirical evidence, but we know far too little to set forth a prescription. Two programs that appear to offer some hope are the Health Visitor's Program and Family-Centered Childbirth. The Health Visitor's Program consists of assigning a health visitor to the family during a pregnancy and for the first two years of a baby's life. Results indicate a significant preventive effect among both families and poor unmarried women. Family-Centered Childbirth constitutes a second programmatic approach to providing families with support to prevent child maltreatment. This effort includes an assessment of the quality of mother–infant relationships in the delivery room and during the first few days after birth. By identifying problematic interaction, practitioners can intervene and prevent abuse. What is interesting about both interventions is that they require that someone supervise the family, that the family to some degree is under surveillance, and that there is an implication of social control.

Prevention strategies need to be tailored to meet the needs of the intended target population (different family structures, minority groups, etc.). Related prevention goals must be stated precisely, and limits set on what can be claimed. In other words, distinction must be made between "reducing incidence and reducing severity" (Garbarino, 1986, p. 153), and evaluation efforts must be planned to document differential effects. As stated in Chapter 6, evaluation should utilize multiple measures; it may be unwise to limit them to measures of reported child abuse. Prevention efforts must also attack the broader environmental and social context. Merely to focus on parenting skills and the parenting unit and to ignore such factors as racial isolation, poverty, and unemployment is to omit a host of societal contributors. As stated earlier in this chapter, many societal stressors can place even a functional family unit under stress and undermine its ability to respond to daily living. The adoption of a transactional perspective forces us to move in this direction.

Primary Prevention and Screening

Attempts to identify potential abusers have been discussed in the literature. It is terribly attractive to think that potential abusers can be identified and intervention provided before abuse takes place. Some research has been conducted with this goal in mind—secondary prevention of child maltreatment (McMurtry, 1985). Although there are some general indicators of persons who might abuse, more research is needed to establish accurate identifying criteria and to determine effective means of intervention to prevent abuse. General indicators include these

1. An economic explanation—related to inequalities and the acceptance of parental use of force—which points toward advocacy of children's rights, redistributive economic policies, and widely embraced social reform.
2. Intrafamilial variables in the appearance of abuse and neglect (role blurring, stress, intergenerational problems, lack of social support).

Preventive interventions that emerge from this view include homemaker services, family therapy, development of social supports, home visitors, and crisis assistance.

3. Lack of preparation for parenthood. Intensive educational interventions to increase public awareness and to educate parents about appropriate behavior management techniques are called for.

McMurtry (1985) conducted a review of published research on secondary prevention of child maltreatment. The conclusion was that although some risk characteristics are evolving, more research is needed to establish and to validate criteria.

To attack the problem of child abuse, the use of prevention and intervention techniques on many levels offers our best hope for success (see Table 7.1). This is congruent with the transactional framework because it focuses attention on the different environments, as well as the individual.

SUMMARY

In Chapter 5, considerable discussion is devoted to an overview of social welfare programs and policies intended to benefit children, adolescents, and their families. It is unfortunate that many of these programs and policies are reactive

---

TABLE 7.1   Multilevel targets for child abuse prevention and intervention

I. **Individual Level**
  - Psychological problems associated with the parent's history of abusive and/or rejecting childhood experiences
  - Limited coping skills of caregivers
  - Stress-related symptoms affecting emotional and physical health
  - Negative attributions for child transgressions
  - Insensitivity to, or neglect of, child's needs and abilities
  - Low self-esteem, poor self-motivation, limited social competence
  - Limited financial and household management skills
  - Child symptoms associated with victimization (fears, affect disturbance, poor peer relations)

II. **Familial Level**
  - Marital discord and conflict, poor problem-solving abilities
  - Low rate of positive interactions between family members
  - Difficult behavior of child

III. **Community Level**
  - Socioeconomic conditions
  - Support and educational services for disadvantaged families
  - Suitable employment opportunities

IV. **Societal and Cultural Level**
  - Acceptance of corporal punishment of children
  - Low priority for parenthood education and preparation
  - Unequal burden of child-rearing responsibilities placed on women

---

SOURCE: Wolfe, D. A. (1987). *Child abuse: implications for child development and psychopathology*, p. 127. Newbury Park, Calif.: Sage Publications. Reprinted with permission.

and come much too late to prevent the stress that is often felt by families. Children and adolescents are often abused and neglected because their parents or guardians can no longer cope.

It appears that multiple interventions may be the appropriate course of action. Wolfe (1987) proposes that such intervention should be used to strengthen protective factors in a child's environment rather than to target a child's behavior. This is perhaps the best course of action because it minimizes blaming the "victim." Targeting the child carries the implicit message that he or she is at fault for the abuse. Wolfe suggests that we (1) modify deleterious characteristics of the target person or family members, (2) reduce family discord and increase the acceptance of the child, and (3) draw upon external agencies to support the family and child (1987, p. 126). Intervention must eliminate the transfer of poor parenting and abuse from one generation to another; provide sufficient economic, social, and other resources (opportunity to learn appropriate parenting) at the community level; and at the societal level work toward changes that would enhance some of the programs and policies described in Chapter 4.

QUESTIONS FOR DISCUSSION

1. What might be some of the coping skills used by abused children and adolescents? How would a practitioner proceed to reduce the use of defense mechanisms to replace them with responses that would promote healthy functioning?

2. Discuss the positives and negatives of using young children to provide testimony about abuse in court.

3. Expand upon the stages of therapy with abused children outlined in this chapter. In your discussion, include specific intervention for each stage that would move the child or adolescent along the continuum of therapy.

4. Explore in more depth the effects of abuse (physical, sexual, and emotional) on functioning in adulthood. How can we break the cycle of intergenerational transmission? Include in your discussion specific interventions (e.g., programs, individual, group), as well as policy.

5. Several case illustrations are presented in this chapter. Review each and address the clinical issues raised, interventions, potential barriers, and other factors.

6. Outline a set of intervention strategies that would address the sexually abused adolescent male or female.

7. Outline a set of intervention strategies that would address the incestuous family.

8. Contact either your local or your state child and family services office that assumes responsibility for responding to reports of abuse. Inquire about the volume and characteristics of cases reported for your geographical area. Compare these statistics to those found in national reports. Discuss the implications of your findings.

9. Do you agree with the seesaw conceptualization of abusive families? Defend your position.

10. Identify and describe the local crisis services available to parents in times of stress. Evaluate the availability and diversity of these services.

ADDITIONAL READINGS

Barth, R., & Howard, D. (1993). Intensive family preservation services with abused and neglected children: An examination of group difference. *Child Abuse and Neglect* 17(2): 213-225.

Barth, R., & Sullivan, R. (1985). Collecting competent evidence in behalf of children. *Social Work* 30: 130-137.

Berliner, L., & Conte, J. (1993). Sexual abuse evaluations: Conceptual and empirical obstacles. *Child Abuse and Neglect* 17(1): 111-125.

Brodzinskey, D. (1993). On the use of psychological testing in child custody evaluations. *Professional Psychology Evaluations: Research and Practice* 24(2): 213-219.

Compher, J. (1983). Home services to families to prevent child placement. *Social Work* 28: 360-364.

Conte, J., Sorenson, E., Fogarty, L., & Rosa, J. (1991). Evaluating children's reports of sexual abuse: Results from a survey of professionals. *American Journal of Orthopsychiatry* 61: 428-437.

Dietrich, D., Berkowitz, L., Kadushin, A., & McGloin, J. (1990). Some factors influencing abusers' justification of their child abuse. *Child Abuse and Neglect* 14: 337-345.

Dormstadt, G. (1990). Community-based child abuse prevention. *Social Work* 35: 487-489.

Draucker, C. (1992). *Counseling survivors of childhood sexual abuse.* Newbury Park, Calif.: Sage Publications.

Engeland, B., & Vaughn, B. (1981). Failure of bond formation as a cause of abuse, neglect and maltreatment, *American Journal of Orthopsychiatry* 51: 78-84.

Gaudin, J., & Kurtz, D. (1985). Parenting skills training for child abusers. *Journal of Group Psychotherapy, Psychodrama and Sociology* 38: 35-54.

Gil, E. (1991). *The healing power of play: Working with abused children.* New York: Guilford Press.

Halpern, R., (1986). Home-based early intervention: Dimensions of current practice. *Child Welfare* 65(4): 387-398.

Hansen, J. (1984). Progress in treating the sexual abuse of children. *Social Work* 29: 258-264.

Hartman, A., & Laird, J. (1983). *Family-centered social work practice.* New York: Free Press.

Jackson, H., & Nuttall, R. (1993). Clinical responses to sexual abuse allegations. *Child Abuse and Neglect* 17(1): 127-143.

Lie, G., & Inman, A. (1991). The use of anatomical dolls as assessment and evidentiary tools. *Social Work* 36: 396-399.

Nasjleti, M. (1980). Suffering in silence: The male incest victim. *Child Welfare* 59: 269-275.

Nelson, K., Landsman, M., & Deutelbaum, W. (1990). Three models of family centered placement prevention. *Child Welfare* 69: 3-21.

Orr, D., & Downs, M. (1985). Self-concept of adolescent sexual abuse victims. *Journal of Youth and Adolescence* 14: 401-410.

Salter, A., Richardson, C., & Kairys, S. (1985). Caring for abused preschoolers. *Child Welfare* 64: 343-356.

Schinke, S., Shilling, R., Kirkham, M., & Gilchrist, L. (1986). Stress management skills for parents. *Journal of Child and Adolescent Psychotherapy* 3: 293-298.

Schultz, L. (1990). Social workers as expert witnesses in child abuse cases: A format. *Journal of Independent Social Work* 5: 69-87.

Subramanian, K. (1985). Reducing child abuse through respite center intervention. *Child Welfare* 64: 501-509.

Thorman, J. (1983). *Incestuous families.* Springfield, Ill.: Charles C. Thomas.

Wayne, J., & Weeks, K. (1984). Groupwork with abused adolescent girls: A special challenge. *Social Work with Groups* 7: 83-104.

Whipple, E., & Webster-Sratton, C. (1991). The role of parental stress in physical abuse families. *Child Abuse and Neglect* 15: 279-291.

REFERENCES

Backhaus, K. (1984). Life books: Tool for working with children in placement. *Social Work* 29: 551-554.

Ballew, J. (1985). The role of natural helpers in preventing child abuse and neglect. *Social Work* 30: 37-41.

Browne, D. (1986). The role of stress in the commission of subsequent acts of child abuse and neglect. *Journal of Family Violence* 1: 289-297.

Champaign-Urbana *News Gazette.* (1986) Illinois child abuse deaths increase 49 percent. September 14, p. A-2.

Child Welfare League of America. (1989). *Standards for services to strengthen families.* Washington, D.C.: The League.

Famularo, R., Barnum, R., & Stone, K. (1986). Court-ordered removal in severe child maltreatment: An association to parental major affective disorder. *Child Abuse and Neglect* 10: 487-492.

Garbarino, J. (1984). Adolescent maltreatment: A guide for practice and policy. *Practice Notes* 20: 1-5.

Garbarino, J. (1986). Can we measure success on preventing child abuse? Issues in policy, programming and research. *Child Abuse and Neglect* 10: 143-156.

Gelles, R. (1984). Applying our knowledge of family violence to prevention and treatment: What difference might it make? Paper presented to the Second National Conference for Family Violence Researchers, August, Durham, N.H.

Goodwill, S. (1987). Dance movement therapy with abused children. *Arts in Psychotherapy* 14: 59-68.

Gratteau, H., & Dold, B. (1986). In only precious few states do abused kids have a friend. *Chicago Tribune,* October 12, Sect. 6, pp. 8-12.

Hecht, M., Foster, S., Dunn, D., Williams, J., Anderson, D., & Pulbratek, D. (April 1986). Non-verbal behavior of young abused and neglected children. *Communication Education* 35: 134-142.

Homebuilders. (1990). *Homebuilders evaluation summary.* Washington, D.C.: Behavioral Sciences Institute.

Illinois Department of Children and Family Services. (1980). The Abused and Neglected Child Reporting Act P.A. 81-1077, pp. 1-20.

Lamphear, V. (1985). The psychosocial adjustment of maltreated children: Methodological limitations and guidelines for future research. *Child Abuse and Neglect* 9: 251-264.

Lindberg, F., & Distad, L. (1985). Survival responses to incest: Adolescents in crisis. *Child Abuse and Neglect* 9: 521-526.

Maluccio, A. (1991). *Teaching family preservation in the social work practice courses.* Storrs: University of Connecticut School of Social Work, Center for the study of child welfare.

McIntyre, T. (1987). Teacher awareness of child abuse and neglect. *Child Abuse and Neglect* 11: 133–135.

McMurtry, S. (1985). Secondary prevention of child maltreatment: a review. *Social Work* 30: 42–48.

Mian, M., Wehrspann, W., Klajner-Diamond, H., LeBaron, D., & Winder, C. (1986). Review of 125 children 6 years of age and under who were sexually abused. *Child Abuse and Neglect* 10: 223–229.

Meter, M. (1986). An alternative to foster care for victims of child abuse/neglect: A university-based program. *Child Abuse and Neglect* 10: 79–84.

Mouzakitis, C. (1984). Characteristics of abused adolescents and guidelines for intervention. *Child Welfare* 63: 149–157.

National Conference on the Sexual Victimization of Children. (1986). Behavioral comparisons of young sexually abused, neglected, and non-referred children. *Journal of Clinical Child Psychology* 17: 53–61.

Ney, P. (1987). The treatment of abused children: The natural sequence of events. *American Journal of Psychotherapy* 41: 391–401.

Ney, P., Moore, C., McPhee, J., & Trought, P. (1986). Child abuse: A study of the child's perspective. *Child Abuse and Neglect* 10: 511–518.

Ostbloom, N., & Crase, S. J. (1980). A model for conceptualizing child abuse causation and intervention. *Social Casework* (March): 164–172.

Paisley, P. (1987). Prevention of child abuse and neglect: A legislative response. *School Counselor* 34: 226–228.

Pless, I., Sibald, A., Smith, A., & Russell, M. (1987). A reappraisal of the frequency of child abuse seen in pediatric emergency rooms. *Child Abuse and Neglect* 11: 193–200.

Reis, J., Orme, J., Barbera-Stein, T., Herz, E. (1987). A multidimensional inventory for assessment of parental functioning. *Evaluation and Program Planning* 10: 149–157.

Schinke, S., Schilling, R., Kirkam, M., & Gilchrist, L. (1986). Stress management skills for parents. *Journal of Child and Adolescent Psychotherapy* 3: 293–298.

Seagull, E. (1987). Social support and child maltreatment: A review of the evidence. *Child Abuse and Neglect* 11: 41–52.

Sink, F. (1986). Child sexual abuse: Comprehensive assessment in the pediatric health care setting. *Children's Health Care* 15: 108–113.

Terrel, M. (1977). Identifying the sexually abused child in a medical setting. *Health and Social Work* 2: 113–129.

Wolfe, D., MacPherson, T., Bolunt, R., & Wolfe, V. (1986). Evaluation of a brief intervention for educating school children in awareness of physical sexual abuse. *Child Abuse and Neglect* 10: 85–92.

Wolfe, D. (1987). *Child abuse: Implications for child development and psychopathology.* Newbury Park, Calif.: Sage Publications.

Wolfe, D., Edwards, B., Manion, I., & Koverola, C. (1988). Early intervention for parents at risk of child abuse and neglect: A preliminary investigation. *Journal of Consulting and Clinical Psychology* 56: 40–47.

Yates, A., (1988). Anatomically correct dolls: Should they be used as the basis for expert testimony? *Journal of the American Academy of Children and Adolescent Psychiatry* 27 (March): 254–257.

Zimrin, H. (1986). A profile of survival. *Child Abuse and Neglect* 10: 339–349.

Zuravin, S. (1986). Residential density and urban child maltreatment: an aggregate analysis. *Journal of Family Violence* 1: 307–322.

chapter **8**

School Failure and Special Populations

Each year, large numbers of school children fail in our nation's educational institutions. Several national reports have called for more attention to education and to factors that undermine educational achievement (National Commission on Excellence in Education, 1983; *Newsweek,* 1983).

According to Allen-Meares, Washington, and Welsh (1986), the persistence of poverty and the attendant problems of inadequate housing, health care, and nutrition, along with insufficient early childhood education programs, affect the quality of learning. Fragmentation of social supports, emotional and psychological problems, poverty, lack of opportunity, and the absence of appropriate role models contribute to unnecessary school failure. Many young people seek employment to supplement inadequate family income, and thus attend school sporadically or drop out. Some find the educational system too structured and stifling and become psychological dropouts.

New terms, such as "at risk," applied to children have become a part of the dialogue on educational reform. Furthermore, change in the structure of schools has been advanced as one of many ways to reform the system. It is encouraging that we are not only looking at the characteristics and life circumstances that contribute to the at-risk status of pupils but also investigating the need for major reform of the school as an institution. In Chapter 4, it is noted that dysfunctional transactions occur because of both the characteristics of youth and the characteristics of the environments in which they must function. In our efforts to achieve functional exchanges, intervention too often targets the youth as the object of change, while ignoring the need for environmental and institutional changes.

This chapter provides a brief overview of select theories that attempt to explain why some youth fail in our nation's schools. In addition, different school

143

populations that warrant special attention (e.g., minority youth, truants, exceptional populations) are discussed. Although it is beyond the scope of this book to discuss each of these populations in detail, groups that tend most often to be the targets of concern are highlighted. Special attention is given not only to the development of social skills and coping skills among youth but also to environmental change strategies.

WHY DO SOME YOUTH FAIL?

A number of different theories address school failure. Neisser (1986) points out that we typically approach school failure as a deficit in the young person. The notion is frequently advanced that this deficit could be caused by dissimilar cultural experiences in early childhood or by genetic factors. In many respects, however, these theories are insufficient and lack adequate empirical support to be accepted as plausible explanations. A transactional framework better explains the phenomenon.

It is well known that if a teacher or adult expects the worst of a child, the child will respond accordingly—a self-fulfilling prophecy has been created. From this perspective, it becomes clear that a child can be set up for failure when positive reinforcements, reasonable expectations, and social approvals are withheld by significant adult figures.

The National Coalition of Advocates for Students (1985) makes it clear that teachers of low-income children tend to emphasize rote learning and minimize discussion that requires children to draw upon their cognitive skills. They track children by drawing upon psychometric tests and place them in low- or high-achievement groups. Tracking children along the lines of their ability has created a caste-like system in our schools.

Neisser (1986) maintains that there are anthropological, political, and educational explanations of why some youth fail. When these explanations are integrated, it creates the impression that American culture produces group differences in terms of achievement. Several components of American culture contribute to this result: the caste system has pernicious effects (e.g., children from lower economic backgrounds typically do less well educationally than their middle-class counterparts); schools are sometimes ineffective institutions (e.g., they do a better job of educating middle-class children than those of low-income minority-group status); differential instruction takes place (e.g., teachers interact differently with certain groups of pupils, minority children, males, females, and poor readers); and there is prejudice and stress within the educational system (e.g., racial minority males are more often placed in special classes for behaviorally disordered pupils, boys excel in math and science while girls do not perform as well).

Ogbu (1986) acknowledges the importance of the environmental explanation in understanding differential achievement among pupils. Because of poverty, inadequate cognitive stimulation in the home (e.g., the lack of reading materials, absence of early childhood education), undereducated parents, and lack of social experiences (e.g., trips to museums, zoos, art galleries, concerts), some children are less prepared to function in school. In addition to these factors, racism, classism, sexism, and the need to change the opportunity structure can all be included in the environmental explanation.

What is often omitted in the environmental explanation is the need to examine the institutional policies and practices of a school that both overtly and covertly discriminate against certain populations of youth. Before it is possible to deal with school failure and differential achievement outcomes, it is imperative to examine the school as a social system and to work toward maximizing equal educational opportunity. A transactional framework directs attention to the school as a social system.

According to Bloom (1976), almost all children can learn if their teachers understand the history of the learners and provide worthwhile instruction and feedback. Bloom's theory of mastery learning suggests that variations in students' achievement, rate of learning, and affective outcome can be equalized. One of the many assumptions undergirding the theory is that the history of the learners (the youths' cognitive experiences, affective characteristics, levels of motivation, and self-esteem) should be understood and taken into consideration. How the school responds to a learner's history may increase or reduce individual differences in school learning. Restructuring the learning task to meet the individual needs of the student, providing corrective feedback, and getting the learner to participate can improve learning outcomes.

Children and Adolescents at Risk

Children at risk of academic failure often belong to one or more of the following groups:

> *Children of racial or ethnic minority status* (e.g., African American, Native American, Latino, Hispanic, and other groups) are more often labeled as underachievers or dropouts. A sociodemographic profile of Hispanics in the United States indicates that this is the most rapidly growing and diverse population. In fact, it is projected that this group will displace African Americans as the country's largest minority group (Raigoza, 1988). Because of both high fertility rates and high immigration, this population is increasing at a dramatic rate. Many Hispanic children who enter school have not mastered basic English; thus they experience considerable difficulty in meeting the expectations of teachers. According to Raigoza, in 1981, 36 percent of Hispanics aged 18 and 19 were high school dropouts, compared with 16 percent for whites and 19 percent for African Americans. Other factors that contribute to educational termination include poverty, overcrowded living conditions, discrimination, schools poorly equipped to meet the bicultural needs of Hispanic students, and early

pregnancy and marriage. A higher percentage of African American and Hispanic families continue to live in poverty.

Children born into a life of poverty, lacking adequate health care services and food, are prime candidates for developmental delays and consequent school failure. Many of these children move from home to home, and some are even homeless. According to the Children's Defense Fund (1985), 22 percent of the homeless in shelters, not including runaway youth, are children under the age of 18. It is estimated that more than 66,000 children live without adequate permanent shelter. These children often live in one-parent families, born to mothers who have had insufficient medical treatment. In 1982, one of every 20 pregnant women of all backgrounds and one of every 10 pregnant black women received either no prenatal care or none until the final three months of pregnancy (Children's Defense Fund, 1985). Less than half the black preschool children are adequately immunized against polio, pertussis, tetanus, and other childhood diseases.

Children who are handicapped or considered exceptional and bear the label mentally retarded, learning disabled (LD), or behaviorally disordered run the risk of being mislabeled and thus miseducated. Though legislation and litigation protect the rights of these children, many are not being educated, some are overplaced in specific categories (e.g., whites are overly represented in the learning-disabled group, whereas racial minorities are overrepresented in the behavior-disordered group), and some receive no services (Allen-Meares, Washington, & Welsh, 1986).

SPECIAL POPULATIONS

Exceptional Children

Although the federal government has attempted to define categories of exceptional children, there remains considerable confusion in daily practice about how to differentiate one group from another (Kauffman, Cullinan, & Epstein, 1987). It appears that in the identification of the various exceptional pupil populations— what school personnel find in the behaviors and characteristics of such children— the federal definition and the terminology are in disagreement. The identification, assessment, and placement of children for these groups is plagued with bias at every step. More males are categorized as severely emotionally disturbed or mentally retarded. Minorities are also overrepresented in these groups (Allen-Meares & Lane, 1983, Allen-Meares, Washington & Welsh, 1986).

Within the federal regulations to govern the Education for All Handicapped Children Act, 1975 (P.L. 94-142), a handicapped child is classified as follows:

1. *Mentally retarded*—a child who is significantly "subaverage in general intellectual functioning existing concurrently with deficits in adaptive behavior, and manifested during the developmental period which adversely affects the child's educational performance."

In one study it was reported that mentally retarded youth demonstrated more conduct problems, disruptiveness, anxiety, and low self-esteem than nonretarded youth and that such problems were more prevalent in males than in females (Polloway, Epstein, & Sullivan, 1985).

2. *Hard of hearing*—a child who suffers "from a hearing impairment, with a permanent, or fluctuation in his/her hearing [which] adversely affects the child's educational performance, but which is not included under the definition of 'deaf.'"
3. *Deaf*—a child "with a 'hearing impairment' so severe that his/her hearing is non-functional for the purposes of educational performance."
4. *Speech-impaired*—a child who experiences a "communication disorder, such as stuttering, impaired articulation, a language impairment, which adversely affects educational performance."
5. *Visually handicapped*—a child with a "visual impairment which, after correction, adversely affects educational performance. The term includes partially seeing and blind children."
6. *Severely emotionally disturbed*—a child who exhibits "one or more of the following characteristics over a long period of time and to a marked degree:
   (1) an inability to learn which cannot be explained by intellectual, sensory, or health factors;
   (2) an inability to build or maintain satisfactory interpersonal relationships with peers or teachers;
   (3) inappropriate types of behaviors or feelings that hinder normal circumstances; and a tendency to develop physical symptoms or fears associated with personal or school problems. The term includes autistic, schizophrenic and emotionally disturbed, but not the socially maladjusted."
7. *Orthopedically impaired*—a child with a "severe orthopedic impairment which adversely affects educational performance. The term includes impairment caused by congenital anomaly (for example, clubfoot, cerebral palsy, and polymyositis)."
8. *Health impaired*—a child who "suffers from limited strength, vitality, or alertness due to chronic or acute health problems, i.e., heart conditions, tuberculosis, rheumatic fever, nephritis, sickle cell anemia, and lead poisoning."
9. *Learning disability*—a child who has a "disorder in one or more of the basic psychological processes involved in understanding or in using

language spoken or written, which may manifest itself in an imperfect ability to listen, think, speak, read, write, spell, or do mathematical calculations. The term includes such conditions as perceptual handicaps, brain injury, minimal brain dysfunction, dyslexia, and developmental aphasia. The term does not include children with learning problems primarily the result of these visual, hearing, or motor handicaps, of mental retardation, or of environmental, cultural, or economic disadvantages."

Defining a learning disabled (LD) student is indeed a challenge. Early on, the LD youth was believed to be a subset of a group of underachievers (Algozzine & Ysseldyke, 1983). Over the years, the definition has undergone a reexamination. A central question that school officials must deal with is how to differentiate an LD student from one who is a general low achiever. One research effort sought to differentiate these two groups using select achievement scores (e.g., on the Wechsler Intelligence Scale for Children, revised; Peabody Individual Achievement Test; and Behavior Problem Checklist; and others), and found that the LD youth did not meet the federal definition as operationalized in the study, while many low-achieving youth were LD by the same guidelines (Algozzine & Ysseldyke, 1983).

10. *Multiple handicaps*—"a child who exhibits two or more impairments, severe either in nature or total impact, which significantly affect ability to benefit from the educational program."

A main goal of educators, who work with exceptional youth is to facilitate the development of self-esteem. Much school failure can be attributed to a learner being negatively reinforced by significant others (e.g., teachers and parents, etc.) and made to feel different.

11. *Gifted children,* according to Durrett and colleagues (1985), represent about 2.5 million students. Many of these students drop out of school, go unidentified, perform two to four grades below ability, endure unrecognized emotional problems, bear such labels as emotionally disturbed or behavior disordered, and sometimes show deficient social skills. These youth can be overly self-critical, given to daydreaming, and very sensitive to world conditions. These characteristics interact with such environmental factors as parents and teachers who may expect too much from these youth; gifted children may be rejected because they do not conform; classroom and home environments may be too rigid or lack the kind of stimulation required for their intellectual precocity; and peers may reject them because they appear to be different (e.g., adultlike, too smart, strange).

Gifted children are typically identified by relying upon formal IQ tests and teacher or parent evaluation data. Though there are other ways to ascertain whether a youth is gifted, the formal method of relying upon test data tends to be the primary mode.

12. *Truants*—compulsory attendance laws are found in all 50 states, the District of Columbia, and Puerto Rico. States and courts, however, have established conditions under which children are exempt from compulsory attendance (e.g., mental, emotional, or physical disability). The absence of pupil transportation is a ground for exemption from compulsory attendance in some states, provided the child resides a specific distance from the school to which he or she is assigned. In some instances, married students are exempt from attendance. In some states, specific language in the school code defines how many days of absenteeism designates one a truant. Factors that contribute to truancy include poverty, alienation, poor achievement, lack of parental involvement, family disorganization, a conflict in value system (lower-class pupils being made to feel inferior in middle-class schools), and apathy.

The following case illustrations highlight two different situations or circumstances that have the same result—the youth is truant from school. These cases accentuate the complex and yet diverse aspects of labeling a youth truant.

CASE ILLUSTRATION—SITUATIONAL TRUANT, AGE 15

Shannon Allen dropped out of school on her fifteenth birthday. She comes from an extremely deprived background. Her father, who was frequently unemployed, left her mother, who raised Shannon and three younger siblings. The mother cleans rooms at one of the local hotels, but several health problems have undermined consistent employment. One of the younger children, age ten, has been identified as behaviorally disordered. The maternal grandparents are unable to assist because they have been seriously ill. Shannon sees herself as the primary helper and doer for the family. Though her grades were above average, they could have been excellent if she had not been so involved in the parenting role.

Shannon decided to leave school and seek employment to provide some economic assistance for the family. Her mother, a school counselor, and her friends repeatedly attempted to convince her that she was making a mistake. After several visits to the house, the school social worker was able to persuade Shannon to visit an alternative school that held classes during the evenings. After the social worker took Shannon to meet the director of the program and some of the other students, Shannon finally decided to enroll. She could work during the day and attend school in the evening. Of course, she will not be able to graduate at the same time as her peers, but at least she will eventually have a high school diploma.

CASE ILLUSTRATION—PSYCHOLOGICAL DROPOUT, AGE 15

John Perkins is a tall, slim, blond student. He comes from one of the more influential families in town. His mother and father are active in the parent teacher association and are volunteers in the school and community. John has traveled extensively in Europe and parts of Asia. He even attended a private school in London. John is 15, and his 12-year-old sister is described as a model child (an A student, always follows through, popular with everyone, loves school, and actively participates in extracurricular activities).

John hates the structure of the school. He has repeatedly complained to his guidance counselor about feeling alone, not caring about doing well, and hating the rigidity of the school environment. "Why do I need to be here at 8 A.M.? I know this stuff. The teacher does not appreciate different points of view. I do not feel as though I belong here."

John's grades continue to deteriorate. He comes to school and then leaves immediately to hang out in the park with his friends. As the year progresses, John becomes involved with drugs, his appearance deteriorates, and he increasingly speaks out in anger. His parents turn to the school for assistance.

INTERVENTIONS

Self-Evaluation and Problem Solving

For some groups of exceptional children and for youths who perform within the normal range of intellectual functioning, self-evaluation and social-skill training programs have been empirically proven to be an effective intervention (Christoff et al., 1985). Many school children and adolescents are rejected by their peer groups because they lack social skills. Shy adolescents can also benefit from social skills and social problem-solving training. Youth can be trained to engage in conversations and to learn the behavioral skills needed to carry on social interactions. In the study by Christoff and colleagues, youths at an average age of 12.8 years who were experiencing shyness showed positive improvement in self-esteem and ability to interact with others, following social skills and social problem-solving training. The subjects, their teachers, and parents validated their improvement in these areas. Training procedures consisted of reviewing problem-solving skills, verbalizing how to apply these skills, and applying them in practice situations. Conversational skills were enhanced by having subjects rehearse conversations on select topics while the therapist modeled appropriate behaviors.

In a report by Polirstok (1987), handicapped students in a mainstreamed environment were taught to use self-evaluation techniques. Through the use of such techniques, students learn to take responsibility for their actions and increase their internal locus of control. As the chairperson of a special education department at a high school, the present author observed the difficulty experienced by mainstreamed handicapped pupils in making friends. Mainstreamed classrooms were less structured and offered less individual attention than small special education classes. Because the peer group was difficult to interact with, the transition was stressful at best. Regular classroom teachers also lacked the special training to respond to the behaviors and other needs of handicapped youths. According to Polirstok, the components of self-evaluation include self-assessment, self-recording, and self-determination and self-administration of reinforcement. Students are taught the parameters of targeted behaviors and how to record them. They are sometimes given a token or a social reinforcer to maintain their interest in self-monitoring. In order to generalize and maintain behaviors, self-selected reinforcers become an integral part of the programming. This technique can be used to supplement other intervention. Essential to this technique is specifying the appropriate behaviors for the youth to monitor.

Intervention with Groups

Group work is being done in schools with different populations and theoretical orientations (e.g., psychotherapeutic, ecological, behavioral and task, etc.). One intervention found to be effective with the educably mentally handicapped is an in-school program of group psychotherapy, which brings about improved self-esteem, competence, and mutual support (Baumhardt & Lawrence, 1983). The groups meet once a week for a school year or longer under the direction of two therapists. They focus on how the participants feel about school and about their lives in general. Both male and female ninth graders were represented in the groups. The rules of the group were that confidentiality would be maintained, that no physical violence would be permitted, and that only one person could speak at a time. Members could be excluded from the group if they broke a rule. Music, drawing, and fantasy were used to expand the acceptable range of ways to communicate. Frequently, the youth would get involved in scapegoating behavior. The meetings provided choice (each member could volunteer for a specific activity), modeling (adult leaders participated in every activity and demonstrated appropriate behaviors at all time), and food (which represented the nurturing aspect of the group). Metaphors were used (at the beginning of each meeting a story was told, and each individual had an opportunity to relate to it from a personal point of view), and power and control resolution were addressed. By the end of these meetings, scapegoating had stopped, members had come to value individualization, and there was more mutual support.

Working with youth in groups is an effective way to capitalize on the experiences of individual members. Growth and healing are fostered, and insight and problem-solving strategies are shared.

Social Skills Training

The goal of social skills programs is to teach children how to interact with peers in a more socially acceptable manner. Structured learning and training are provided. This approach draws upon such procedures as role plays, modeling of appropriate ways to interact, social reinforcement (e.g., encouragement by a significant other), corrective feedback, and opportunities to demonstrate newly learned skills in a safe environment. The practitioner may use a one-on-one approach with a child or, depending upon the functioning of the child, provide instruction in a group setting.

In a study by Oden and Asher (1977), socially isolated third and fourth graders were coached in social skills. The coaching included instruction from an adult in social skills relevant to friendship making, game playing with peers to practice social skills, and a postplay review session. The results of this experimentally controlled study were very positive. The pretest–posttest sociometric assessment of the four-week intervention indicated that the play sociometric rating of the coached group increased significantly. A follow-up assessment one year later found continued progress.

An effort that targeted moderately mentally impaired students (Lane et al., 1985) reinforced the importance and generalizability of using this intervention (see Table 8.1). This effort drew upon a collaborative team model involving school personnel representing different disciplines and professions. The team model for social skills training has several benefits: It offers a balanced emphasis and multiple perspectives, enhances the basic components of social skill training programs, and maximizes support for the members of the team and their efforts. This approach was used with moderately mentally impaired students. The characteristics of these students and their implications for social skills training are shown in Table 8.1.

The successful use of social skills training requires an understanding of the complex nature of four major components: assessment, planning, training techniques, and outcome evaluation.

No universally accepted specification or definition of appropriate social skills exists (Foster & Ritchey, 1979). However, there are competing definitions that reflect several significant similarities:

1. Social skills are situational, that is, the nature of appropriate behavior varies from one situation to another.
2. An effective social skills repertoire includes verbal and nonverbal response components.
3. Social skills and their various components are learned-response capabilities; thus, when specific skill deficits are identified, they can be remediated.
4. Effective social skills are adaptive rather than maladaptive and they result in maximization of reinforcement from others (Van Hasset et al., 1982, p. 415).

Although few consistent empirical data specify and operationalize the components of social skill, it is clear that social skill is a highly complex multidimensional phenomenon that involves an interactive process adjustment of the child. What defines competent behavior? What knowledge or rules will lead to a

TABLE 8.1 Learning characteristics of moderately mentally impaired students

Characteristics	Implications for Training
1. They have difficulty retaining short-term memory	Need frequent practice and repetition of skills
2. They are cognitively delayed and have poor abstract thinking skills	Use concrete objects or examples to increase problem-solving behaviors
3. They attend to irrelevant stimuli because they lack adequate discrimination skills	Emphasize and teach relevant situational stimuli or cues
4. They have low levels of motivation and functional incentives to achieve (external locus of control)	Provide instructions with a lot of reinforcement and set reasonable goals to guarantee success
5. Basic expressive and receptive language concepts are severely delayed	Use language concepts at student level (for example, instead of "why?" ask "what?")
6. Low levels of adaptive behavior (i.e., independent functioning, personal and social responsibility)	Provide training with role playing, modeling, behavior rehearsal techniques
7. They lack the ability to generalize from situation to situation, person to person, and skills to skills	Provide instruction and feedback across settings, situational cues, and/or persons

From "A Collaborative Team Approach to Social Skills Training for Moderately Impaired Students" by B. Lane, A. Ahn, S. Jerschow, and J. Petru (unpublished paper) presented at the third National Conference on School Social Work, New Orleans, January 31–February 3, 1985.

competent performance? What are the relevant processing, developmental, cognitive, and behavioral characteristics of the trainees? To what extent is the social skill deficit a product of intraindividual skill or performance deficits? To what extent are the student's interpersonal relations characterized by isolation, neglect, rejection, or acceptance by others? How is the individual's knowledge assessed? What is the best teaching technique? Here is a suggested planning sequence for social skills training:

Assessment
1. Problem is identified and defined as one involving social skills deficit.
2. Essential functional social skills and skill prerequisites associated with problem areas are identified.
3. Specific learner characteristics of the trainees are identified (e.g., cognitive levels, speech and language levels, behavioral attributes, physical limitations).
4. Multiple social skill assessment techniques are selected and modified to accommodate specific learner or environmental characteristics.
5. Social skill performance levels are assessed in training and natural settings.
6. Ecological assessment of current and predicted subsequent environments is conducted.

7. Specific skill deficits are identified for training program.

Intervention
8. Multiple training techniques (or curriculum utilizing multiple techniques) are selected.
9. Selected training techniques are adapted to the learner characteristics of the trainees (e.g., increased level of concreteness of material and demonstrations, significant cues highlighted, continuous repetition and numerous examples added, language strategies included, behavior management strategies for increasing attention and motivation added).
10. Generalization strategies are selected and integrated into training approach.

Outcome Evaluation
11. Outcome evaluation methods are planned for ongoing skill performance levels, generalization, and environmental reaction.

Planning
12. Ongoing planning regarding program implementation and team functioning issues is conducted once program is implemented.

Social skill trainers need to use carefully developed guidelines to plan and select intervention strategies that fit the nature of the child's need and utilize the most effective method for teaching a particular skill (see Tables 8.2 and 8.3).

An extremely helpful list of selection and evaluation criteria for social skill training curriculum has been outlined:

1. Does the curriculum promote social competence?
2. Does the curriculum accommodate the learning characteristics of the students?
3. Does the curriculum target the unique needs of the population served?
4. Does the curriculum incorporate teaching methodologies found to be effective with the target population?

Intervention with Parents in Homes

A child's behavioral problems, unless determined to be medically related, are often a result of dysfunctional family interactions and behaviors (Farber, Felner, & Primavera, 1985). Social workers employed in the school setting frequently work with families. Intervention is often used to stabilize problematic living arrangements and interpersonal difficulties or to identify resources to assist a family in functioning. The following case illustration depicts a combination of interventions that target home, guardians, school, and child.

TABLE 8.2 Social skills sequential framework

Antecdent Social Situation

Place

Social and physical cues
Existing norms and expectations for behavior
Level of tolerance and support

Response

Person

Physiological and developmental status
Perception (e.g., auditory, visual, kinesthetic)
Cognitive processing (e.g., discrimination, sequencing, memory, concept development)
Behavior
  Nonverbal (e.g., eye gaze, gestures, body languages)
  Verbal (e.g., questions, statements)

Consequent Social Situation

Place

Reinforcing or nonreinforcing
Accepting or rejecting
Self-concept building or devaluing
Interaction promoting or inhibiting

From "A Collaborative Team Approach to Social Skills Training for Moderately Impaired Students" by B. Lane, A. Ahn, S. Jerschow and J. Petru (unpublished paper) presented at the third National Conference on School Social Work, New Orleans, January 31–February 3, 1985.

CASE ILLUSTRATION—MARCUS, AGE 12

Marcus is currently on Ritalin for hyperactivity. He is in a self-contained classroom for behaviorally disordered pupils.

He has an extremely interesting history. Marcus has been in several foster homes and attended six schools. His other siblings live in foster homes 25 miles from him. Marcus and the other children were removed from their home because the mother had left the children unsupervised for short periods or left them with her boyfriend, who physically abused them. If the boyfriend was not available, she would handcuff the children to the bed so they could not leave the house. The mother, who suffered from periodic episodes of depression, had been clinically diagnosed as being suicidal. Referrals to the appropriate social service agencies enabled the mother to get psychological counseling. The biological father could not be located.

Marcus's teachers described him as too physically aggressive with the other children; he could concentrate for only short periods, he could not sit still,

TABLE 8.3   Social skills training techniques

Direct Teaching. Providing verbal instruction regarding rules for appropriate social behavior given specific social situations.

Modeling: A physical demonstration highlighting the essential features of a particular skill allowing students to learn observationally.

Symbolic Modeling. Video or Audio presentation of a modeling example.

Behavior Rehearsal. Verbal and/or nonverbal practice of the essential features of a particular social skill or sequence of skills.

Role Play. The practice of spontaneously performed appropriate social skills within a simulated social situation.

Role Reversal. The switching of roles during role play training to enhance a student's empathy and understanding of the thoughts, feelings and actions of others in a given situation.

Reinforcement & Shaping. Providing social, activity or tangible reinforcers for the appropriate performance or successive approximation of social skills during training and nontraining times.

Manipulation of Antecedents. Structuring the situation following a social skill training response to assure reinforcement of an appropriate response and extinction of an inappropriate response.

Cognitive Behavioral Training. Teaching students a sequence of normal voice verbal statement, soft voice verbal statement, and internally thought statement of rules for social behavior to improve internalized verbal mediation skills.

Homework. Assigned practice of social skills in natural environments (e.g., home, community, other school settings), with or without the assistance of confederate peers or adults to monitor effectiveness.

Feedback/Correction Procedures. Verbal and physical cues, prompts or guiding procedures which help students perform training skill in an appropriate manner.

From "A Collaborative Team Approach to Social Skills Training for Moderately Impaired Students" by B. Lane, A. Ahn, S. Jerschow and J. Petru (unpublished paper) presented at the third National Conference on School Social Work, New Orleans, January 31–February 3, 1985.

he interfered with other children who were on task, he sought them out for attention for minor problems, and he found it difficult to follow rules.

An Individualized Educational Program (IEP) staffing included the foster parents, the school psychologist, the school social worker, the behavioral disorder teacher, and the school administrator, among others. The school psychologist noted that despite his many negative life experiences, appropriate intervention could help Marcus become an average student. The youth was in desperate need of nurturing and appropriate discipline.

Some of the objectives established for Marcus included the following:

1. Marcus will continue to take Ritalin as prescribed.
2. Marcus will complete school assignments with 80 percent accuracy.
3. Foster parents will positively reinforce Marcus for appropriate behaviors at home and use social approval as the primary reinforcer (social reinforcers will be used by teachers as well).
4. Foster parents will work with Marcus for 45 minutes each evening on his reading. The teacher will provide instruction on how the parents should conduct these sessions.

5. Marcus will have two visits per month with his mother and other siblings.
6. Marcus will remain in his seat for 20 minutes per class hour, followed by five minutes of an activity that allows him to move around the classroom. The in-seat time will be gradually increased until he can remain seated for the entire class period.
7. Marcus will participate in social skills training to be directed by the school social worker (see Table 8.3).

According to Kurtz and Barth (1989) considerable evidence documents that when parents are involved in their children's education, academic performance tends to be better. They found in a study of 253 school social workers that the following pupil problems, in rank order, were in need of services: handicapping conditions, discipline, academic progress, mental health, and truancy. Parent conferences were the most commonly used intervention. Referral was the intervention most often employed for serving parents of students with mental health problems. Crisis intervention was used for truancy, discipline, and mental health problems. Most parents came from low-income backgrounds and few resources were available to them. When services are not available in one's agency, many practitioners draw upon the referral process to get the appropriate services for such families and youth.

The referral process involves several essential steps (Johnson, 1979):

1. Assessment of the situation to determine which agency or institution is most appropriate to receive the referral. This is critical.
2. Ascertaining whether a formal or an informal referral is required by the receiving agency. A formal referral may require an intake staffing and presentation of assessment materials about family and child, whereas an informal referral may merely involve suggesting to the parent that a mental health worker is available for counseling and assistance.
3. In most cases a release of information is needed to initiate the referral. Typically, this arrangement requires that the client sign a form indicating that agency A can share information with agency B. It is essential at this stage that the practitioner have explored the fears of the clients related to the referral and responded to any questions or concerns that could result in early termination or in the client refusing to participate in the referral. Sometimes the practitioner may accompany the client to the agency to minimize fear and potential dropout.
4. Follow up with the client and the agency is important once the client has had at least one meeting. Clients sometimes feel abandoned by the referring agency. Thus, it is important to indicate to the client that postreferral contacts will be made to ascertain progress.

Margolis and Brannigan (1986) offer several strategies to help professionals build a trusting relationship with parents. Practitioners need to initiate cooperation rather than demand it, be open to the points of view of the parents, and demonstrate acceptance. In addition, workers must be clear about the objectives of the relationship and the respective roles of all parties and allow sufficient time to nurture trust, respect, and a real discussion of the issues. The eco-map can serve as a tool to facilitate sharing (see Chapter 4; Hartman, 1978).

Both research and many demonstration projects have shown that the development of family–community–school networks designed to increase parental involvement in a child's education is an effective intervention (London, Molosti, & Palmer, 1984). Practitioners sometimes use behavioral contracts with individual children, as well as a home intervention plan or program, so that parents respond to the child in a consistent manner. Appropriate reinforcers are identified, their selection being dependent upon the child or youth's development and cognitive ability. Of course individual psychotherapy and family therapy drawing upon many different theoretical points of view can be used, reflecting the client's needs and practitioners' strengths.

Parent effectiveness training (PET) (Gordon, 1970) is a humanistic way of training parents in active listening, communication skills, and conflict resolution. Typically, parents participate in small group sessions, lasting for about eight to ten weeks, conducted by a trained lead. The primary goal of PET, like that of other parent training programs is to instruct parents on more appropriate ways to communicate with their children.

School-Based Programs and Services

There is a continuum of services for special or exceptional children. These services typically include moving the youth from a special class to a regular classroom setting or to a modified or resource room where he or she receives special instructional help. There are also community-based treatment programs, special day schools, and residential schools or hospitals (Swan, Brown, & Jacob, 1987). Service options typically move from the more restrictive self-contained programs, in which the youth is isolated from nonhandicapped peers, to mainstreaming in regular classes, the least restrictive option. The reintegration of youth with emotional or behavioral problems is often the outcome goal specified on their individual educational programs (IEP). An IEP is the product of a staffing that often includes special educators; regular educators; parents or guardians; and school administrator or other school personnel deemed knowledgeable about a youth's current social, educational, and psychological functioning (Allen-Meares & Pugach, 1982).

An IEP contains the following information: the youth's present level of educational functioning; annual goals, including short-term instructional objectives; specific educational and related services to be provided and the extent to which he or she will be able to participate in regular education; time of initiation and duration of services; and criteria for determining at least annually whether objectives are being achieved. The IEP is the primary vehicle for ensuring quality education for the handicapped. Essentially, there are five steps in the development of the IEP: identification of the learning problem, referral to the multidisciplinary team, diagnosis or evaluation, statement of the IEP, and evaluation and monitoring of the IEP (Allen-Meares, Washington, & Welsh, 1986). Information presented at the IEP staffing often includes a social developmental study, psychometric test data, an evaluation of the youth's adaptive behavior, teacher and parent observation data, and other relevant details.

Empowering Minority Youth through Environmental Intervention

One theoretical framework for empowering minority youth, in particular African Americans who experience school failure, assigns considerable importance to intergroup power relations between schools and minority communities (Cummins, 1986). The central position of the framework is that the dominant society can empower or disable youth and that the interaction between minority youth and their communities and schools has been dysfunctional. The status of minority groups in the society promotes a disabling mentality because schools are primarily white middle-class institutions that lack sensitivity to life circumstances particular to minority-group life. Students with similar physical characteristics and ways of behaving tend to perform well and to be reinforced to learn. Students who are socially or linguistically different from the majority can be disempowered or disabled because of the lack of understanding and reinforcement conducive to learning. Furthermore, the communities from which minority students come have also been disempowered by interaction with a larger society that is both racist and oppressive. Thus equal opportunities are denied by both the societal and the educational communities. In the classroom, minority children are frequently viewed as less able than white children. To empower minority youth in order to promote learning and achievement, schools must move from majority orientation to one that includes cultural diversity and recognizes the strengths of youth who are culturally different. Parental and community involvements should be integral aspects of school's objectives. The educational staff should reflect the diversity of the larger society, so that youth have role models within the school. In other words, all youth need to experience environments where their cultural identity is reinforced. Collaboration between parents and the educational staff should take place on a consistent basis, and meaningful learning experiences should be provided that are drawn from the richness of the youths' cultural backgrounds.

This theoretical framework confirms the importance of the ecological perspective and social systems concepts and reinforces the notion that a child's total world consists of integrated and overlapping subsystems or environments. The quality of transactions among those subsystems can determine the developmental outcome for youth. Thus parents, community, and school as subsystems in which the child interacts are important targets of intervention.

Intervention that targets larger systems (schools, communities, and ethnic or racial groups) requires collaborative structures among relevant persons, groups, and institutions that share similar interests, goals, and objectives. For example, working with Hispanic parents, their church, and local community groups could result in a cohesive effort to institutionalize bilingual educational programs and structure a means to encourage parental involvement in the schools to enhance the educational performance of their children. Several other kinds of environmental interventions hold relevance for this discussion:

1. To develop new programs within social services agencies that will assist children and their families and schools.
2. To restructure programs and institutional policies (e.g., develop modified educational schedules for children who have difficulty functioning in school all day or who have jobs).
3. To develop new programs for children in the school (e.g., project recapture—to bring truants back into the educational system; in-school programs for pregnant or adolescent parents; prevention programs that target at-risk behaviors such as drug use and sexual behaviors that could result in pregnancy or venereal disease).

SUMMARY

This chapter describes several target groups of pupils, their characteristics, and the factors that contribute to their at-risk status. It reaffirms the need to use interventions that target the particular individual, group, and the family or home, as well as those subsystems or environments in which they function that contribute to their difficulties.

QUESTIONS FOR DISCUSSION

Please read the case of Christopher and respond to the questions that follow:

CASE: CHRISTOPHER

You are a school social worker serving the special preschool program Christopher attends (approximately 30 children) and the elementary school Kevin and Samantha attend.

Christopher is three and one-half years old. He has autism and moderate mental retardation. He is the third of four children: Kevin, age seven; Samantha, age six; and Garth, age one and one-half. Kevin is in the second grade and receives speech therapy for his serious language delays. He takes Dilantin and phenobarbital which control his epileptic seizures fairly well. Samantha was identified as a gifted child in kindergarten and is now achieving well in the first grade. Garth was recently evaluated in a comprehensive developmental disabilities clinic. He has pervasive developmental delays and many autistic-like behaviors.

The parents of these children are Louise and Bill. They were married in a Mormon temple eight years ago, and they are active in the Church of the Latter Day Saints.

Louise graduated from college with a degree in home economics. Bill completed two years of college and then went to work in the family dairy business. He drives a milk delivery truck. Your primary contacts have been with Louise who brings Garth with her when she comes to the preschool to work with Christopher and his teacher in the classroom. Louise is bright, attractive, friendly, and very conscientious. She is also tearful and frequently seems overcome with sadness.

You make a home visit to help her implement a behavior program at home with Christopher. While you are there, Louise breaks down and cries as she tells you Bill has left her and moved back in with his family. He has not slept in their home during the last month. He has filed for divorce. She herself sought legal counsel this week. It is obvious to you as you sit in her home that Louise is overwhelmed by the needs of her four children, and you quickly realize the absurdity of expecting her to implement a behavior change program with Christopher at this time.

Case prepared by Professor K. Moroz, Department of Social Work, University of Vermont. Used with permission.

1. **a.** What would be your priorities for this case? Give a rationale for each.
   b. Discuss possible interventions that could prove useful in addressing the needs of the parents and the child of primary concern.
   c. What might be some of the strengths of this family?
   d. Draw an eco-map of the family's situation, identifying potential resources and conflicts that a practitioner needs to consider.

2. Identify a vulnerable group of children or adolescents of interest to you that is experiencing problems in functioning (e.g., those who are abused, neglected, or sexually exploited; truants; the emotionally disturbed; the behaviorally disordered; the school phobic; runaways, etc.). Review the available literature on this vulnerable group. What interventions (individual, group, or programmatic appear to be most effective? What are the major gaps in the literature?

3. Visit a mental health program or agency that has a unit devoted to children and families at risk. Talk with the practitioners concerning their caseloads, ask them to identify other community agencies they work with, and ask them to evaluate the quality of services available to parents and children in the area of mental health.

4. Analyze the network of community services available to school children and their families. Which agencies include prevention programs? Analyze these preventive programs. What characteristics do they have in common?

ADDITIONAL READINGS

Band, B., & Weisz, J. (1988). How to feel better when it feels bad: Children's perspectives on coping with everyday stress. *Developmental Psychology* 24: 247–253.

Barth, R. (1986). *Social and cognitive treatment of children and adolescents.* San Francisco: Jossey-Bass.

Campbell, S. (1990). *Behavior problems in preschool children: Clinical and developmental issues.* New York: Guilford Press.

Canfield, J., & Wells, H. (1976). *One hundred ways to enhance self-concept in the classroom: A handbook for teachers and parents.* Englewood Cliffs, N.J.: Prentice-Hall.

Clark, R. (1983). *Family life and school achievement: Why poor black children succeed or fail.* Chicago: University of Chicago Press.

Clarke, G., Hawkins, W., Murphy, M. & Sheeber, L. (1993). School-based primary preventing of depressive symptomatology in adolescents: Findings from two studies. *Journal of Adolescent Research* 8(3): 193–204.

Eder, D. (1981). Ability grouping as a self-fulfilling prophecy: A microanalysis of teacher-student interaction. *Sociology of Education* 54: 151–162.

Franklin, C., McNeil, J., & Wright, R. (1991). The effectiveness of social work in an alternative school for high school dropouts. *Social Work with Groups* 14: 59–73.

Freeman, E., & Pennekamp, M. (1988). *Toward a child, family, school, community perspective.* Springfield, Ill.: Charles C. Thomas.

Hawkins, M. (1985). *Achieving educational excellence for children at risk.* Washington, D.C.: National Association of Social Workers.

Jernberg, A. (1979). *Theraplay.* San Francisco: Jossey-Bass.

Kurtz, P. (1983). Identifying handicapped preschool children. *Social Work in Education* 5: 213–228.

Pfeifer, G. (1993). The therapist use of self and cultures in children's psychotherapy groups. *Journal of Child and Adolescent Group Therapy* 3(2): 89–102.

Stanger, C., & Lewis, M. (1993). Agreement among parents, teachers, and children on internalizing and externalizing behavior problems. *Journal of Clinical Child Psychology* 22(1): 107–115.

Strauss, J., & McGann, J. (1987). Building a network for children of divorce. *Social Work in Education* 9: 96–105.

Weinstein, R., Soule, C., Collins, F., Cone, J., et al. (1991). Expectations and high school change: Teacher-researcher collaboration to prevent school failure. *American Journal of Community Psychology* 19: 333–363.

Yasseldyke, J., & Regan, R. (1980). Non discriminatory assessment: A formative model. *Exceptional Children* 46: 465–466.

REFERENCES

Algozzine, B., & Ysseldyke, J. (1983). Learning disabilities as a subset of school failure: The oversophistication of a concept. *Exceptional Children* 50: 242–246.

Allen-Meares, P., & Lane, B. (1983). Assessing the adaptive behavior of children and youth: A basic approach for social workers. *Social Work* 27: 297–301.

Allen-Meares, P., & Pugach, M. (1982). Facilitating interdisciplinary collaboration on behalf of handicapped children and youth. *Teacher Education and Special Education* 5: 30–36.

Allen-Meares, P., Washington, R., & Welsh, B. (1986). *Social work services in schools.* Englewood Cliffs, N.J.: Prentice-Hall.

Baumhardt, L., & Lawrence, S. (1983). Transforming negatively labeled students groups into support groups. *Social Work in Education* 5: 229–240.

Bloom, B. (1976). *Human characteristics and school learning.* New York: McGraw-Hill.

Children's Defense Fund. (1985). *A children's defense budget: An analysis of the president's FY1986 budget and children.* Washington, D.C.: The Fund.

Christoff, K., Scott, W., Kelley, M., Schlundt, D., Baer, G., & Kelly, J. (1985). Social skills and social problem-solving training for shy young adolescents. *Behavior Therapy* 16: 468–477.

Cummins, J. (1986). Empowering minority students: A framework for intervention. *Harvard Educational Review* 56: 18-36.

Durrett, J., Dawson, S., Patterson, M., & Gray, V. (1985). Group work with gifted children: A school resource. In M. Hawkins, ed., *Achieving educational excellence for children at risk*, pp. 7-20. Silver Spring, Md.: National Association of Social Workers.

Farber, S., Felner, R., & Primavera, J. (1985). Parental separation/divorce in adolescence: An examination of factors mediating adaptation. *American Journal of Community Psychology* 14: 2-4.

Foster, S., & Ritchey, W. (1979). Issues in the assessment of social competence in children. *Journal of Applied Behavior Analysis* 12: 623-627.

Gordon, T. (1970). *Parent effectiveness training: The program for raising responsible children.* New York: Petter A. Wyden.

Hartman, A. (1978). Diagrammatic assessment of family relationships. *Social Casework* 59: 463-476.

Johnson, M. (1979). The referral process. Unpublished handout, University of Illinois, Urbana.

Kauffman, J., Cullinan, D., & Epstein, M. (1987). Characteristics of students placed in special programs for the seriously emotionally disturbed. *Behavioral Disorders* 12: 175-184.

Kurtz, P., & Barth, R. (1989). Parent involvement: Cornerstone of school social work practice. *Social Work* 34: 407-413.

Lane, B., Ahn, A., Jerschow, S., & Petru, J. (1985). A collaborative team approach to social skills training for moderately impaired students. Paper presented at the Third National Conference on School Social Work, New Orleans, January-February.

London, C., Molosti, P., & Palmer, A. (1984). Collaboration of family, community, and school in a reconstruction approach. *Journal of Negro Education* 53: 455-463.

Margolis, H., & Brannigan, G. (1986). Building trust with parents. *Academic Therapy* 22: 71-74.

National Coalition of Advocates for Students. (1985). *Barriers to excellence: Our children at risk.* Boston: The Coalition.

National Commission on Excellence in Education. (1983). *A nation at risk: The imperative for educational reform.* Washington, D.C.: U.S. Department of Education.

Newsweek. (1983). "Can schools be saved?" May 9, pp. 58-59.

Neisser, U., ed. (1986). *The school achievement of minority children: New perspectives.* Hillsdale, N.J.: Erlbaum.

Oden, S., & Asher, S. (1977). Coaching children in social skills for friendship making. *Society for Research in Child Development* 48: 495-506.

Ogbu, J. (1986). The consequences of the American caste system. In U. Neisser, ed., *The school achievement of minority children*, pp. 19-56. Hillsdale, N.J.: Erlbaum.

Polirstok, S. (1987). Training handicapped students in the use of self-evaluation techniques. *Journal for Remedial Education and Counseling* 3: 9-17.

Raigoza, J. (1988). U.S. Hispanics: A demographic and issue profile. *Population and Environment* 10: 95-105.

Swan, W., Brown, C., & Jacob, R. (1987). Types of service delivery models used in the reintegration of several emotionally disturbed/behaviorally disordered students. *Behavior Disorders* 12: 99-109.

Van Hassett, V., Hersen, M., Whitehill, M., & Bellock, A. (1982). Assessment and training for children: An evaluation review. *Behavior Research and Therapy* 17: 410-417.

chapter 9

Substance Abuse

The Office for Substance Abuse Prevention, created by federal legislation in 1986, was charged with providing leadership to develop comprehensive strategies for dealing with problems of alcohol and other drugs. The word "comprehensive" included prevention strategies and involved the family, the whole community, and other related institutions (Resnik, 1990). Because it includes both the person and the environment, this approach is consistent with the transactional framework. At present there is intense national concern for what some believe to be an epidemic. With the rise in drug use, a war on drugs has been launched. Americans consider drug use among its various subpopulations to be the country's most serious problem. Billions of dollars are being spent on law enforcement strategies to reduce the use and spread, while fewer dollars are being invested for treatment and preventive strategies.

Some states, such as Illinois, have launched drug-free initiatives to prevent substance abuse. For example, monies have been earmarked to develop statewide systems intended to prevent perinatal addiction and to expand youth and rural programs (Illinois Department of Alcoholism and Substance Abuse, 1990). One special initiative that targets youth is the substance abuse screening project. Its intent is to develop screening tools that accurately and efficiently predict whether a youth entering a social service agency needed substance abuse assessment. Special workshops and training are being made available to human service providers who come into contact with youth who might abuse drugs.

At this time, no single strategy has demonstrated long-term impact on the reduction of substance abuse. The drug crisis has drawn more attention to prevention that focuses both on environmental, social, and cultural realities and on the need for strong, responsive legislation (Wallach & Corbett, 1990). Communities throughout the United States are agitating for the eradication of drug use, and some have even organized to confront pushers. To some degree, the focus of attention has moved from the individual to the broader context—the situations that promote use. There has been a shift away from blaming the victim; and a transactional perspective now offers a more appropriate point of view. In the broader context, environmental conditions tend to reinforce addictive behavior. For example, advertising and the mass media constantly urge the American public to smoke, to drink, and to indulge in other consumer-oriented thrill-seeking behavior. Through the media and the contradictory behaviors of adult role models, the environment sends mixed messages to today's youth.

This chapter deals with substance abuse among adolescents and theories that attempt to explain their dependency. It explores the traditional strategies of treatment and the newer preventive ones that appear to be gaining attention.

CHARACTERISTICS AND PREVALENCE

By the time they reach seventh or eighth grade, many youth have experimented with either alcohol or marijuana; and seemingly more and more youth are involved in early drug use (Fraser, 1987). Table 9.1 contains data about drug use and alcohol patterns of high school students and youth in Illinois. In terms of racial or ethnic differences, it is difficult to get a reliable account of substance abuse, because social class, education and income compound the statistics. A 1988

TABLE 9.1   Drug and alcohol use patterns of high school seniors, college students, and young adults, 1988 (percentages)

	High School Students		College Students		Young Adults	
Drug	*Actual*	*Monthly*	*Actual*	*Monthly*	*Actual*	*Monthly*
Marijuana/Hashish	33.1	18.0	34.6	16.8	30.8	17.5
LSD	4.8	1.8	3.6	1.1	2.7	0.7
Cocaine	7.9	3.4	10.0	4.2	13.8	5.7
Heroin	0.5	0.2	0.2	0.1	0.2	0.1
Other Opiates	4.6	1.6	3.1	0.8	2.6	0.6
Stimulants	10.9	4.6	6.2	1.8	7.0	2.7
Sedatives	3.7	1.4	1.5	0.6	2.0	0.8
Barbiturates	3.2	1.2	1.1	0.5	1.9	0.7
Methaqualone	1.3	0.5	0.5	0.1	0.5	0.1
Tranquilizers	4.8	1.5	3.1	1.1	4.3	1.4
Alcohol	85.3	63.9	89.6	77.0	88.4	73.7
Cigarettes	NA	28.7	36.6	22.6	37.3	28.9

NA: Data not available.
SOURCE: Illinois Department of Alcoholism and Substance Abuse: *Confronting Tomorrow, Today. A Comprehensive Plan for Alcohol/Other Drug Services,* 1990. Reprinted with permission.

high school survey conducted by the University of Michigan, with a sample of 16,000 high school seniors, found a variety of chemical substances was used at a high rate. In fact, one of five high school seniors had used marijuana in the month prior to the survey, three of ten had used cigarettes, and nearly two-thirds had consumed alcoholic beverages (Wallach & Corbett, 1990). Alcohol is the most widely used drug among youth: among 14 to 17 year olds, one in five is a problem drinker, one in every 20 high school seniors uses alcohol daily; about two-thirds of American teens try an illicit drug before they finish high school; one in six families is affected by alcoholism; the leading cause of death of young persons ages 15 to 24 is alcohol-related traffic accidents; one of six youth has tried crack cocaine (Carle Pavilion; 1990).

Youth also smoked cigarettes often, in fact daily for many (Wallach & Corbett, 1990). Other drugs that had been used in the past 30 days included stimulants, (4.6%) and cocaine (3.4%). The legal drugs alcohol and tobacco were used more often by this group. Since 1978, the use of marijuana, stimulants, and barbiturates has declined. Though this latter finding may serve as the basis for some celebration, these statistics are still alarming. Fraser (1987) points out

TABLE 9.2 Prevalence of drug use among high school seniors, classes of 1987 and 1988

Drug	Percentage Ever Used		Percentage Used Last 12 Months		Percentage Used Last 30 Days		Percentage Used Daily	
	1987	1988	1987	1988	1987	1988	1987	1988
Marijuana/Hashish	50.2	47.2	36.3	33.1	21.0	18.0	3.3	2.7
Inhalants	17.0	16.7	6.9	6.5	2.8	2.6	0.1	0.2
Hallucinogens	10.3	8.9	6.4	5.5	2.5	2.2	0.1	0.0
LSD	8.4	7.7	5.2	4.8	1.8	1.8	0.1	0.0
PCP	3.0	2.9	1.3	1.2	0.6	0.3	0.3	0.1
Cocaine	15.2	12.1	10.3	7.9	4.3	3.4	0.3	0.2
Crack	5.6	4.8	4.0	3.1	1.5	1.6	0.2	0.1
Heroin	1.2	1.1	0.5	0.5	0.2	0.0	0.0	0.0
Other Opiates	9.2	8.6	5.3	4.6	1.8	1.6	0.1	0.1
Stimulants	21.6	19.8	12.2	10.9	5.2	4.6	0.3	0.3
Sedatives	8.7	7.8	4.1	3.7	1.7	1.4	0.1	0.1
Barbiturates	7.4	6.7	3.6	3.2	1.4	1.2	0.1	0.0
Methaqualone	4.0	3.3	1.5	1.3	0.6	0.5	0.0	0.1
Tranquilizers	10.9	9.4	5.5	4.8	2.0	1.5	0.1	0.0
Alcohol	92.2	92.0	85.7	85.3	66.4	63.9	4.8	4.2
Cigarettes	67.2	66.4	NA	NA	29.4	28.7	18.7	18.1

NA: Data not available.

SOURCE: Illinois Department of Alcoholism and Substance Abuse: *Confronting Tomorrow, Today. A Comprehensive Plan for Alcohol/Other Drug Services,* 1990. Reprinted with permission.

that males tend to use drugs more frequently and to use larger quantities of drugs than females.

The findings of a study that sought to differentiate youth who used drugs and alcohol or tobacco from those who did not suggest that invulnerable individuals, or nonusers, reported generally better physical and mental health and academic performance (Marston et al., 1988). The sample consisted of 843 youths in the ninth through twelfth grades (379 boys, 464 girls). Of the sample, only 43 girls and 34 boys were identified as nonusers. Nonusers were found to be generally happier; they reported daydreaming and being concerned about their futures. Users were tense and hyperactive and showed less concern about their futures.

DRUGS AND THEORIES OF DEPENDENCY

It would be beyond the scope of this book to discuss fully the different kinds of drugs, their influence on behavior, their effects on mental health, and their withdrawal symptoms. Table 9.3 presents some of this information.

Chemical dependency in this book refers to dependency on alcohol or other drugs. It is a chronic, progressive addiction characterized by loss of control and feelings of powerlessness. Though many youth do not lose control or feel powerless, they still may be at risk of problems with substance abuse (e.g., accidents or health risks). Chemical dependency is treatable. It has a variety of signs and symptoms specific to youth, including decline in academic performance, loss of interest in friends and activities, bragging about using drugs, memory problems, and rejection and withdrawal from family members, in addition to changes in values, argumentativeness, deterioration of physical appearance, disregard for curfews, and stealing.

Theories of Addiction

Although many different theories attempt to explain addiction, according to Alexander (1987) there are two fundamentally different views of addiction as an illness. The first is the *disease model,* which suggests that there are causal links or processes that lead to addiction or makes an individual susceptible to it. A person may have either a genetic predisposition to addiction, or vulnerability attributable to childhood trauma, environmental stressors, or exposure to drugs. The second view, known as the *adaptive model,* also identifies several causal factors, starting with environmental stressors (e.g., family breakdown, ghetto life, pressures of employment, failure to achieve) and lack of self-confidence attributable to negative environmental reinforcers (e.g., pressure from peers) that result in the maladaptive response known as addiction. Whereas the disease model locates the problem in the individual or family, the adaptive model locates much of the problem in the environment.

TABLE 9.3 Chemical substances and their effects

Chemical or Drug	Behavior Changes	Withdrawal Symptoms
Alcohol	Slurred speech, flushed face, mood lability, impaired judgment and physical coordination	Headaches, tremors, vomiting, delusions
Amphetamines	Pupillary dilation, elevated blood pressure, perspiration, psychomotor agitation, grandiosity	Fatigue, insomnia, or hypersomnia
Caffeine (coffee, tea, cola, chocolate)	Restlessness, nervousness, flushed face, diuresis, muscle twitching, gastro-intestinal problems	Headaches, sleeping difficulty, anxiety
Cocaine	Pupillary dilation, elevated blood pressure, nausea or vomiting, euphoria, grandiosity	Dysphoric mood, insomnia or hypersomnia, depression
Hallucinogens (hashish, marijuana, LSD, mescaline)	Pupillary dilation, sweating, blurred vision, tremors, anxiety or depression, paranoid ideation	Hallucinations, visual distortions, chronic or recurrent psychosis, mood swings
Inhalants (paints, paint thinners, polishes)	Dizziness, slurred speech, unsteady gait, depressed reflexes, apathy, assaultiveness	Depression, anxiety, sleeping difficulties
Nicotine (cigarettes)	Irritability, anger, restlessness, decreased heart rate	Weight gain, craving of nicotine
Phencyclidine (PCP)	Increased blood pressure or heart rate, muscle rigidity, seizures, psychomotor agitation, impaired judgment	Sweating, sleep difficulties, muscle problems
Opiates	Drowsiness, slurred speech, impairment in attention or memory, psychomotor retardation	Craving, muscle aches, pupillary dilation, yawning
Sedatives, hypnotics (Librium, Valium, Quaalude)	Slurred speech, unsteady gait, memory problems, mood changes	Vomiting, tremors, seizures

Adapted from materials developed by Carl Pavilion, 809 W. Church St., Champaign, Ill.

Empirical evidence can be found to support each concept. Alexander (1987) believes that it is appropriate to combine both models into one framework rather than attempt to evaluate each as separate hypotheses. Tarter and Edwards (1987) offer a diathesis stress model to explain addiction, which also suggests that genetic vulnerabilities combined with external factors (e.g., family socialization or environmental conditions) lead to addiction.

Sometimes omitted in discussions of these theories are the developmental factors associated with youth growing into adolescence and young adulthood. Youth tend to feel that they are invulnerable and therefore unlikely to die from drugs or even become addicted. The "It will not happen to me" attitude and the desire to experiment with high-risk activities (thrill-seeking behavior) contribute to adolescents' vulnerability. These factors also interact with cognitive development. Depending upon their age, many youths have a "here and now" orientation. They are unable to fully understand and comprehend the long-term consequences of their actions. They develop counterarguments or rationales to justify their actions, and tend to be egocentric.

Stages of Drug Involvement

Fraser (1987) offers two social perspectives on the use and abuse of substances by adolescents. Each has some empirical validation. The first focuses on separate stages of drug involvement, and the second tries to identify risk factors for different kinds of substances. For the first model, there is the assumption that drug involvement begins with experimentation, which usually precedes use, which is followed in turn by abuse. There is also a progression of the substances that are used. For example, young people frequently begin with alcohol then proceed to marijuana use. Some think that marijuana is the gateway drug that leads to other illicit substances. Thus, the stages of addiction are as follows:

Stage 1. Experimentation with drugs—occasional tobacco or alcohol use.

Stage 2. Regular use of alcohol and tobacco.

Stage 3. Use of marijuana in conjunction with alcohol and/or tobacco.

Stage 4. Use of multiple drugs or what is referred to as polydrug use. Many youth do not reach this stage. (Fraser, 1987, p. 23).

This author believes that family environment and other environmental conditions interact to affect the progression of drug abuse by most youth. For example, an alcoholic parent, drug-using peer groups, and poor school conditions, such as lack of a nurturing learning environment, can propel a youth deeper into drug abuse.

The risk-factor perspective suggests that there are many paths to drug use. For example, a youth with low self-esteem, poor grades, family dysfunction, a stressful lifestyle, depression, destructive peer group affiliations, and parents who use drugs may be prone to drug use. Some of these factors are more highly correlated with drug use than others. In other words these conditions make some youths more vulnerable than others. To some degree, it is difficult to claim that chemical dependency is genetic. It could be that youth emulate the behaviors of parents or significant others and model what they see.

In an exploratory study of alcoholic black women who were raised in alcoholic families, Brisbane (1986) noted some interesting gender differences. Although these women tended to view their mothers' alcoholism with disgust, they were more protective of alcoholic fathers. Although alcoholic themselves, the subjects felt that their mothers' drinking had a greater negative impact. In terms of their own alcoholism, the interventions that appeared to be most effective in reducing drinking were a confrontation about drinking with one of their own children, often the son, their faith in God, and their faith in themselves.

CASE ILLUSTRATION—JAMES, AGE 16

James is a white male living in an upper-middle-class community. The youngest of four children, he is the only one remaining in the household. His father, an executive in a major company, has done well over the years in terms of promotions. The mother, though educated as an elementary school teacher, has remained at home to raise the children. She has been hospitalized for alcoholism and depression several times. She attributes her depression to the facts that she has sacrificed her own personal development to raise a family and that her children are slowly abandoning her. Her relationship with the father has also been problematic. She claims that he has ignored the children and her for his career. She no longer has the stamina to raise James, who presents a real challenge.

James has had a series of school-related problems (underachievement and disruptive behavior, etc.). His previous peer group has rejected him, and he is now associated with young people who drink and steal. His mother has warned him that this group is "no good" and has begged his father to speak with him.

James begins to drink beer with his friends on weekends, and then he finds himself drinking during the week as well. He denies that his drinking is a problem. He has been absent from school and no longer takes an interest in his appearance.

INTERVENTION AND PREVENTION

Intervention strategies can be divided into insight-oriented approaches (e.g., individual, family, and group treatment); behavioral methods (e.g., assertiveness and cognitive approaches), and self-help groups (e.g., Alcoholics Anonymous, Al-A-Teen, Al-Anon, etc.). Age, sex, ethnicity, and degree of environmental supports have much to do with which approach is most appropriate.

Because the roots of drug abuse among young people today are multiple, no single approach or intervention is likely to be effective for the entire population. The following discussion describes interventions that move from a micro or individual level to a macro or environmental and societal level (see Tables 9.4 and 9.5). As stated previously, youth take drugs for many reasons: because we are a drug-oriented society, out of curiosity, in response to peer pressure and need for approval, to resolve identity crises, to fill the urge for instant gratification, to satisfy psychosomatic needs, and to deal with family and personal problems. It has become clear to this author that after-the-fact intervention must be replaced with a more anticipatory and preventive approach, one tailored to the needs of this diverse population.

Individual Interventions

Social Competency Approach and School-Based Intervention. One approach that is being advocated teaches adolescents the social skills to prevent substance abuse (Caudill, Kantor, & Ungerleider, 1990). A more detailed discussion of developing social skills in youth is presented in Chapter 8. Positive outcomes in the prevention of drug use among adolescents have also resulted from training in skills to resist peer pressure.

The Life Skills Training Program (Dusenbury, Botvin, & James-Ortiz, 1990) emphasizes self-improvement of personal, as well as social, skills. The program, designed for use in schools, provides adequate information on substance abuse and promotes an anti–substance abuse attitude. In the first four sessions, this curriculum provides factual information about cigarettes, alcohol, and marijuana. These sessions cover myths and facts, so that the adolescent can have the correct information for decision making. The short- and long-term consequences of drug use are presented. The next four sessions cover decision-making skills, and the five steps to effective decision making are presented. The sessions then turn to self-image and how to enhance self-esteem so as to promote a sense of control. Students develop goal statements and then make behavioral plans to make their goals into reality.

At each session, students give progress reports on their efforts to make their goals reality. Coping with anxiety is also a part of the program. Youth are taught skills in anxiety reduction, drawing upon three cognitive behavioral techniques, and then they practice them: self-directed relaxation, diaphragmatic (or deep) breathing, and mental rehearsal. Audiotapes are used to induce relaxation. In its final stage, the program addresses basic communication skills, social skills, and assertiveness. Teachers use a manual that covers the 15 to 18 sessions; booster curricula are taught once the youths have had the initial program. Typically the program targets seventh graders. This program has been evaluated using an experimental design and found to be effective over time.

Children of alcoholics have been identified in the literature as a high-risk population for eventual problems in social functioning and substance abuse

TABLE 9.4 FY89 admissions to residential treatment by age, sex, race, primary drug of choice, and route of administration

	Total		Detox		Short-Term Rehab		Long-Term Rehab		Halfway House		Residential Methadone	
	Number	Pct.	Number	Pct.	Number	Pct.	Number	Pct.	Number	Pct.	Number	Pct.
Total	42,323	100.0%	31,724	100.0%	7,219	100.0%	1,639	100.0%	1,609	100.0%	132	100.0%
Age												
0–17	1,195	2.8%	314	1.0%	568	7.9%	313	19.1%	0	0.0%	0	0.0%
18–64	40,204	95.0%	30,634	96.6%	6,514	90.2%	1,322	80.7%	1,603	99.6%	131	99.2%
65+	538	1.3%	479	1.5%	52	0.7%	0	0.0%	6	0.4%	1	0.8%
Unknown	386	0.9%	297	0.9%	85	1.2%	4	0.2%	0	0.0%	0	0.0%
Sex												
Male	34,656	81.9%	27,014	85.2%	5,172	71.6%	1,207	73.6%	1,186	73.7%	77	58.3%
Female	7,281	17.2%	4,413	13.9%	1,962	27.2%	428	26.1%	423	26.3%	55	41.7%
Unknown	386	0.9%	297	0.9%	85	1.2%	4	0.2%	0	0.0%	0	0.0%
Race												
White	21,077	49.8%	14,878	46.9%	4,395	60.9%	632	38.6%	1,134	70.5%	38	28.8%
Black	18,802	44.4%	15,021	47.3%	2,433	33.7%	825	50.3%	432	26.8%	91	68.9%
Hispanic	1,740	4.1%	1,283	4.0%	250	3.5%	168	10.3%	36	2.2%	3	2.3%
Nat. Amer.	108	0.3%	85	0.3%	17	0.2%	5	0.3%	1	0.1%	0	0.0%
Asian	117	0.3%	109	0.3%	4	0.1%	3	0.2%	1	0.1%	0	0.0%
Other	81	0.2%	44	0.1%	30	0.4%	2	0.1%	5	0.3%	0	0.0%
Unknown	398	0.9%	304	1.0%	90	1.2%	4	0.2%	0	0.0%	0	0.0%
Primary Drug of Choice												
Alcohol	24,854	58.7%	19,316	60.9%	4,113	57.0%	284	17.3%	1,139	70.8%	2	1.5%
Cocaine	12,998	30.7%	9,786	30.8%	2,000	27.7%	842	51.4%	319	19.8%	51	38.6%
Marijuana	1,579	3.7%	717	2.3%	568	7.9%	225	13.7%	69	4.3%	0	0.0%
Narcotics	1,437	3.4%	929	2.9%	188	2.6%	217	13.2%	38	2.4%	65	49.2%
Sed./Hyp.	271	0.6%	205	0.6%	39	0.5%	2	0.1%	22	1.4%	3	2.3%
Halluc.	155	0.4%	61	0.2%	63	0.9%	28	1.7%	3	0.2%	0	0.0%
Other	323	0.8%	259	0.8%	33	0.5%	14	0.9%	17	1.1%	0	0.0%
Unknown	706	1.7%	451	1.4%	215	3.0%	27	1.6%	2	0.1%	11	8.3%
Route of Administration												
Oral	25,368	59.9%	19,653	61.9%	4,211	58.3%	323	19.7%	1,179	73.3%	2	1.5%
Smoking	10,246	24.2%	7,519	23.7%	1,698	23.5%	812	49.5%	193	12.0%	24	18.2%
Inhalation	2,115	5.0%	1,168	3.7%	613	8.5%	191	11.7%	137	8.5%	6	4.5%
Intramuscular	164	0.4%	149	0.5%	10	0.1%	0	0.0%	1	0.1%	4	3.0%
Intravenous	3,399	8.0%	2,604	8.2%	362	5.0%	282	17.2%	66	4.1%	85	64.4%
Unknown	1,031	2.4%	631	2.0%	325	4.5%	31	1.9%	33	2.1%	11	8.3%

SOURCE: Illinois Department of Alcoholism and Substance Abuse: *Confronting Tomorrow, Today: A Comprehensive Plan for Alcohol/Other Drug Services,* 1990. Reprinted with permission.

TABLE 9.5 FY89 Total admissions to both categories and residential and outpatient by age, sex, race, primary drug of choice, and route of administration (detoxification removed)

	Both		Residential		Outpatient	
	Number	*Pct.*	*Number*	*Pct.*	*Number*	*Pct.*
All Admissions	48,955	100.0%	10,599	100.0%	38,356	100.0%
Age						
0–17	6,111	12.5%	881	8.3%	5,230	13.6%
18–64	41,319	84.4%	9,570	90.3%	31,749	82.8%
65+	550	1.1%	59	0.6%	491	1.3%
Unknown	975	2.0%	89	0.8%	886	2.3%
Sex						
Male	34,339	70.1%	7,642	72.1%	26,697	69.6%
Female	13,641	27.9%	2,868	27.1%	10,773	28.1%
Unknown	975	2.0%	89	0.8%	886	2.3%
Race						
White	33,236	67.9%	6,199	58.5%	27,037	70.5%
Black	12,201	24.9%	3,781	35.7%	8,420	22.0%
Hispanic	2,873	5.9%	457	4.3%	2,416	6.3%
Nat. Amer.	77	0.2%	23	0.2%	54	0.1%
Asian	60	0.1%	8	0.1%	52	0.1%
Other	162	0.3%	37	0.3%	125	0.3%
Unknown	346	0.7%	94	0.9%	252	0.7%
Primary Drug of Choice						
Alcohol	29,192	59.6%	5,538	52.3%	23,654	61.7%
Cocaine	7,393	15.1%	3,212	30.3%	4,181	10.9%
Marijuana	4,884	10.0%	862	8.1%	4,022	10.5%
Narcotics	3,011	6.2%	508	4.8%	2,503	6.5%
Sed./Hyp.	499	1.0%	66	0.6%	433	1.1%
Hallucinogens	368	0.8%	94	0.9%	274	0.7%
Other	2,204	4.5%	64	0.6%	2,140	5.6%
Unknown	1,404	2.9%	255	2.4%	1,149	3.0%
Route of Administration						
Oral	30,514	62.3%	5,715	53.9%	24,799	64.7%
Smoking	8,226	16.8%	2,727	25.7%	5,499	14.3%
Inhalation	3,047	6.2%	947	8.9%	2,100	5.5%
Intramuscular	53	0.1%	15	0.1%	38	0.1%
Intravenous	3,389	6.9%	795	7.5%	2,594	6.8%
Unknown	3,726	7.6%	400	3.8%	3,326	8.7%

SOURCE: Illinois Department of Alcoholism and Substance Abuse: *Confronting Tomorrow, Today. A Comprehensive Plan for Alcohol/Other Drug Services,* 1990. Reprinted with permission.

(Emshoff, 1990). There are an estimated 28 million children of alcoholics in this country. Families of alcoholics share some general characteristics that appear to be fairly pervasive although they differ in severity. For example, there is an air of secrecy, a negative mood or tone in the family environment, rigidity, role blurring, and lack of social order and organization. The effects on children can be devastating. Children of alcoholics may have lower cognitive abilities, increased rates of antisocial behaviors, and poor school performance. They may assume parenting roles that are not appropriate, engage in substance abuse, and have fewer friends (Emshoff, 1990).

Intervention is used to reduce the risk that these children will become alcoholics. Developing positive self-esteem and having significant adults to respond to their emotional needs can moderate or ameliorate the negative consequences of being raised in an alcoholic family. One school-based program addresses the needs of this special population (Emshoff, 1990). It provides factual information then turns to the students' social competence and problem-solving or coping skills. Refusal skills—how to say no—are also developed. Developing a social network or social support system is essential. The first step in implementing the program is to obtain administrative support and to decide on the sequence and content of the various sessions. Recruiting students and making them aware of the consequences of substance abuse for individuals as well as families are the next steps. Parents give parental consent for those youth who are interested in participating. Students are then surveyed to ascertain their levels of knowledge and understanding. In a quasi-experimentally designed evaluation of 200 students, those who participated in the program established stronger social relations, sense of self-control, and self-concept. The intervention seemingly gave students a greater sense of internal locus of control, and participants reported very low levels of alcohol usage. The program consisted of 18 sessions, each lasting about 50 minutes, with about seven or eight students per group. Sessions, conducted once or twice a week, consisted of didactic information, skill building, role plays, audiovisual materials, demonstrations, and group exercises. In the first session, rules and norms were usually decided upon; the second and third sessions were devoted to the dissemination of information about alcohol; the fourth and fifth sessions focused on factors that can influence alcoholism and on vulnerability factors. Other sessions were devoted to roles, behaviors, and the problems and embarrassment experienced by the children of alcoholics. Social activities were included to increase bonding among group participants; and attention was given to communication skills on how to build rapport with friends, parents, and others. The relationship with the nonalcoholic parent was an important focus. Several sessions were devoted to the development of coping skills and anxiety-reducing skills to help the youth respond effectively to difficult situations at home and in school (e.g., relaxation training, assertiveness skills, etc.). Simulations and role plays focused on how to respond to different crises—violence, drinking and driving. The last sessions were devoted to termination of the group and the next steps. A representative from Al-A-Teen provided helpful information and offered support to facilitate termination.

Family Interventions

Problem-Solving Approach.   Family problem-solving training was tried with three adolescents to decrease drug use and school failures over a three-to-four-month period with positive outcome (Bry, Conboy & Bisgay, 1986). The subjects—

one female and two male—came from white middle-class intact families. The specific intervention consisted of weekly and biweekly one-and-one-half-hour meetings in a university psychology clinic. Each adolescent and his or her family met for three to four months to learn problem-solving techniques. The intervention consisted of identifying specific changes desired by the youth, assessing potential variables that maintain problematic behaviors by observing the family as a system, focusing and monitoring areas that have been consistently reported as problematic at each meeting to ascertain progress, and providing positive reinforcement for changes when they occurred. The families were encouraged to draw upon the problem-solving procedures at home and to incorporate them into their interactions. Intervention lasted until each family had no additional complaints. All grades and drug data demonstrated that improvement did occur from the preintervention stage to the end of the follow-up. Targeted behaviors were still improving at follow-up, and the families' newly learned problem-solving skills had generalized beyond the training sessions.

The most highly rated strategy for combating substance abuse problems for youth is the involvement of parents in both education and treatment (Caudill, Kantor, & Ungerleider, 1990). When parents are informed about drug use and its consequences and when they are involved in family therapy that treats dysfunctional communications and patterns within the family system, results are most positive.

State Initiative.   Project Safe, known as Substance and Alcohol-Free Environment, is an initiative supported by a federal demonstration grant provided by the Department of Health and Human Services. The Illinois Department of Children and Family Services, in cooperation with the Illinois Department of Alcoholism and Substance Abuse (DASA), has implemented the project in Illinois. The intent of the initiative is to develop, demonstrate, evaluate, and disseminate an innovative model of providing services to neglectful mothers who abuse drugs. Diagnosis and treatment of the parent are the primary goals of the initiative.

Group Intervention

Group intervention can be used both as an independent approach and in conjunction with several other approaches to address chemical dependency and drug use among adolescents. For example, group counseling, family therapy, individual counseling, education, and support groups may be combined.

Many of the individually oriented techniques transfer readily to the group situation. Work with adolescents in groups is effective for several reasons: There can be mutual sharing of experiences and insights among group members; youth tend to value the opinions and views of peers over those of adults; and the group relationships can act as a support system during the group process and in postgroup life.

Logan, McRoy, and Freeman (1987) offer useful guidelines to be considered in the development of group intervention. They found that homogeneity among group members, the structure of the group, the use of group treatment as an adjunct to other forms of treatment, the opportunity for role modeling by the group leader, and the use of the group to deal with transference issues were all important for a successful outcome.

Many years ago the author organized and led a group of tenth- and eleventh-graders who were involved in substance abuse. The typical procedures and principles for organizing a group were followed. Members were interviewed, and parental permission sought. The goals of the group were dealt with, as were the content to be discussed per session and the group composition. Nevertheless, to some degree, the group turned out to be a failure. Though the youth enjoyed the group, attended regularly, participated to a high degree, and attended a few more of their academic classes, they also shared too much information about how to get high, which drugs to use, how to hide drug use, and similar matters. This essentially defeated the purpose of the group. It also raised some important questions about group composition. Although group members were interviewed and each expressed a desire to do better in school and to attend more classes, there was no real commitment to terminating drug use. In the author's opinion, they lacked positive role models. Too many of them were involved in outsmarting their parents, teachers, and other adults. This experience suggests that there needs to be a commitment to end drug use and a greater diversity of group composition of the (e.g., presence of youths who could serve as role models by moving away from reliance on drugs, participation of adults to supply positive role models, such as those who had undergone treatment for substance abuse).

PREVENTION—SCHOOLS AND COMMUNITIES

Although schools and communities can take active roles in the treatment of substance abuse among adolescents, they are also excellent environments in which to launch preventive efforts. Prevention tends to be tied to education and drug awareness. We must target the very young. We also need to institute harsher social controls and support constructive socialization patterns on the part of parents and primary institutions, such as the schools. Promoting competence and mobilizing community resources and awareness are important elements for success (Gullota & Adams, 1982). Preventive intervention can target several subsystems or environments in which youth function (e.g., school, community, family, etc.). Fraser (1987) argues for targeted preventive intervention and suggests that we not adopt a generic preventive stance; instead generic and targeted intervention can supplement each other.

Attempts have been made to organize the available prevention efforts in our nation's schools into three groups: information (education programs), social resistance or inoculation intervention, and personal and social coping skills training programs. Assumptions underlying each of these prove to be very interesting (Forman & Linney, 1988). For instance, many education programs are based on the assumption that presenting facts and information will discourage use.

Generally, this approach alone should be considered ineffective. Social resistance programs target the social and assertiveness skills of young people so that they can say no effectively to the pressures of peers and otherwise cope. These programs are considered inoculations against drug use, and there is some evidence that they can change certain correlates of later drug use. Coping skills, sometimes known as life skills, have been shown to be effective in preventing drug use (Gilchrist & Schinke, 1985).

In implementing preventive programs in a school or community, it is important to know not only whether the intervention selected is empirically validated but also whether there is a commitment to its basic principles from key school officials and groups (parents, school administrators, teachers, and students). According to Forman and Linney (1988), the development of multiintervention approaches that target personal and environmental variables leading to substance abuse is perhaps the best course of action. Thus, in the development of school-based intervention–prevention programs, it is essential to keep this principle at the heart of planning.

In one article, an intervention called Project Impact is described as an effective approach using a variety of professionals and resources to prevent substance abuse among adolescents. School administrators and other personnel were trained by multidisciplinary Impact Core teams. Project Impact was most effective when the school, community, and parents worked together as a team to prevent substance abuse (Caudill, Kantor, & Ungerleider, 1990). Core teams established in each high school were responsible for coordination of all the interventions and referrals of families and students to appropriate community-based services. These teams raised the level of sensitivity on the part of school personnel and enabled them to identify youth who were abusing alcohol and detect factors that contributed to chemical dependency. Individuals trained by the Impact teams made more referrals of students for assistance.

"Here's Looking at You, Too" is a comprehensive drug education program for kindergarten through grade 12 (Green & Kelley, 1989). The program offers several important features. One component is parenting education, which draws attention to family substance abuse problems. In addition, a student assistant program identifies youth at risk, and an absenteeism prevention program identifies youth who are chronically absent and works with them, as well as their families, to encourage attendance. A student leadership program is intended to empower youth. Teachers and other school officials participate in a training program so that a drug curriculum can be included in the classroom. The goals of this initiative are similar to those of prevention programs already described. They aim to promote self-esteem, improve coping skills, develop effective decision-making skills, and provide the facts about drugs and the consequences of their use. A quasi-experimentally designed evaluation of this program found statistically significant gains in knowledge about drugs at all grades over all years. However, the findings on improvement in decision-making and coping skills were not as impressive, probably because these skills are determined by many situational variables that are not easily controlled.

The Student Attitudinal Inventory (SAI) has been used to evaluate students' attitudes toward drug abuse prevention programs (Kim, 1981). It measures or assesses the effectiveness of various prevention programs that target adolescents. It is a self-administered 70-item instrument using a Likert-scale format. Scale items include such dimensions as drug attitude, school value, student–teacher affinity, self-esteem, family cohesiveness, social attitude, and rebellious attitude. This scale is under revision to improve its reliability.

Community-Based Services

Developing preventive intervention beyond the walls of the school is essential if we are to reduce substance abuse among youth. Community-based services are desperately needed to supplement other intervention in a positive way. Unfortunately, too few programs target the youth population. In one report on the relationship to treatment outcome of specific characteristics of outpatient programs that provided treatment for adolescent drug users, it was found that the provision of special services, such as vocational programming, recreational opportunities, and birth control, had more to do with the effectiveness of treatment outcome than the type of therapy (e.g., Gestalt, crisis intervention, music and art, group confrontation) or the size of the program (Friedman & Glickman, 1988).

SUMMARY

Approaches to addressing substance abuse among children and adolescents are on the increase. We are experimenting with a variety of approaches because we are still trying to sort out what works best with whom. It is clear that there is a role for prevention and that this direction is most promising. It is also clear that our targets of change must be the person, as well as the environment.

QUESTIONS FOR DISCUSSION

1. Locate the community-based drug rehabilitation center funded by public dollars in your community. Visit the center and ask the following questions of a staff member who knows the breadth of services provided: What services are provided for adolescent drug users? If there are such services, what drugs are most often used, and are there specific patterns of use for males and females, minorities and nonminorities, low income and middle and upper-middle income individuals? Which intervention strategies are used most often, and why? Do services provide for family intervention, long-term follow-up, and preventive measures? How do you evaluate outcome?

2. Visit a residential drug rehabilitation center that is funded primarily by private dollars. Raise the same questions that are listed in question 1. What are the differences? What are the similarities?

3. Select one of the interventions discussed in this chapter and conduct an extensive review of the literature. Identify the theoretical roots of the intervention. What research has been done specific to the intervention? Critique the scientific method of the study.

4. Discuss some difficulties specific to the development of preventive strategies to reduce the incidence of substance abuse.

5. Identify other community and school-based programs that have gained attention in the reduction of substance abuse among adolescents. Critique them in terms of comprehensiveness and involvement of the adolescents' significant others.

ADDITIONAL READINGS

Bell, C., & Battjes, R., eds. (1985). *Prevention research: Deterring drug abuse among children and adolescents.* (DHHS Publication No. 6). Washington, D.C.: U.S. Government Printing Office.

Bueger, D. (1984). Behavioral family therapy for delinquent and substance abusing adolescents. *Journal of Drug Issues* 14: 403–418.

Capto, R. (1993). Volatile substance misuse in children and youth: A consideration of theories. *International Journal of the Addictions* 28(10): 1015–1032.

Clayton, R., & Ritter, C. (1985). The epidemiology of alcohol use among adolescents. *Advances in Alcohol and Substance Abuse* 4(3): 33–51.

Downs, W., & Robertson, J. (1990). Referral for treatment among adolescent alcohol and drug abusers. *Journal of Research in Crime and Delinquency* 27: 190–209.

Eggert, L., & Herting, J. (1991). Preventing teenage drug abuse. *Youth and Society* 22: 482–524.

Forster, B. (1984). Upper-middle-class adolescent drug use: Patterns and factors. *Advances in Alcohol and Substance Abuse* 4(2): 27–31.

French, L. (1990). Substance abuse treatment among American Indian children. *Alcoholism Treatment Quarterly* 7: 63–76.

Glynn, T. (1984). Adolescent drug use and the family environment: A review. *Journal of Drug Issues* 14: 271–295.

Johnson, G., Shantz, F., & Locke, T. (1984). Relationships between adolescent drug use and parental drug behaviors. *Adolescence* 19: 295–299.

Lecca, P. (1993). *Preschoolers and substance abuse: Strategies for prevention and intervention.* New York: Haworth Press.

Lohrman, D., & Fors, S. C. (1986). Can school-based educational programs really be expected to solve the adolescent drug abuse problem? *Journal of Drug Education* 16: 327–339.

Murray, D., & Perry, C. (1985). The prevention of adolescent drug abuse: Implications of etiological, developmental, behavioral and environmental models. In C. Jones & R. Battjes, eds., *Etiology of drug abuse: Implications for prevention* Rockville, Md.: National Institute on Drug Abuse.

Oshudin, C. (1984). Designing a health education program to reduce use of drugs in a secondary setting. *Journal of Alcohol and Drug Education* 29: 1–7.

Penney, A., & Garfield, E. (1984). Parent groups in drug abuse prevention: Is this the consistency we've been waiting for? *Journal of Primary Prevention* 4: 173–179.

Poulin, T. (1991). Racial differences in the use of drugs and alcohol among low income youth and young adults. *Journal of Sociology and Social Welfare* 18: 159–166.

Tarker, R. (1990). Evaluation and treatment of adolescent substance abuse: A decision tree method. *American Journal of Drug and Alcohol Abuse* 16: 1–46.

Tarter, R., Blackson, T., Martin, C., & Loeber, R. (1993). Characteristics and correlates of child discipline practices in substance abuse and normal families. *American Journal on Addictions* 2(1): 18-25.

VanHanselt, V., Null, J., Kempton, T., & Bukstein, O. (1993). Social skills and depression in adolescent substance abusers. *Addictive Behaviors* 18(1): 9-18.

Wodarski, J. (1990). Adolescent substance abuse: Practice implications. *Adolescence* 25: 667-688.

REFERENCES

Alexander, B. (1987). The disease and adaptive models of addiction: A framework evaluation. *Journal of Drug Issues* 17: 47-63.

Brisbane, F. (1986). Divided feelings of black alcoholic daughters: An exploratory study. *Alcohol Health and Research World* 11: 48-50.

Bry, B., Conboy, C., & Bisgay, C. (1986). Decreasing adolescent drug use and school failure: Long-term effects of targeted family problem-solving training. *Child and Family Behavior Therapy* 8: 43-59.

Carle Pavilion. (1990). *New choice: Alcohol and drug treatment.* Champaign, Ill.: Carle Foundation Hospital.

Caudill, B., Kantor, K., & Ungerleider, S. (1990). Project impact: A national study of high school substance abuse intervention training. *Journal of Alcohol and Drug Education* 25: 61-74.

Dusenbury, L., Botvin, G., & James-Ortiz, S. (1990). The primary prevention of adolescent abuse through the promotion of personal and social competence. *Prevention in Human Services* 7: 201-225.

Emshoff, J. (1990). A preventive intervention with children of alcoholics. *Prevention in Human Services* 7: 225-252.

Forman, S., & Linney, J. (1988). School-based prevention of adolescent substance abuse: Programs, implementation and future directions. *School Psychology Review* 17: 550-558.

Fraser, M. (1987). Reconsidering drug involvement among youth and young adults: Implications for targeted primary prevention. *Journal of Sociology and Social Welfare* 14: 21-48.

Friedman, A., & Glickman, N. (1988). Program characteristics for successful treatment of adolescent drug abuse. *Journal of Nervous and Mental Disease* 174: 869-879.

Gilchrist, L., & Schinke, S. (1985). Preventing substance abuse with children and adolescents. *Journal of Consulting Clinical Psychology* 53: 121-235.

Green, J., & Kelley, J. (1989). Evaluating the effectiveness of a school drug and alcohol prevention curriculum: A new look at "Here's looking at you, too." *Journal of Drug Education* 19: 117-132.

Gullotta, T., & Adams, G. (1982). Substance abuse minimization: Conceptualizing prevention in adolescent and youth programs. *Journal of Youth Adolescence* 11: 409-424.

Illinois Department of Alcoholism and Substance Abuse (1990). *Confronting tomorrow, today: A comprehensive plan for alcohol/other drug services—building a drug free Illinois.* Chicago, Ill.: The Department.

Kim, S. (1981). Student attitudinal inventory for outcome evaluation of adolescent drug abuse prevention program. *Journal of Primary Prevention* 2: 91-100.

Logan, S., McRoy, R., & Freeman, E. (1987). Current practice approaches for treating the alcoholic client. *Health and Social Work* 12: 178-186.

Marston, A., Jacobs, D., Singer, R., Widaman, K., & Little, T. (1988). Adolescents who apparently are invulnerable to drug, alcohol, and nicotine use. *Adolescence* 23: 593-597.

Resnik, H., ed. (1990). *Youth and drugs: Society's mixed messages.* Rockville, Md.: U.S. Department of Health and Human Services.

Tarter, R., & Edwards, K. (1987). Vulnerability to alcohol and drug use: A behavior-genetic view. *Journal of Drug Issues* 17: 67-81.

Wallach, P., & Corbett, K. (1990). Illicit drug, tobacco, and alcohol use among youth: Trends and promising approaches in prevention. In H. Resnik, ed., *Youth and drugs: Society's mixed messages,* pp. 5-23. Rockville, Md.: U.S. Department of Health and Human Services.

chapter **10**

Issues of Adolescent Sexuality, Premature Parenthood, and Prostitution

Adolescent sexuality is a complex developmental process strongly affected by family and by social and cultural conditions (Chilman, 1989). Major research findings regarding adolescent coitus, contraception, and childbearing present a very complicated picture. The author's own assessment of this research suggests that more emphasis needs to be placed on the positive aspects of adolescent sexuality, on the interaction of social and cultural conditions, and on intervention that facilitates the healthy sexual development of youth.

Adolescence is that period in a person's life that stretches from the onset of puberty to young adulthood. Puberty is the first phase of adolescence, when sexual maturation becomes evident; and reaching the age of 18 usually signals the end of adolescence, although entry into young adulthood is less easily defined these days. Adolescence is often divided into two major stages. The first stretches from the onset of puberty to about the age of 14 to 16; psychologically it is characterized by the push for independence from parents and an attempt to develop peer group identification. Although a childish dependency persists, there is a dire need for separation from adult figures. The second stage is marked by the search for a mature identity and the quest for a mate; the exploration of different sets of values and the definition of occupational and other life goals are of primary interest. Throughout adolescence, sexuality is one of several major themes. What is often disregarded in this country is that sexuality pervades virtually every aspect of human life.

Puberty also brings the completion of two processes that start earlier; solidification of sexual identity as male or female and the realization of sexual preference. Typically, males see themselves as boys growing into men and females see themselves as girls growing into women. However, some youth develop a preference for same-sex relationships or respond bisexually. Homosexuality is discussed in more detail at a later point.

Diamond and Diamond (1986) revealed that adolescents often have both severe knowledge gaps concerning venereal disease and birth control and a desire for more information about sexuality. Although physical changes indicate movement into the next stage of development toward womanhood or manhood, there are no universal rituals to signal the transformation. According to these and authors, the biological events of puberty are the same the world over; but the cultural events marking this transition vary enormously. Some societies have dramatic initiation rights in which the individual is welcomed to adulthood. At present, in the United States and Europe, the transition period of adolescence is protracted, and methods of certifying adulthood are deficient. When is one a woman? When is one a man? Teenage pregnancy, truancy, smoking, alcohol drinking, and running away from home are often negative attempts to prove adulthood. Earning merit badges, contributing to family income, driving a car, or volunteering hours to a worthy cause are positive attempts to attain adult status.

SEXUAL DEVELOPMENT

Physical Changes

During puberty, development is characterized by disproportionate growth of various parts of the body (e.g., fat is deposited before muscle mass increases, feet grow before legs, the nose may increase disproportionately to the rest of the face, and one side of the body may develop before the other). There are marked differences in growth patterns between males and females.

In girls the earliest signs of puberty are changes in body shape first noted between the ages of eight and ten. The hips begin to widen, and fat deposits soften the skin and round out the body. The onset of breast development typically follows the accumulation of hip-fat deposits. During this period, the breasts develop, and pubic hair becomes more plentiful. Many aspects of breast development are a source of worry for a teenage girl. There is a concern that she will be completely flat chested. The most common worry is that her breasts will fail to grow large enough or that one breast seems to be growing differently from the other. Girls whose breasts grow larger than they desire are often concerned with the attention they draw and become ashamed and fearful.

For many girls, the hymen—a thin membrane that usually covers part of the opening of the vagina in a virgin—has already ruptured spontaneously and all but disappeared prior to puberty (Diamond & Diamond, 1986). Although the presence of the hymen was once taken as a sign of virginity, its presence or absence cannot attest either to virginity or to sexual activity. It may be absent in virgins and virtually intact in those who have had a great deal of sexual experience. Vaginal wetting is common from birth and increases during times of sexual excitement. This is to be expected. Menarche (the onset of the menstrual cycle) is not necessarily accompanied by ovulation. There is a period during which the organs associated with reproduction—ovaries, uterus, hypothalamus, pituitary, oviducts—adjust to working in concert. Thus, with the onset of menstruation, some period of time is required for the female body to develop the necessary association of organs to achieve fertility. Because sexual activity at this time does not usually result in pregnancy, the resulting infertility is often mistakenly construed by young girls as a lifelong condition or superstitiously associated with the belief that "it will not happen to me." Many young adolescent females who experiment with sexual intercourse begin to feel that they will never become pregnant because something protects them from this condition.

Puberty starts later in boys. The first signs are usually fat deposits on their chests and abdomens; considerable increase in physical activity; spurts in height; replacement of fat deposits by muscle mass; and growth of the testes, scrotum, and penis. As the testes grow, so does the production of male hormones, mainly testosterone (Diamond & Diamond, 1986). These hormones spur development of males' secondary characteristics: extension of long bones, increase in penis size, growth of pubic hair (and later of chest and other body hair), and enlargement of the larynx with a deepening of the voice. Growth spurts start in the male at about ten or 11 years; the genitals do not reach adult size until about the age of 15 or 16.

Unfortunately for many males, concern with penis size starts during puberty and remains throughout adult life. However, very young males can be found touching and exploring their genitals. Spontaneous erections, which begin during fetal development, now occur with increasing—often embarrassing—frequency. Masturbation increases in frequency and vigor, about 90 percent to 95 percent of American boys have begun to masturbate by the end of puberty, compared with 50 percent to 60 percent of American girls. This is the most likely time for the development of mature sperm and the first ejaculation. Nocturnal emissions (wet dreams) generally follow soon after (Diamond & Diamond, 1986).

Socialization Agents

Media.   As adolescents move into adulthood, they are confronted with mixed messages from society. For example, adolescents are told by society to curb their sexuality; but their peers (and often their fathers as well) exult when they "score." Girls are told to be modest and reserved, yet their peers (and often their mothers) achieve popularity by being just a little sexy. These contradictory messages are also reinforced by the media. For example, several studies have noted the increased role of the media in a sexual socialization process that influences not only information about sex but also sex role behaviors (Harrison & Pennell, 1989). Typically, television programs and popular music affect the development of sexual attitudes and behaviors. This is not surprising, given that many young people spend more time watching television than in any other activity except sleep (National Institute of Mental Health, 1982). Unfortunately, adolescents are heavy viewers of prime-time programming, music television, soap operas, and commercials; they also consume radio programs, films, and music; and they are exposed to advertisements from all media sources. Their consumption of the mass media has been enhanced by access to VCRs, boom boxes, and cable television, including pay channels offering explicit sexual programming. Much of this material depicts distorted sexual stereotypes and presents unreliable messages about sexuality. It creates unrealistic images of physical attractiveness, and violence within the sexual relationship is common. The media generally portray men as aggressive and powerful figures in a relationship, whereas women are depicted in passive, submissive roles. Morgan and Rothchild (1983) found that the amount of television consumption by adolescents was positively associated with traditional sexual stereotypes, particularly for adolescents with few peer affiliations. Adolescents have been shown to use physically attractive media figures as sexual role models. Strouse and Fabes (1985) found that the consumption of sexually oriented media, such as soap operas and MTV, may have some influence on sexual permissiveness. Larson and Kubey (1983) found that an adolescent's familiarity with popular music was also associated with greater peer involvement and less family involvement. Although direct causal links between the effect of media on adolescent sex roles and sexual behavior have not been firmly established, there is some suggestion that youths receive mixed sex role messages.

Family.   Richmond-Abbott (1983) recognizes the important role of parental and family influence in sex role development. Parents exert considerable influence through their own model behavior, their levels of acceptance of their children's behavior, and their responses to external socialization forces. For example, accepting parents seem to foster less traditional sex roles (androgyny) in their children, whereas greater parental control is related to more traditional sex roles. Richmond-Abbott found only a few differences between children raised by single parents and children raised in two-parent homes. When differences did exist, the father's absence had typically occurred before the child was five years old. Most of the research has been done on custodial mothers and absent fathers, and the effects were similar to those found in two-parent households with low father availability. A single parent, whether mother or father, is more likely to model androgynous behavior (perhaps out of necessity) and may expect the same from the children. Although some single custodial mothers may be concerned about the lack of masculine role models for their sons, there is some evidence to suggest that fatherless boys are not entirely lacking in role models. For example, such models can be found on television and in institutions beyond the family. As another example, some adolescent daughters of mothers employed outside the home have been found to be more assertive and independent and to have more positive career plans of their own. Seemingly, a mother's attitude toward work and her employment outside the home set a different tone for an adolescent girl. Women who are satisfied in their employment may encourage more independence and communicate more positive messages about work roles for women. Although the importance of parental influence is beyond question, no longer is the family the primary sex role socializer.

We do know, however, that many parents do not assume the responsibility of communicating information about sexuality, sexually transmitted diseases, and contraception to their adolescents (Allen-Meares & Shapiro, 1989). Many are uncomfortable with the subject and lacked role models in their own lives to emulate appropriate interactions with their children. When adolescents sense their parents' discomfort, they often respond with such familiar statements as, "We learned that in school," or, "I already know about sex."

Peer Groups.   During adolescence, peer groups often replace families as the dominant socialization force. Adolescents are more likely to adhere to the suggestions and advice of their peer groups than those of family figures or other adults in sexual matters. According to Harrison and Pennell (1989), peer pressure on male teens relates to qualities that are traditionally masculine and even macho. To feel tough, it is important for the adolescent male to engage in athletic achievement; he must also be cool—showing little or no emotion and no fear of danger. For females, the sexual norms are more ambiguous and less consistent, incorporating both traditional and nontraditional gender behaviors. For both sexes, there is stress in attempting to conform to these pressures. Adolescent girls face tremendous peer pressure to be physically attractive and popular and to be achievement oriented (Masters, Johnson, & Kolodny, 1988). Their achievements can be traditional (e.g., cheerleading) or nontraditional for women (e.g., sports or academics). Pressures related to achievement and to being popular can be at odds with one another in many settings (Newcomer, Udry, & Cameron, 1983). The importance a girl places on being popular may consume a considerable amount of her time and undermine the amount of energy spent on academics.

FIRST SEXUAL ENCOUNTER

In a study of 202 adolescent boys and 255 adolescent girls, Ostrov and colleagues (1985) found that 54 percent of the boys and 37 percent of the girls reported having sexual intercourse by their seventeenth birthday. The upsurge in sexual activity and conception among middle-class white girls indicates that teenage parenthood and early sexual intercourse can no longer be said to occur mainly in low-income and minority populations. Other studies of teenage sexuality indicate an increasing trend in premarital intercourse since 1967 (Finkel & Finkel, 1975; Jessor & Jessor, 1975; Zelnik & Kanter, 1980). Accompanying this increase has been a steady decline in the average age at first intercourse (Gibbs, 1986).

The social and cultural factors that have been found to influence adolescent sexual attitudes and behaviors are ethnicity, socioeconomic status, parental marital status, religious attitudes, and community size (Reiss, 1970; Udry, Bauman, & Morris, 1975). Sexual activity among adolescent females has been correlated with deviant behavior, substance abuse, educational underachievement, and peer group influence, as discussed earlier. According to Gibbs (1986), there has been an increase in rates of sexual intercourse and in risk of out-of-wedlock pregnancies in the early adolescent group, but their motivation and ability to employ effective contraceptive strategies have apparently not kept pace with their heightened sexual activities. In a study of 3,500 inner-city junior and senior high school students, Zabin and colleagues (1984) found that females 15 years old and younger were less likely to use contraception in a dating relationship, whether it was weak or strong, than were girls 16 years old and older. Although most of the students in the study expressed sexually responsible values and attitudes, these were not consistent with their sexual behavior or their contraceptive practices. Study after study has concluded that adolescents are generally ineffective contraceptors. In a recent review of the literature, Morrison (1985) identified some important demographic factors—such as younger age, low socioeconomic status, and minority-group membership—associated with the failure of adolescent females to use contraceptives effectively. Other correlates of ineffective contraception were noncommitted relationships, lack of access to confidential family planning services, and inaccurate information about actual contraception. Allen-Meares (1984) found that low-income African-American girls have more negative attitudes toward birth control and are less effective contraceptors than low-income white girls. A study conducted by Zelnik and Shah (1983), however, found that in a sample of 936 adolescents, African-American females were more likely than whites to use a prescription method of birth control or some other method under their own control. Furthermore, African-American females who had been exposed to sex education were more likely than similarly exposed whites to use some method of contraception. This suggests that differences in contraceptive practices between African-American and white adolescents may be related to educational opportunities and access to contraceptive services rather than to ethnicity (Gibbs, 1986). Some studies point out that African-American adolescents have a younger mean age at first intercourse than whites—a difference of 0.6 years in 1971 and 0.7 years in 1976 (Zelnik, Kantner, & Ford, 1981).

It is perhaps unfortunate that in the discussion of age at first sexual intercourse and sexual activity, adolescent males are frequently forgotten. In one study (Zelnik, Kantner, & Ford, 1981), initiation of sexual activity occurred in African-American males at a mean age of 18.1 years, whereas among whites it occurred at 19.3 years. The males in this study reported that their first premarital sexual acts usually occurred in their parents' homes or the homes of friends or relatives. There was little difference in this respect between blacks and whites.

A variety of pressure statements between adolescent males and females encourage sexual experimentation and, perhaps, exploitation. Such statements might include, "If you love me you will do it!" "I'll go crazy if I don't have it!" "Let's make love!" "I want you to have my baby!" "I want to have your baby!" "If you get pregnant by him, he will be yours forever." According to Gelman (1990), many youths today do not get accurate information to make the decision whether to engage in sexual activity. However, given the dangerous increase of AIDS, as well as gonorrhea and other venereal diseases, early experimentation with different sexual partners, and the inconsistency in sexual behaviors, adolescent sexual activity becomes a life and death matter.

In the author's experience, many public high schools offer sex education courses. Their content is usually included in the health curriculum. The topic most commonly covered by sex education teachers, however, is venereal disease; the topic least often discussed is sexual techniques; and information about contraception. Nevertheless, adolescents' sexual activities are frequently spontaneous and unplanned; unfortunately they fail to incorporate even the limited knowledge presented in sex education classes.

PREMATURE PARENTHOOD

Teenage pregnancy is a growing social problem in the United States. By the end of the 1970s, 12 million of the 29 million adolescents in America had had sexual intercourse, with sexual activity among unmarried female adolescents rising by two-thirds during the decade. The epidemic of teenage pregnancy—one American adolescent out of every ten becomes pregnant every year—is no longer news. Of great concern is that this rate persisted for a decade since it was first brought to the attention of the American public (Dryfoos, 1985). Of equal significance is the reality that of the 1.2 million adolescents who become pregnant each year, fully three-quarters do so unintentionally. Thus, births to married teens have dropped significantly, and an increasing proportion of births to adolescents now takes place out of wedlock.

The statistics highlighting birth and abortion rates by age in the United States parallel other sex-related concerns for adolescents. About 6 percent (62 per 1,000) of U.S. girls ages 15 through 17 either gave birth or had an abortion in 1981, as did 14 percent (144 per 1,000) of 18 and 19 year olds. The younger teens had about the same number of births as abortions, while older adolescents were more likely to continue pregnancies to birth. Finally, although both the media and social service agencies have given great attention to the fertility of girls under the age of 18, statistically this population accounts for a very small percentage of births and abortions. In 1981–82, about 28,000 pregnancies were reported among girls 14 and younger, with fewer than 10,000 resulting in births (Dryfoos, 1985).

A comparison and analysis of adolescent fertility rates in the United States with those of other countries indicates that this is indeed an alarming problem. The rate from 1979 through 1980 was higher in the United States than in any other country except Iceland, Greece, Hungary, and Romania. Even when one factors out for differences among racial groups in the United States, the rate for whites was higher than in every country except East Germany, Iceland, Yugoslavia, Greece, Czechoslovakia, Hungary, Poland, and Romania. Rates in Western European countries were one-fifth to one-half the U.S. rates, and in Japan the rate was one-twelfth. A more recent cross-cultural study conducted by the Alan Guttmacher Institute (1986), though heavily debated, points to an even more

TABLE 10.1   Teen birth rate

Both the number of births to young women under age 20 and the teen birth rate increased in 1988. Of particular concern is the birth rate among teens aged 15 to 17, which rose by 10 percent between 1986 and 1988. This increase follows a decade in which the birth rate among teens stayed fairly stable.

Rate of Births per 1,000 Females

Age	1980	1985	1986	1987	1988
Under 15	1.1	1.2	1.3	1.3	1.3
15–17	32.5	31.1	30.6	31.8	33.8
18–19	82.1	80.8	81.0	80.2	81.7
15–19	53.0	51.3	50.6	51.1	53.6

Number of Births to Teens

Age	1980	1985	1986	1987	1988
Under 15	10,169	10,220	10,176	10,311	10,588
15–17	198,222	167,789	168,572	172,591	176,624
18–19	353,939	299,696	293,333	289,721	301,729
Total under 20	562,330	477,705	472,081	472,623	488,941

The number of marital births to teens dropped dramatically during the 1980s, while the number of non-marital births increased steadily. In 1988, 66 percent of all births to teens occurred outside of marriage.

From "Facts at a Glance" by Kristin A. Moore. Washington, D.C.: Child Trends, Inc. Reprinted with permission.

alarming situation for adolescents in America, where individual barriers are broken down.

According to Shapiro (1980), the recognition that adolescent sexual activity is widespread should not preclude encouraging adolescents to consider abstinence as an acceptable behavior. Efforts to prevent adolescent pregnancies must nevertheless also emphasize the importance of contraception for adolescents who choose to be sexually active.

On a more positive note, Rodgers espouses an optimistic view:

In general, the sexual attitudes and behaviors of today's youth hold good prospect for future sexual relationships. They talk about sex more openly and are more accepting of themselves sexually than former generations. Also, instead of the sexes exploiting each other or males looking on females as sex objects, most young people have come to utilize sex as a means of communication between mutually respecting persons. The results should be healthier and more satisfying marriages. (1981, p. 209)

Consequences of Adolescent Childbearing

Adolescent childbearing can have unfortunate consequences: reduced opportunities for education, unemployment, poverty, welfare dependency, large family size, and babies often placed at risk of developmental delays (Furstenberg, 1976).

Although much has been written about the consequences of childbearing for the adolescent female, only recently has the literature begun to address the consequences for the male. Marsiglio (1987) has provided some helpful information about teenage fathers in his analysis of data from the National Longitudinal Survey of the Labor Experience of Youth. According to his analysis, 7 percent of young men ages 20 to 27 in 1984 said that they had fathered a child as teenagers. Marsiglio warns that this figure may be inaccurate because some respondents may have been less than candid. More than two-thirds of the children of these young fathers were born outside marriage. Many of the fathers were also high school dropouts. Young African-American men were especially likely to be responsible for nonmarital births. Only 15 percent of these young, black, unmarried fathers said they lived with their partners after the child's birth, compared with 48 percent of Hispanics, 58 percent of disadvantaged whites, and 77 percent of advantaged whites. Allen-Meares (1984) found that many adolescent fathers felt that social service agencies and professionals excluded them from involvement in the planning of the birth of a baby. These young men complained that their partners' and their partners' parents rejecting attitudes excluded them.

Interventions

School-Based Intervention.   Programs to help adolescent parents and their offspring avoid the negative consequences of premature childbearing often include a comprehensive approach. Such programs are intended to enhance adolescent parents' motivation, as well as their ability to avoid further pregnancy. Many of the programs come much too late, after the birth, and many fail to include the adolescent father.

In New York, the governor developed a program called Teen Pregnancy Initiative. This program consists of the following elements: (1) prevention, (2) curriculum on family life education in the public schools, (3) outreach and coordination of services, (4) partnership with the private sector, and (5) development of life skills and opportunities for self-sufficiency. Along with these elements, education, job training, employment, child care, parenting, and health care were included (Randolph & Gesche, 1986).

The Baltimore Prevention Program includes a clinic located across the street from the school and a sex education program within the school. Small-group counseling sessions for adolescents are held, and sex and health education is infused in select courses (Hardy, 1987). The major thrust of the program is to encourage personal responsibility and goal setting so that students will postpone sexual activity until they are older and more mature. Students taking part in the program showed substantial gains in knowledge pertaining to reproduction and contraception and students in an experimental control group showed no significant gains in these areas. Members of the experimental group also began to use more effective means of birth control and to have intercourse seven months later than those in the control group. No change was observed in the control students' age at first intercourse. There was also a 30 percent decrease in the pregnancy rate for those girls who had participated in the experimental program for three years. In comparison, a 57.6 percent increase in pregnancy rate was noted among control students during this time.

Another program that combines sex education with a clinic was initiated in St. Paul, Minnesota. This program involves offering health services at clinics in four of the city's schools. Along with sex education, parenting classes were offered (Bogar, 1985). Throughout the school year, 50 percent of the students visited the clinics, and the fertility rate declined. In 1976–1977 there were 59 births per 1,000 female students; in 1983–1984 this had decreased to 26 births per 1,000; a reduction of more than 50 percent.

Interdisciplinary Community Intervention. Interdisciplinary community-based programs that work in tandem with school, families, and religious institutions can be important. One such program involves the public high school, mental health department, public health, and a community-based day-care program designed to assist adolescent parents (Allen-Meares, 1979). This in-school program for adolescent parents is characterized as consumer oriented, preventive, comprehensive, accessible, and coordinated. The program focuses primarily on the prenatal and postnatal phases. During the prenatal phase, adolescent parents participate in in-school prenatal classes that include attention to nutrition, Lamaze instruction, fetal development, signs of labor, delivery, health care, and related topics. Special resource persons are brought into the class from the community (e.g., public health nurses, day care representatives). During the postpartum period, the adolescent mother receives instruction at home so that little course work is missed. The postnatal phase of the program consists of attention to family planning to reduce the likelihood of repeat pregnancies, child development and parenting, child care arrangements, career choices, and long-range planning (Bogar, 1985). A multidisciplinary team, consisting of representatives from nursing, social work, special education, mental health, and home economics, among others, meets periodically to coordinate the program and to monitor the progress of each student. The school social worker is the team leader. Representatives from the Department of Children and Family Services, Planned Parenthood, Public Aid have participated. Because of this program, the school administration became more concerned about prevention and thus supported the inclusion of more content on sexuality and reproduction in the health education curriculum. All students must take the health education course.

Individual and Group Intervention. A cognitive behavioral approach that targets individuals and small groups of adolescents also appears to be effective. This approach, which draws upon theories of cognition and learning, is the basis for constructing measures for avoiding pregnancy. It is founded on the premise that adolescents lack relevant information and the necessary skills to employ that information in daily situations. Because peers exert enormous pressures and adolescents lack assertiveness skills, young people engage in "risky behaviors" like unprotected intercourse. Schinke, Gilchrist, and Small (1979) have outlined a four-step process for implementing this approach:

1. *Information access.* Youth need current knowledge of sexuality, reproduction, and the consequences of sexual experimentation.
2. *Perception, comprehension, and storage of the information.* Once the
   facts are presented, the adolescent must learn to perceive, comprehend, and store this knowledge for use. The primary modality for trans-
   mitting knowledge is small group sessions that allow the development
   of role playing.
3. *Decision making.* The next step involves the active employment of
   knowledge and behaviors in daily situations. Being able to understand
   that sex without birth control has many negative consequences calls
   on young people to transform abstract concepts into everyday reality.
   Adolescents must personalize information and not merely store it, and
   they must use it when the appropriate situations confront them. Typically, this step is taught by drawing upon simulated role plays that
   take place in small groups, so that the adolescent can experiment with
   newly learned skills and receive feedback. The pressure statements
   described earlier in this chapter that are frequently used by adolescent
   males and females are explored in the small groups. These pressure
   lines are not the sole property of adolescent males. Females use them
   as well. "I want to have your baby." "You are cute." "Let's make a baby."
   These are familiar pressure lines that adolescent females use. Adolescents must be prepared to say no; but if they say yes, they must plan
   to take the necessary precautions. In other words, they must learn
   self-assertion.
4. *Decision implementation.* In the last stage, the newly learned behaviors must be put into action. A part of the cognitive behavioral approach is the inclusion of interpersonal skills training so that the youth
   can be assertive. For example, a youth may say, "I am not ready for
   sex," or "If we have sex we must use a condom and the pill. I do not
   want to be exposed to AIDS."

Other intervention methods that appear to hold promise with this population include the use of case managers to coordinate a variety of services (Brindis,
Barth, & Loomis, 1987) and the development of responsive support systems that
include the paternal and maternal grandparents, as well as the parents, and
involve the adolescent father.

HOMOSEXUALITY IN ADOLESCENCE

Not much has been written about homosexuality in the adolescent. Sullivan and
Schneider (1987) argue that when homosexuality emerges in adolescence, it must
be viewed from a developmentally nonpejorative perspective. Unfortunately, when
adolescents describe themselves as gay or lesbian, many adults around them are
likely to reject the statement as either a phase of development, attention-getting

behavior, or an adjustment reaction. Rather than acknowledging the self-statement, many helping professionals typically ignore it.

> Homosexual fears and fantasies abound in adolescence. A boy experiences an erection while alone with a male friend and concludes he is homosexual. . . . Reassurance that an unplanned, uncontrolled erection is a normal phenomenon in adolescence goes a long way to calm an anxious 14-year-old boy. (Grace, 1981, p. 82)

According to Ricketts:

> We do not know if homosexual behaviors in adolescence always continue into adulthood or, if they do, what form they take. Similarly, we cannot say with assurance that heterosexual behavior in adolescence will continue as an exclusive adult pattern. No matter how difficult it is, we must refrain from telling adolescents that we know that their behavior or feelings will or will not mean that they will behave heterosexually or homosexually in adulthood. (1986, p. 45)

Becoming aware of one's same-sex preference and making it known to others is called "coming out," which is described in the literature as "the developmental process through which gay people recognize their sexual preferences and choose to integrate this knowledge into their personal and social lives" (DeMonteflores & Schultz, 1978, p. 59). In an earlier chapter, it is mentioned that all adolescents face developmental tasks and that the environment can be rejecting. Gay adolescents must develop self-esteem in the context of a society and environment that reject their sexual preference; they must learn social skills that permit them to negotiate and live within a rejecting society (Sullivan & Schneider, 1987).

According to Chilman (1989), it appears that homosexual contacts are most common before age 15 and that the incidence is higher for boys than for girls. Sex play involving such behaviors as exhibitionism, voyeurism, and mutual masturbation occurs frequently in groups of boys (eight to thirteen years old), and about 5 percent of girls may engage in same-sex relations during early adolescence.

The few studies that do exist typically ask why some persons become homosexual while others do not. These studies primarily examine older subjects. Classical analytic, behavioral, and biological theories have all been used to explain same-sex attraction. Regardless of the theory or research, however, and whether one is young or old, to be homosexual in a homophobic society is particularly difficult. Deciding to expose one's sexual preference, or coming out, may be even more difficult for the adolescent because of hormonal and physical changes and the need for peer acceptance. Youth are often laden with feelings of shame, confusion, and constant worry about family and peer rejection. The following case illustration accentuates these concerns and issues. The author does not mean to imply that abused children become gay. These are the facts in this particular case, which is presented here to highlight peers' responses to those who demostrate this sexual orientation.

CASE ILLUSTRATION—JOHN

John Smith was a tenth grade white student living in a group home. John was physically and emotionally abused from infancy throughout childhood until he was removed from his home. His parents had beaten him so that one arm did not develop normally and was much smaller than the other. John had decided that he was homosexual and that he did not care what his peers felt. He sometimes carried a purse to school. His behavior invited the attention of male students, who repeatedly pushed, hit, and subjected him to verbal abuse. In response, he typically sought refuge in the school social worker's office. The staff at the residential home was providing individual casework services.

What is your assessment of John's situation? Why do you think he brings attention to himself? How would you proceed to maximize his self-determination? How would you proceed to make the school environment more conducive to him?

Intervention

Some youth go to practitioners with a preferred sexual orientation for the same sex, while others come with fear and uncertainty about their sexuality. If a youth's uncertainty is based on the remarks of more masculine or feminine adolescents who call the youth "gay" or "lesbian" and if he or she does not identify with such labels, then the practitioner should assist the youth in developing more traditional masculine or feminine behaviors and the appropriate social skills. The youth will need to learn self-assertion.

This latter practice principle can also be applied to youths who have pronounced themselves as gay or lesbian. They will need to learn to assert themselves, communicate their identities to others, and learn to accept that others may reject them because of their sexual orientation. In other words, adolescents may need help with coming out, especially with significant others. Intervention, according to McKinley, Kelly, and Patterson (1977), may also include helping adolescents learn how to handle social situations, how to respond decisively and effectively to negative remarks and demands. The goal of counseling or any intervention should be to help the adolescent develop a positive self-concept. In fact, the practitioner could be one of only a few individuals with whom the adolescent can experience acceptance. The practitioner should also focus on anxiety reduction, provide information to prevent exposure to AIDS, and offer support.

ADOLESCENT PROSTITUTION

Heightened attention is being paid to the escalating number of homeless and runaway youth. In 1983, it was estimated that between 773 thousand and 1.3 million children ran away from home each year (Adolinks, 1984). Many of them are under 18. It is believed that many of them run away to escape an environment of physical and sexual abuse, to escape poverty, to look for adventure, to solicit parental attention, and to satisfy a variety of other needs. There is evidence that many runaways become involved in prostitution. It is estimated that there are over 600 thousand juvenile prostitutes ranging in age from six to 16 years. Most engage in prostitution to sustain themselves on the streets. Children do not choose freely to become prostitutes; and they face terrible risks (as AIDS, torture, and violence).

Another reason often cited as the cause of adolescent prostitution is chemical dependency. Some believe that chemical dependency and prostitution are behavioral indicators of an endless cycle of victimization, disturbed family backgrounds, hopelessness, helplessness, and psychological paralysis (McMullen, 1986; Sibert, Pines, & Lynch, 1982).

Differentiation between adolescent male and female prostitutes is also found in the literature. Male prostitutes, though they may share some similar characteristics (e.g., they have been abused and neglected, they are runaways), differ from females in that their primary contacts are almost always homosexual. There also appears to be a more organized social network for females on the streets than for males (Schaffer & DeBlassie, 1984).

The relationship between the pimp and the youth is one of dependency and security. The process of transferring dependency needs onto the pimp is an area that practitioners need to give their immediate attention. If a child prostitute is very young, dependence needs are often greater; and even older youth who have not been nurtured properly are desperate for closeness and protection.

Intervention

There is little, if any, empirically validated intervention for this population. A high proportion of adult child abusers (those who exploit youth sexually and physically) are known to have been abused themselves as children and youth. To break the cycle of abuse, these adults must be targeted. Furthermore, victimized youths must be exposed to adults who model appropriate behaviors. Too many of these youth assume that something unique to themselves causes abuse. In a safe therapeutic environment, they can be made to realize that they are not responsible for adults who abuse. Because this mobile population is difficult to identify, many cities and towns offer safe houses for youth on the streets. Counseling, food, and shelter are often the direct services provided. Programming typically focuses on building self-esteem, locating significant adult role models in the youth's life (McMullen, 1987), and enhancing life skills through education or vocational training. Additional information on AIDS and the prevention of other sexually transmitted diseases is included in the programming of the safe houses. Ultimately, adolescent prostitutes must be viewed as victims, not as offenders.

SUMMARY

A variety of interventions that target both prevention and remediation efforts is presented in this chapter. The sexual activities of adolescents can be life-threatening given the escalating spread of AIDS and other sexually transmitted diseases. Youth need to have knowledge of the facts, the procedures to protect themselves, and the social skills to employ when confronted with various situations. Schools, parents, youth-related community services, and religious institutions should coordinate their efforts and take the lead in this area. Programming and intervention efforts must be based in a variety of settings if we are to intervene effectively to prevent pregnancies and prostitution. There is considerable variance within these populations; programming and intervention must reflect this variance and not be based on generalizations.

QUESTIONS FOR DISCUSSION

1. What additional interventions would you use to reduce the negative consequences of premature parenthood among adolescents?
2. How would you inform parents of the importance of AIDS awareness for their adolescents?
3. Critically evaluate the appropriateness of cognitive intervention as a prevention strategy with the wide spectrum of adolescents who either are sexually active or are being pressured to engage in sexual activity.
4. Discuss additional emotional and psychological issues that might arise in clinical practice with a gay or lesbian adolescent.
5. Design a community-based program that would target adolescent male prostitutes.

ADDITIONAL READINGS

Billy, J., & Udry, J. (1985). The influence of male and female best friends on adolescent sexual behavior. *Adolescences* 20: 21-32.

Bour, D., Young, J., & Henningsen, R. (1984). A comparison of delinquent prostitutes and delinquent nonprostitutes on self-concept. *Journal of Offender Counseling Services and Rehabilitation* 9 (Winter): 89-101.

Bower, B., Fullilove, M., & Fullilove, R. (1990). African-American youth and AIDS high-risk behavior: The social context and barriers to prevention. *Youth and Society* 22: 54-66.

Cervera N., & Videka-Sherman, L., eds. (1989). *Working with pregnant and parenting teenage clients.* Albany: Family Service of America and Rockefeller College Press.

Combs-Orme, T. (1993). Health effects of adolescent pregnancy: Implications for social workers. *Families in Society* 74(6): 344-354.

Dryfoos, J. (1991). Adolescents at risk: A summation of work in the field: programs and policies. *Journal of Adolescent Health* 12(8): 630-637.

Freeman, E. (1987). Interaction of pregnancy, loss, and developmental issues in adolescents. *Social Casework* 68: 38-46.

Hendricks, L. E. (1983). Suggestions for reaching unmarried adolescent fathers. *Child Welfare* 53: 141–146.

Hunter, J. (1990). Violence against lesbian and gay male youths. *Journal of Interpersonal Violence* 5: 1295–1300.

Inciardi, J., Potlieger, A., & Forney, M. (1991). Prostitution, IV drug use, and sex for crack exchanges among serious delinquents: Risks for HIV infection. *Criminology* 29: 221–235.

Males, M. (1992). Adult liaison in the epidemic of teenage birth, pregnancy, and venereal disease. *Journal of Sex Research* 29(4): 525–545.

Paik, S. (1992). Self-concept of pregnant teenagers. *Journal of Health and Social Policy* 3(3): 93–111.

Pleak, R., & Meyer-Bahlburg, H. (1990). Sexual behavior and AIDS knowledge of young male prostitutes in Manhattan. *Journal of Sex Research* 27: 557–589.

Resnick, M., Chambliss, S., & Blum, R. (1993). Health and risk behaviors of urban adolescent males involved in pregnancy. *Families in Society* 74(6): 366–374.

Santon, B., Black, M., Kaljee, L., & Ricardo, I. (1993). Perceptions of sexual behavior among urban early adolescents: Translating theory through focus groups. *Journal of Early Adolescence* 13(1): 44–66.

Schneider, M., & Tremble, B. (1985/1986). Gay or straight? Working with the confused adolescent. *Journal of Social Work and Human Sexuality* 4: 71–83.

Sullivan, M. (1993). Culture and class as determinants of out-of-wedlock childbearing and poverty during late adolescence. *Journal of Research on Adolescence* 3(3): 295–316.

REFERENCES

Adolinks. (1984). *Prostitution: A symptom of abuse.* St. Louis: Washington University, Center for Adolescent Health.

Alan Guttmacher Institute. (1986). *Teenage pregnancy in developed countries.* New Haven: Yale University Press.

Allen-Meares, P. (1979). An in-school program for adolescent parents: Implications for social work practice and multidisciplinary teaming. *School Social Work Journal* 3(2): 66–77.

Allen-Meares, P. (1984). Sexually active adolescents: Implications for social work intervention and family planning services. *Journal of Social Work and Human Sexuality* 3: 17–26.

Allen-Meares, P., & Shapiro, C., eds. (1989). Adolescent sexuality: New challenges for social work. *Journal of Social Work and Human Sexuality* 8: 1–71.

Bogar, A. (1985). Selected programs in other states relating to adolescent pregnancy prevention. *Wisconsin Legislative Council Staff Information Memorandum* 3: 1–11.

Brindis, C., Barth, R., & Loomis, A. (1987). Continuous counseling: Case management with teenage parents. *Social Casework: The Journal of Contemporary Social Work* 68: 64–172.

Chilman, C. (1989). Some major issues regarding adolescent sexuality and childbearing in the United States. In P. Allen-Meares & C. Shapiro, eds., *Adolescent sexuality: New challenges for social work,* pp. 3–27. New York: Haworth Press.

DeMonteflores, C., & Schultz, S. (1978). Coming out: Similarities and differences for lesbians and gay men. *Journal of Social Issues* 34: 180–197.

Diamond, M., & Diamond, G. (1986). Adolescent sexuality: Biosocial aspects and intervention strategies. In P. Allen-Meares & D. Shore, eds., *Adolescent sexualities overviews and principles of intervention,* pp. 3–15. New York: Haworth Press.

Dryfoos, J. C. (1985). Adolescent pregnancy prevention services in high school clinics. *Family Planning Perspective* 12: 6-14.

Finkel, M., & Finkel, D. (1975). Sexual and contraceptive knowledge, attitudes and behaviors of male adolescents. *Family Planning Perspectives* 7: 156-160.

Furstenberg, F., Jr. (1976). *Unplanned parenthood: The social consequences of teenage childbearing.* New York: Free Press.

Gelman, D. (1990). A much riskier passage. *Newsweek,* 116(26): 10-16.

Gibbs, F. (1986). Psychosocial correlates of sexual attitudes and behaviors in urban early adolescent females: Implications for intervention. *Journal of Social Work and Human Sexuality* 5: 81-97.

Grace, E. (1981). Areas of sexual misunderstanding among adolescents. *Medical Aspects of Human Sexuality* 15: 81-82.

Hardy, J. (1987). Preventing adolescent pregnancy: Counseling teens and their parents. *Medical Aspects of Human Sexuality* 16: 32-46.

Harrison, D., & Pennell, R. C. (1989). Contemporary sex roles for adolescents: New options or confusion? In P. Allen-Meares & C. Shapiro, eds., *Adolescent sexuality overviews and principles of intervention,* pp. 27-46. New York: Haworth Press.

Jessor, S., & Jessor, R. (1975). Transition from virginity to non-virginity among youth: A social psychological study over time. *Developmental Psychology* 11: 473-484.

Larson, R., & Kubey, R. (1983). Television and music: Contrasting media in adolescent life. *Youth and Society* 15: 13-31.

Marsiglio, W. (1987). Adolescent fathers in the United States: Their initial living arrangements, marital experience and educational outcomes. *Family Planning Perspectives* 19: 240-251.

Masters, W. H., Johnson, V. E., & Kolodny, R. C. (1988). *Human sexuality,* 3rd ed. Glenview, Ill.: Scott, Foresman.

McKinley, T., Kelly, J., & Patterson, J. (1977). Teaching assertive skills to a passive homosexual adolescent: An illustrative case study. *Journal of Homosexuality* 3: 163-169.

McMullen, R. (1986). Youth prostitution: A balance of power. *International Journal of Offender and Comparative Criminology* 30: 237-244.

Morgan, M., & Rothchild, N. (1983). Impact of the new television technology: Cable TV, peers, and sex role culturation in the electronic environment. *Youth and Society* 15: 33-50.

Morrison, D. (1985). Adolescent contraceptive behavior: A review. *Psychological Bulletin* 98: 538-568.

National Institute of Mental Health. (1982). *Television and behavior: Ten years of scientific progress and implications for the eighties,* Department of Health and Human Services Publication No. ADM 82-1195. Washington, D.C.: U.S. Government Printing Office.

Newcomer, S., Udry, J., & Cameron, F. (1983). Adolescent sex and behavior and popularity. *Adolescence* 18: 515-522.

Randolph, L., & Gesche, M. (1986). Black adolescent pregnancy: Prevention and management. *Journal of Community Health* 11: 10-19.

Reiss, I. (1970). Premarital sex as deviant behavior: An application of current approaches to deviance. *American Sociological Review* 35: 78-87.

Richmond-Abott, M. (1983). *Masculine and feminine sex roles over the life cycle.* Reading, Mass.: Addison-Wesley.

Ricketts, W. (1986). Homosexuality in adolescence: The reunification of sexual personalities. *Journal of Social Work and Human Sexuality* 5: 35-50.

Rodgers, D. (1981). *Adolescents and youth,* 4th ed. Englewood Cliffs, N.J.: Prentice Hall.

Schaffer, B., & DeBlassie, R. (1984). Adolescent prostitution. *Adolescence* 19: 689-696.

Schinke, S., Gilchrist, L., & Small, R. (1979). Preventing unwanted adolescent pregnancy: A cognitive-behavioral approach. *American Journal of Orthopsychiatry* 49: 56-81.

Shapiro, C. (1980). Sexual learning: The short-changed adolescent male. *Social Work* 25: 489-495.

Sibert, M., Pines, H., & Lynch, T. C. (1982). Substance abuse and prostitution. *Journal of Psychoactive Drugs* 14: 193-197.

Strouse, J., & Fabes, N. (1985). Formal vs. informal sources of sex education: Competing forces in the sexual socialization of adolescents. *Adolescence* 20: 251-263.

Sullivan, T., & Schneider, M. (1987). Development and identity issues in adolescent homosexuality. *Child and Adolescent Social Work* 4: 13-23.

Udry, J., Bauman, K., & Morris, N. (1975). Changes in premarital coital experiences of recent decades of birth cohorts of urban America. *Journal of Marriage and the Family* 37: 783-787.

Zabin, L., Hirsch, M., Smith, E., & Hardy, J. (1984). Adolescent sexual attitudes and behavior: Are they consistent? *Family Planning Perspectives* 16: 181-185.

Zelnik, M., & Kanter, J. (1980). Sexual activity, contraceptive use, and pregnancy among metropolitan area teenagers: 1971-1979. *Family Planning Perspectives* 9: 55-73.

Zelnik, M., Kantner, J., & Ford, K. (1981). *Sex and pregnancy in adolescence.* Beverly Hills, Calif.: Sage.

Zelnik, M., & Shah, F. (1983). First intercourse among young Americans. *Family Planning Perspectives* 15: 64-70.

part IV

Coordinating Services and Evaluating Practice

Part IV is devoted to a discussion of case management as a developing method of service coordination and accountability in delivering human services on behalf of children and adolescents. The many roles of the case manager and an advocacy model are discussed.

Related, and very important to the delivery of services, is the evaluation of outcome. Those in daily practice too often forget to assess the effects of interventions. This section contains useful and important information about measurement, research designs, and tools used to assess outcome. Considerable discussion is devoted to the question of why professionals must be accountable. It is the position of the authors that this is part of their professional obligation. This information informs practice, redefines priorities, and contributes knowledge to the professional literature. The growing requirements to be more accountable to funders is obvious to all.

chapter 11

Case Management and Coordination of Child and Youth Services

Elizabeth Segal and Paula Allen-Meares

Human services workers involved with children, adolescents, and their families strive with limited resources to provide necessary services for those most in need. The struggle to balance needed services and available resources has led practitioners to search for management tools that can help them in the delivery of services. One method that is gaining attention and is often used in social work practice with children and adolescents is case management. Much of the literature on case management is descriptive: Concern for tasks, roles, and discussions of demonstration models are primary topics.

The literature on case management could be considered in its infancy. According to Weil and Karls, "Case management is a developing method of service coordination and accountability in the human services. It is a series of actions and a process to assure that clients and human services systems receive a service, treatment, care, and opportunities to which they are entitled. . . . It is a set of logical steps and a process of interaction within a service network which assure that a client receives needed services in a supportive, effective, efficient and cost-effective manner" (1985, p. 2). Case management can be an effective way to monitor services and ensure that clients receive a level of individualized assessment that allows an efficient use of limited resources. Case management is useful in all forms of social work practice, but it is particularly helpful in child and adolescent settings. It is employed in a variety of settings to assist different populations. For example, it has been used with autistic students in special treatment programs (Garrels, 1983) and with hospitalized adolescents who have anorexia nervosa (Colligan, Ferdinande, & Rasmussen, 1984). The setting of the agency has a strong influence on how the management system operates. The structure, goals, and resources of the agency influence the way case management is implemented. There are a number of case management models: generalist, service broker, primary therapist, interdisciplinary team, comprehensive service center, family as case manager, supportive care manager, and volunteer as case manager (Weil & Karls, 1985).

According to Rubin (1987), evidence of the effectiveness of case management programs is accumulating. The literature includes a variety of research approaches and purposes, including the evaluation of community-based service programs, several experimental evaluation studies of case management and its use with different populations, and even quasi-experimental studies on its cost effectiveness.

The reality of work with children and adolescents, the bulk of which is delivered through public agencies, is that a significant amount of time is spent facilitating the provision of concrete services (Gibelman, 1983). Practitioners often find children and adolescents in crisis situations who need specific services such as health care, housing, food, clothing, day care, court protection, or temporary foster placement. Because there is rarely enough time or resources for a clinically oriented approach, case management has become an appropriate intervention strategy (O'Neil & Wilson-Coker, 1986).

THE ROLE OF THE CASE MANAGER

Regardless of the setting or population, case management entails the basic activities of assessing, planning, linking, monitoring, recording, and evaluating (Rubin, 1987). These tasks differ from those of a direct service provider. Rather than being responsible for the delivery of a specific service, the case manager takes an overall perspective on the needs of the child and family. Bertsche and Horejsi (1983) have suggested that a case manager's function could be split into a diagnostic service and a managerial role. Case coordinators must understand the availability of services within the community or their clients' immediate environments and have sufficient time to draw upon them to enhance services for those clients. Case coordinators essentially bring together different systems on behalf of their clients. They must deal with the gaps in services. Upon receiving a case, their first step is assessment, followed by planning or identifying the services needed and monitoring and evaluating progress of the case. The real challenge to the case manager is keeping everyone in the delivery system informed of the status of the client.

The initial phase of case management is the period of assessment. Although others may do the actual intake, the case manager must be aware of the child or adolescent's personal history, the family's history, its strengths, previous services received, and the perceptions of those involved. The strengths perspective moves case management away from the medical or psychopathological point of view and assumptions to embrace the following principles:

1. One should focus on individual strengths rather than pathology.
2. Case manager–client relationship is primary.

3. Intervention should be based on client self-determination.
4. The community is viewed as an oasis of resources.
5. Aggressive outreach is the preferred mode.
6. People (children and adolescents) can learn, grow, and change (Rapp, 1991, p. 46).

The case manager must continue to follow the progress of the client in order to assess changes in needs and services.

The information gathered through assessment enables the case manager to develop a case plan. In a sense, the case manager is also a program planner. Usually this requires a complete awareness of which services are appropriate and available for the client. The case manager must keep an updated file on services available in the community so as to develop a service plan that will serve the individual needs of the child and his or her family. Especially when working with children and adolescents, case coordination functions can become a part of or intertwined with intraagency agreements.

In Chapter 1, which addresses the transactional perspective and the role of environment, the importance of assessment is stressed. Here too, assessment of client and environmental conditions or systems that either support or inhibit growth and service delivery becomes essential. For example, knowing the capacity of a youth's parents to fulfill their role and act as collaborators in advocating special services to respond to the child's handicap can be important in charting a case management plan. If the parents are lax about the parenting role or lack the necessary skills to follow up, more of the work of advocacy is likely to fall to the case manager.

The next step in case management is linking the client and the family with the services. Once the necessary services are identified, the client must be linked to the providers. This can be as simple as a phone call, or it can demand a stronger means of advocacy. Agencies may be reluctant to take new clients, especially those that appear to require significant attention, and clients may be apprehensive about or uninterested in receiving services. Thus, the case manager becomes both an advocate and a broker. For example, in child abuse cases, families are often ordered by a court to receive services, such as counseling. The case manager can serve as a broker between the court and the family and between the service agency and the family.

Serving in a management role rather than being a direct service provider or an enforcer allows the case manager to monitor the progress of a client. The case manager can be objective about the effectiveness and quality of services because he or she is not providing them. The client also can turn to an outside advocate while receiving services. Most important, the client has someone following his or her progress from identification of the problem through service delivery. In the maze of social services, clients all too often get lost and never receive the services they need. A striking example of this can be seen in the numerous cases of children and adolescents placed in foster care for years, living in many different foster homes, and often leaving the system only when they reach the age of 18.

Without case management, it is difficult to follow the changes in a child's needs and life situation, and services can be either totally absent or duplicated. Case managers can assess the needs of clients, plan for appropriate service, connect clients to services, and monitor the process from beginning to end. The use of case management can be extremely effective in child and youth services, but only when it is implemented properly. Large caseloads and unrealistic expectations of workers can produce negative results. Overloaded workers are prone to stress and burnout. Thus, in implementing case management for child and adolescent work, it is imperative that great thought and care be used to determine the realistic role and number of cases for each case manager.

In one report involving case managers working with adolescent parents (Brindis, Barth, & Loomis, 1987), the amount of contact was three hours per client per month, and the caseload per worker was 30 to 35. Activities performed by these workers included one-to-one counseling, group work, and family mediation. Case managers worked with these parents to involve them as partners in the delivery of assistance, and they operated as brokers and advocates in linking these clients with community services. The case managers complained that their heavy caseloads denied them sufficient time to make new referrals and contacts on behalf of their clients. When the managers were asked what knowledge and skills were most useful, they mentioned counseling and communication skills, knowledge of the population they were serving, knowledge of available resources, and inter- and intraorganizational skills. Establishing a good rapport with the client was also identified as the foundation upon which other activities were built.

DEVELOPMENT OF CASE MANAGEMENT

In the development of a case management program, several factors should be kept in mind (Weils & Karls, 1985): First, the program must meet the needs of the client it intends to serve. Thus, the manager must be informed about gaps in service for that population. Second, the case management system must fit the organizational context in which it exists. Goals and objectives of the system must be considered. Typically, the more complex the organization, the more complex the case management system. Staff needs must also be taken into account. The system must be able to respond to the storage and retrieval of information. It must have the capacity to revise and redirect itself; in other words, a system of corrective feedback is required if the system is truly going to be responsive to changing needs and environmental conditions. Accountability and the evaluation of the system's effectiveness and efficiency are central considerations in the implementation and continuation of a responsive system. Documenting client progress, as well as length of time required in service to achieve goals established for client and agency objectives, should be a part of the evaluation and accountability system.

A MODEL FOR CASE MANAGEMENT IN CHILD AND ADOLESCENT PRACTICE

When case management is utilized with children and adolescents, there are some differences in its implementation. For example, the degree of involvement on the part of the child may vary from intense to negligible, given the child's age and maturity level. Typically, with adults who function in the normal range of social and psychological levels, the case manager seeks to empower and involve them at the very beginning. In working with children and adolescents, managers attempt to empower by organizing appropriate resources that foster optimal development. More work is done on behalf of children and youth because they lack the maturity, resources, and mobility to connect with agencies and services independently.

Rose (1992) elaborates an ordinary model intended to empower clients. It is very interesting about this approach that it not only requires the case manager to deliver direct services to the client but it also requires the worker to challenge dysfunctional service delivery systems. Implicit in this approach is the message that if the service delivery systems were operating in a functional manner there would be no need for a case management approach. The advocacy and empowerment model seeks to give each client maximum involvement in the process; thus it is "client driven rather than service driven" (p. 271). Rose outlines several assumptions on which this model is based: case management clients are seen as whole human beings living in a social context; people grow and develop when provided with the necessary material and support to do so; growth and movement occur in the context of relationships that are characterized by clarity of goals and shared action; and diagnosis does not determine a client's entire future development or deny the capacity to live more fully than providers' roles permit (see pp. 273–276).

An intriguing aspect of this model is its heavy reliance upon the use of informal resources and networks in the development of service plans. This is of particular importance in work with children and adolescents, who are especially vulnerable because both their parents or guardians and the social service delivery system have failed them—the parents for a host of personal, economic, and other reasons; the system because of poorly coordinated services, ill defined service planning, insufficient services that mistarget their needs, lack of comprehensive services, and the lack of advocates on their behalf. Though it may be difficult to generalize completely the notion of empowering children or adolescents, they can surely be allowed to participate in the various stages of case management in a manner approporiate to developmental age and readiness. For example, many youngsters become captives of the foster care system and spend their entire childhoods and adolescence in the system, living with different families or in different situations. The Center of the Study of Social Policy (1987) describes a 13-year old boy who had been placed in six foster homes over a five-year period and attended four different public schools. The need for someone to advocate and coordinate the different systems on behalf of this youth is self-evident. The youth was experiencing academic difficulty and had been identified as someone who needed special educational services.

Most service providers interact with a family in regard to a specific activity over a limited time. Historically, the role of the case manager has been confined to the structure of a specific program, such as foster care, or an agency, such as a department of children's services or a mental health agency. This does not need to be the case. For the case management advocacy model, the role of the worker is separate from both the actual services and the assigned agency. With an advocacy approach, the case management relationship develops between the worker and the family over time and lasts for the duration of all different services received. This can allow a worker to serve as a "family advocate," both guiding and empowering the family.

The model centers around four key aspects as have been outlined in the following list:

Case Management Advocacy Model*

Complete Case Assessment	Data on family history, employment status, environment assessment, prior services
	Utilize knowledge of child development, family, organization, and behavior
Worker Access to Services	Contact departments of children's services, health, and education; judicial system; public and private child welfare agencies
	Identify resources to process services
Authority	Utilize legislative and financial backing of state and local governments
Evaluation and Follow-through	Evaluate services, monitor agencies and quality of providers
	Evaluate progress of family and use of services

The case manager first conducts a complete assessment of the family. This includes doing a family history—checking the family's community involvement, employment, living environment, and use of prior services. A transactional framework is helpful for the assessment; it requires that the worker have a good knowledge both of child and adolescent development and of the various systems in which the child functions, including the family. The second and third components of the model require that the worker have both access to services and the ability

---

*Prepared by professor Elizabeth Segal, School of Social Work, Ohio University, Columbus, Ohio.

to procure them for the family. This means obtaining the resources and authority to actually enroll a family in a service once the need is identified. This statement could be considered somewhat idealistic, given that agencies frequently place limits on caseload sizes and have extensive intake procedures. The case manager must be well versed in the network of child welfare services and be backed legislatively, ideally by both state and local governing bodies. The final component of the model is the need to evaluate and provide follow-up to the services provided. In addition to monitoring the progress of the client, the case manager should also monitor the effectiveness and quality of the services offered.

The effectiveness of this model depends in large part on manageable caseloads and the backing received from authorities. Workers often have difficulty carrying out their jobs because they are responsible for large numbers of clients. For the case management advocacy model to work, case managers must be assigned a reasonable number of families, and the caseload should be adjusted to reflect the severity of the cases.

CASE MANAGEMENT IN CHILD WELFARE ON A MACRO LEVEL: AN ILLUSTRATION

The Child Welfare and Adoption Assistance Act of 1980 (P.L. 96-272) was designed to improve and reform the child welfare system. In particular, it stressed the prevention of unnecessary and prolonged placement of children in foster care and the improvement of services for children requiring foster care. Some of its key components:

1. Expanded the role of the courts to ensure that "reasonable efforts" have been made to prevent removal of a child and to reunify the family
2. Provided for case review of each child in foster care at least once every six months
3. Called for a hearing after 18 months to plan for permanent placement
4. Required a written case plan for each child

These mandates encouraged states to develop and implement case management techniques in their child welfare systems in order to receive federal funds. In response to this law, 34 states have enacted statutory requirements for written case plans, 38 states have required court reviews, 21 states have required administrative reviews, and 13 states have credited citizen review boards (Robison, 1987). However, in no state is there a comprehensive system for case management that follows a child and his or her family throughout service delivery and acts as an advocate for the family.

Although the reforms that stemmed from the 1980 act gave rise to some improvements in the child welfare system, child advocates are once again calling for legislation to improve the system. Following enactment of P.L. 96-272, case reviews and written plans seemed to help keep many families intact and provided needed services. Today, the system is once again overloaded with an increasing number of cases and families with more severe problems (Children's Defense Fund, 1989). At the same time, workers are burdened with large caseloads that make true case management impossible. In many cities, each worker carries an average of 50 or 60 cases, with some carrying as many as 100 cases (House Subcommittee on Human Resources, 1989). Case management can be a good model for service delivery, but it must be done with reasonable caseloads, legislative support, and adequate resources. Because of increased numbers, severity of cases, and overloaded workers, the child welfare system is again in need of reform. Nevertheless, by knowing what is going on in the primary client's life, the manager remains better able to plan and intervene. Such planning can meet the individual needs of the client, enhance continuity of service, and in some instances empower the client. Given all this, however, there are nevertheless a number of disadvantages to case management.

ADVANTAGES AND DISADVANTAGES OF CASE MANAGEMENT

Case management creates a broader view of the client and includes his or her living environment over time. Thus, a case manager can see to it that a client receives more comprehensive services. In the long run, the approach is both effective and efficient. It eliminates inappropriate services and duplication, and it deals more adequately with family resistance and agency inaccessibility. It also provides continuity of services by having the worker follow the client throughout the course of service delivery. And finally, the model provides a higher level of accountability.

The case management approach also frequently requires one person to play such a great variety of roles that the issue of burnout among professional case managers is gaining recognition (Kemp, 1981). Barriers to case management include administrative inertia, heavy caseloads, agency policies that inhibit the assignment of personnel, and the lack of consistent monitoring and recording (Wells, 1985). Effective case management is contingent upon the availability and degree of cooperation of services. Problems in the coordination of services, issues of invested interests, difficulties associated with public and private agencies working together, scarcity of resources, and role confusion are only a few of the obstacles. Uncooperative attitudes can affect interagency relations, leading to staff conflicts about responsibility for clients and distrust and misunderstanding between state facilities and community agencies. Poor information exchange and lack of agreement between staff members can also hinder success. Many agencies and staff are ill equipped to utilize the latest technological advancements, and lack of computer capability is an issue that needs to be addressed. The time needed to record and document outcome is often given insufficient attention.

SUMMARY

The research on case management is flawed with a host of methodological problems. In part, there has been a lack of definition or agreement on what defines case management, what outcome measures are appropriate, and what the nature of the evaluation ought to be (Fisher, Landis, & Clark, 1988). Nevertheless, it appears to be an approach that is widely accepted and growing in popularity.

QUESTION FOR DISCUSSION

1. Visit a local human service agency providing services to children, adolescents, and families that has embraced case management as an interventive tool. Interview one of the case managers and raise the following questions: What is the worker's opinion of the advantages and disadvantages of case management? How would the worker describe the agency's case management system (e.g., complex, opportunities for evaluation and corrective feedback are present, effective and efficient, and so on). What changes would he or she make in the present management system and why?

ADDITIONAL READINGS

Benjamin, M., & Ben-Daskan, T. (1982). Case management: Implications and issues. In C. Sanborn, ed., *Case management in mental health services.* New York: Haworth Press.

Cheung, K., Stevenson, R., & Leung, P. (1991). Competency-based evaluation of case management skills in child sexual abuse intervention. *Child Welfare* 70: 425–435.

Homonoff, E., & Maltz, P. (1991). Developing and maintaining a coordinated system of community-based services to children. *Community Mental Health* 27: 347–358.

Johnson, P., & Rubin, A. (1983). Case management in mental health: A social work domain. *Social Work* 28: 49–55.

Kisthkardt, W. (1991). A strengths model of case management: The principles and functions of a helping partnership with persons with persistent mental illness. In D. Saleebey, ed., *The strengths perspective in social work practice.* White Plains, N.Y.: Longman.

Lamb, R. (1980). Therapist–case manager: More than brokers of services. *Journal of Hospital and Community Psychiatry* 31: 762–764.

Rapp, C., & Chamberlain, R. (1985). Case management for the chronically mentally ill. *Social Work* 30: 417–432.

Rapp, C. A., & Wintersteen, W. T. (1989). The strengths model of case management: The results of twelve demonstrations. *Journal of Psycho-Social Rehabilitation* 13: 23–32.

Sandborn, C., ed. (1983). *Case management in mental health services.* New York: Haworth Press.

REFERENCES

Bertsche, A., & Horejsi, C. (1983). Case manager. In H. Weissman, I. Epstein, & A. Savage, eds., *Agency-based social work: Neglected aspects of clinical practice.* Philadelphia: Temple University Press.

Brindis, C., Barth, R., & Loomis, A. (1987). Continuous counseling: Case management with teenage parents. *Social Casework* (March): 164-172.

Center for the Study of Social Policy. (1987). *A framework for child welfare reform.* Washington, D.C.: The Center.

Children's Defense Fund. (1989). *A vision for America's future.* Washington, D.C.: The Fund.

Colligan, R., Ferdinande, R., & Rasmussen, N. (1984). Anorexia nervosa: Academic-behavioral management and mainstream dismissal planning for hospitalized adolescents. *Residential Group Care and Treatment* 2: 45-55.

Fisher, M., Landis, D., & Clark, K. (1988). Case management service provision and client change. *Community Mental Health Journal* 24: 134-141.

Garrels, D. (1983). Autism, the ultimate learning disability: A case management approach. *Journal of Child Care* 1: 23-35.

Gibelman, M. (1983). Social work education and the changing agency practice. *Journal of Education for Social Work* 19: 23-34.

House Subcommittee on Human Resources. (1989). *Child welfare system: Foster care and adoption programs.* Washington, D.C.: U.S. Government Printing Office.

Kemp, B. (1981). The case management model of human service delivery. *Annual Review of Rehabilitation* 2: 212-238.

O'Neil, M., & Wilson-Coker, P. (1986). The child welfare specialist: An interdisciplinary graduate curriculum. *Child Welfare* 65: 102-117.

Rapp, C. (1991). The strengths perspective of case management with persons suffering from severe mental illness. In D. Saleebey, ed., *The strengths perspective in social work practice.* White Plains, N.Y.: Longman.

Robison, S. (1987). *State child welfare reform: Toward a family-based policy.* Washington, D.C.: National Conference of State Legislatures.

Rose, S. M. (1992). *Case managements—An advocacy/empowerment design in case management: Social work practice.* S. Rose, ed., pp. 271-297. White Plains, N.Y.: Longman.

Rubin, A. (1987). Case management. In *Encyclopedia of social work,* 18th ed., pp. 213-222). Silver Spring, Md.: National Association of Social Workers.

Weil, M. & Karls, J., eds. (1985). *Case management in human service practice.* San Francisco, Calif.: Jossey-Bass.

Wells, S., (1985). Children and the child welfare system. In M. Weil & J. Karls, eds., *Case management in human service practice,* pp. 119-144. San Francisco, Calif.: Jossey-Bass.

chapter 12

Evaluating Social Work Practice with Children and Adolescents

Vanessa G. Hodges and Betty J. Blythe

Social work practice with children and adolescents presents many challenges to practitioners, among them a desire to provide appropriate and effective interventions. This chapter examines measurement and research methods that will help practitioners evaluate progress when working with children and adolescents. The research techniques suggested here are generic and applicable to practice in all settings and with all populations.

The chapter begins with a discussion of the importance of data collection in terms of client and agency accountability. Next, the concept of measurement is explored, including a description of the different types of measurement tools and a discussion of problems practitioners sometimes face in trying to implement various measures. The third section describes various research designs for evaluating practice, including case studies, single-case, and experimental and quasi-experimental designs. The chapter concludes with a discussion of procedures for analyzing client outcome data, including visual and statistical procedures.

THE IMPORTANCE OF DATA COLLECTION

Data collection serves several important functions in service delivery. First, collecting assessment data influences the type and sequence of interventions the practitioner will use. Specific information about the onset, level, and nature of a child's problem allows a worker to tailor an intervention plan to meet the needs of the child.

A second, albeit related, function of data collection is to allow workers to routinely examine if a child's goals are being achieved. Collecting periodic information about the existence, frequency, duration, or severity of a problem indicates whether clients are making progress in the desired direction. Thus, monitoring the progress of specific intervention activities provides a decision-making tool to assist workers in determining whether to modify, continue, or terminate an intervention plan. Ultimately, these data assess the effectiveness of the intervention plan.

A third reason for collecting data is one of accountability to the client, agency, and external funders. Accountability to clients involves using interventions that have empirical support, whenever possible, and routinely monitoring client progress once an intervention has been initiated (Ivanoff, Robinson, & Blythe, 1987). On a broader level, practitioners are accountable to their agencies and funding sources to provide efficient, cost-effective interventions.

Finally, data collection may contribute to expanding the social work knowledge base on effective interventions with children. By accumulating facts and information over time, data collection can suggest which interventions are effective with which children, thereby increasing the knowledge base of the profession (Blythe & Briar, 1985).

MEASUREMENT

During assessment and intervention, practitioners systematically collect information about behaviors, thoughts, feelings, and significant aspects of a child's environment. For example, as a practitioner collects assessment data to begin work with a withdrawn child, he or she observes the child's interaction at school and in the home. The practitioner collects data describing how this child interacts with peers, as well as adults, attempting to identify both strengths and weaknesses (or areas needing improvement). The practitioner determines whether the child sees himself or herself as withdrawn and how the child feels about his or her interactions. Finally, the practitioner makes a careful assessment of the child's environment to determine if there are persons or situations either encouraging and supporting this dysfunctional behavior or potentially helpful in changing it. This information is used to specify the problem, design intervention plans, and monitor progress on goals and objectives. Practitioners, however, need a system for organizing and drawing conclusions based on this information. Measurement is the process of categorizing and assigning labels or numbers to information (Bostwick & Kyte, 1988). Measurement concepts and principles facilitate practitioners' efforts to make objective assessments of client progress.

Four fundamental concepts are central to measurement: reliability, validity, sensitivity, and directness. Although these concepts are discussed briefly, readers are referred to other sources for a more detailed discussion (See Barlow & Hersen, 1984; Grinnell, 1993; Rubin & Babbie, 1993; Marlow, 1993).

Reliability refers to the likelihood that a measure will produce similar results at two different points in time (Corcoran & Fischer, 1987). A measure with high reliability would provide the same results at measurement intervals 1 and 2, assuming no change had taken place. Whenever possible, practitioners should select measures with high degrees of reliability and administer them in a manner that enhances reliability. This insures that change on the measure is more likely attributable to the intervention than to some other factor. For example, if you rate a child's social skill level on a monthly basis, a reliable measure will provide the same results at measurement intervals 1 and 2, assuming no skills training or improvement in social skill has occurred.

Validity refers to the extent to which an instrument measures what it claims to measure and, ultimately, to how well these measures can be generalized to other measures or predictions about a client's behavior (Blythe & Tripodi, 1989). Different types of validity include predictive (the ability to predict behavior from a current score or observation), concurrent (the correlation between two standardized measures, assessing similar information, gathered at the same time), construct (the degree to which constructs, such as self-esteem or depression, are accurately represented by the measure), and content (the degree to which all dimensions of a target problem are represented by the measure).

A measure that is sensitive can detect client change easily, even when change is slow and occurs in small increments (Bloom & Fischer, 1994). A measure that can identify small changes is desirable because it can give the worker and client more information about client progress. As an example, direct observation is an excellent way to measure minute changes. A frequency count tells immediately how often a child helps with chores. An increase from six to seven would be a small change in the desired direction, but a checklist with categories, helps with chores (a) 1-5 times per week and (b) 6-10 times per week, would not reflect this slight progress. If a measure fails to indicate client progress, the client and the worker may both become discouraged, and the worker may prematurely change the intervention.

A final concept central to a discussion of measurement is directness. This refers to how closely the measure approximates the true target problem (Bloom & Fischer, 1982). Practitioners should attempt to select measures that are as direct as possible. For example, it is more desirable to measure a child's social skills by actually observing the child interacting with peers than by interviewing the child's parent. The former option is likely to yield a more accurate reflection of social skills. Indirect measures leave much more room for error through interpretation.

Specifying Problems and Goals

After completing the formal assessment of the client and the family, the worker formulates an intervention plan. This plan is a blueprint that outlines the goals and objectives and the treatment methods to accomplish these objectives. Goals that reflect the desired outcomes for the family are stated in measurable terms. For example, Beverly will see a physician one time per month to monitor the dosage of her retalin medication. Objectives are smaller steps that lead to the achievement of the goal. In the above goal, objectives might include (a) scheduling the appointment, (b) arranging transportation, and (c) actually keeping the appointment. Finally, the intervention plan should include specific suggestions about how the goals and objectives are to be achieved. In this example, the treatment plan might include problem solving for transportation and reinforcement for keeping the appointment.

Types of Measures

Approaches to measurement vary widely depending on the individual child or adolescent, the family, the environment, and the nature of the target problem. While a discussion of specific measurement alternatives for each of the problem areas addressed in this book is not possible here, general measurement approaches are discussed, and the advantages and disadvantages of each are considered. The following measurement strategies are reviewed: standardized measurement, observation, and self-report. These strategies were selected because they fit well with social work practice with children, are appropriate for measuring a variety of different problem situations, and are easily implemented.

Standardized Measures.   Standardized measures include questionnaires, rapid assessment instruments (RAI), checklists, personality tests, interview schedules, and sentence completion tests, to name the most common examples (Edelson, 1985; Corcoran & Fischer, 1987).

There are literally hundreds of standardized measures, and practitioners may find it difficult to select appropriate instruments. Practicality, purpose, measurement error, reliability, validity, and availability of norms are important considerations when evaluating different measures (Blythe & Tripodi, 1989). Practicality refers to the time required to complete the measure, the degree to which test items are understandable, the costs of the measure, and the amount of training necessary to complete the instrument accurately. Ideally, measures should take less than 10 minutes to complete, be clearly written, and require minimal training.

Practitioners must carefully evaluate the purpose of the instrument and the types of results the measure will yield. For example, some standardized measures are not designed to be given to clients at repeated frequent intervals. While they are of some benefit during the initial assessment process, these types of measures are of little use for evaluating client progress when repeated measurement is necessary.

Measurement error reduces the reliability and validity of the instrument. Practitioners should evaluate test items for potential sources of bias and estimate the extent to which this bias will misrepresent the problem being measured.

Standardized measures should contain content validity and data on the appropriate type of reliability. Measures that have low reliability are of little value. Furthermore, if the concept measured by the instrument is not valid, the information will not be useful.

Finally, measures that have normative data for a population similar to that of the client are preferable. Norms provide a summary of how a similar group, representative of a larger population, completed the instrument. For example, the Stanford-Binet IQ test has information on how institutionalized, developmentally disabled children typically score on the test. A practitioner working with such a child would compare the client with the demographic information presented for the normative data of other developmentally disabled children. If the client is similar in age, sex, race, and type of institutional placement, the normative data would allow the practitioner to compare the client with a similar population to determine whether the client performs at the same level, higher, or lower than his or her peers.

CHILD'S ATTITUDE TOWARD MOTHER (CAM)   Today's Date _____

Name _____

This questionnare is designed to measure the degree of contentment you have in your relation-ship with your mother. It is not a test, so there are no right or wrong answers. Answer each item as carefully and accurately as you can by placing a number beside each one as follows:

1   Rarely or none of the time
2   A little of the time
3   Some of the time
4   A good part of the time
5   Most or all of the time

Please begin.

1. My mother gets on my nerves.   _____
2. I get along well with my mother.   _____
3. I feel that I can really trust my mother.   _____
4. I dislike my mother.   _____
5. My mother's behavior embarrasses me.   _____
6. My mother is too demanding.   _____
7. I wish I had a different mother.   _____
8. I really enjoy my mother   _____
9. My mother puts too many limits on me.   _____
10. My mother interferes with my activities.   _____
11. I resent my mother.   _____
12. I think my mother is terrific.   _____
13. I hate my mother.   _____
14. My mother is very patient with me.   _____
15. I really like my mother.   _____
16. I like being with my mother.   _____
17. I feel like I do not love my mother.   _____
18. My mother is very irritating.   _____
19. I feel very angry toward my mother.   _____
20. I feel violent toward my mother.   _____
21. I feel proud of my mother.   _____
22. I wish my mother was more like others I know.   _____
23. My mother does not understand me.   _____
24. I can really depend on my mother.   _____
25. I feel ashamed of my mother.   _____

FIGURE 12.1 Sample standardized measure

SOURCE: Hudson, W., WALMYR Assessment Scale Scoring Manual (1992), WALMYR Publishing Co., P.O. Box 24779, Tempe, Arizona 85285-4779. Reprinted with permission from the author.

Standardized measures have some disadvantages. Because they are more generalized to fit a range of individuals, they often fail to address the specific target problem of a given client. For example, a practitioner may gain a general understanding of sibling rivalry by administering a standardized measure on sibling relationships. If the target problem is intense jealousy, however, a measure on sibling relationships may not be sensitive enough to this particular aspect of the relationship. Another potential disadvantage in using standardized measures is the norming process. These measures are usually normed on a large population and then averaged to yield a single representative score. Comparing an individual child's score to the average normed score may not result in a legitimate comparison. For example, if the client is a child with multiple handicaps and the normative group has few or no children with disabilities, it may be erroneous to compare the client to this norm, especially if the measure was not designed to assess some significant aspect of this particular client's problem. Another disadvantage is that standardized measures require a certain reading and understanding level (Corcoran & Fischer, 1987). A standardized measure will yield unreliable and inaccurate information if the client has a low reading level or is functionally illiterate yet attempts to complete the measure. This is an especially important consideration when children complete such measures because their reading levels vary greatly. Instructions for some measures allow or suggest that the practitioner read and record responses for the client. In such cases, practitioners should follow the instructions accompanying the standardized measure carefully because interpreting scores is based on strict adherence to the instructions.

Observation.   Observational data consist of direct and indirect data about a client's behavior collected by the worker or a designate (e.g., teacher or parent, sibling), rather than the client (Barlow, Hayes, & Nelson, 1984). Direct observation can be made in a therapeutic setting or in the client's natural environment (e.g., home, school, neighborhood, or work). These measures represent actual samples of the target behavior. Indirect observational measures, sometimes called secondary data, consist of information previously collected for other purposes, such as school, hospital, or police records.

When collecting data through observation, the worker begins by defining the behavior in operational terms so as to be clear about what should be counted and what should be ignored (Cormier & Cormier, 1991). For instance, if a parent is recording data on a child's "back talk" to his mother, it is important to define "back talk" operationally. Does it involve *any* comment made after an instruction or directive is given? Does it involve only refusal or negotiations after an instruction is given? Should it be counted only if profane language is involved? The operational definition must also specify which dimensions of the target behavior will be recorded. Frequency, duration, discrete occurrences, and physiological conditions are possible dimensions to consider. Frequency, which involves the number of times a target behavior occurs, typically is used when the behavior occurs often. For example, a teacher may record the frequency of unexcused absences, or the parent of an adolescent may record the number of nights the teenager returns home after curfew. Duration specifies the length of time for each episode of the behavior (Ciminero, Nelson, & Lipinski, 1977). For instance, a parent may record the number of minutes a temper tantrum lasts. A third observational measure is discrete occurrence or nonoccurrence of a behavior. This dimension involves recording the presence or absence of the behavior. For example, a case manager could use a discrete measure to record whether or not a family followed through with a referral to a community mental health center to be evaluated for family therapy. Finally, physiological measures include measures of heart rate, pulse, blood pressure, and skin temperature. As an illustration, a practitioner using biofeedback to reduce stress and anxiety in an adolescent could measure the increase in skin temperature as a measure of the success of biofeedback in reducing anxiety.

While observation is most commonly used to collect information about an individual child, it actually occurs in the child's natural environment, such as a classroom, playground, home, residential treatment center, or recreational center. These settings give the practitioner a more realistic picture of the target behavior and decreases the chance of distortion or bias when data are collected indirectly. For instance, if a practitioner is trying to increase family interaction, a home visit is an appropriate way to assess opportunities for increased family communication. Home observation is preferable to data provided by parents or children describing a typical meal-time conversation or the furniture arrangement of the dining area. Simple environmental changes, such as a specified meal time with no television, radio, or telephone interruptions, might facilitate more interaction during meals. A different furniture arrangement in the adjoining family room might discourage television viewing and encourage more conversation. These types of environmental manipulations are difficult, if not impossible, without the opportunity to observe the home directly.

Observation, one of the most popular forms of data collection, offers many advantages to the practitioner. First, it is a direct measure of the behavior. It represents actual samples of the target behavior and eliminates the need for the practitioner to make inferences. Observational measures collected in the natural environment also provide the practitioner with information about the context in which the behavior takes place. This type of information is critical in intervention planning. In many instances, intervention may more appropriately be directed to the environment than to the child or other family members. Second, observational measures are sensitive measures insofar as they can record small, almost minute, changes, as well as larger changes, in the target behavior. A third advantage of observational measures is that scores are easily quantified and compared to previous scores so that patterns of behavior over time can be discerned. Finally, observational data are generally simple to collect, as long as the worker does not get carried away with designing the measure.

The major disadvantage of observational measurement is the inability to measure thoughts and feelings. Other measurement tools are available to tap these covert processes, although they are less direct and thus more open to interpretation.

Wilson Family   Date: _____

                                                       Rater: _____

Behavior observed: Number of "I" messages used during 60-minute family therapy session.

                    4:00   4:15   4:30   4:45

Mrs. Wilson

Mary

John

Sid

FIGURE 12.2   Sample observational recording form

A second disadvantage of observational measurement is the potential for reactivity, or changes in behavior caused by measurement (Foster & Cone, 1980; Haynes & Horn, 1982; Barlow, Hayes, & Nelson, 1984). People generally behave differently if they know they are being observed. For example, if a student knows that the teacher will be counting each time he interrupts his classmates, his interrupting behavior is likely to decrease somewhat. If a father knows that a practitioner is observing his delivery of time-out to his son, he is likely to behave differently than he would if the practitioner were not observing. Initially, reactivity has a positive effect insofar as behavior changes in the desired direction (Corcoran & Fischer, 1987). However, this change is temporary and eventually begins to deteriorate unless an intervention directed at more permanent change is instituted. A third disadvantage of observational measurement is that it often is time consuming. As much as possible, workers should try to limit the amount of information the observer must record.

Self-Reports.   These measures include frequency counts by clients, client logs and diaries, self-anchored rating scales, and interviews. Unlike data obtained by observation, data for these measures are always provided by the client. Self-report measures offer an important tool for collecting data on client thoughts and feelings. For example, a child with performance anxiety could use a diary to enumerate negative thoughts before giving a class report.

Client logs and diaries include journal-type entries of significant events that affect or relate to the target problem. Logs and diaries are highly individualized, with the client helping to define the content to be included, the frequency with which entries are recorded, and the format for recording (Bloom & Fischer, 1994). They are also helpful as an exploratory measure when clients are having difficulty defining target problems or identifying their antecedents and consequences.

Self-anchored rating scales are Likert-type scales. Ideally, these scales are designed with each point anchored or labeled for a specific client. The scales

Sandy's Body-Image Log

DIRECTIONS: This is a log to record my feelings about my body. I will record each time I am feeling unhappy, nervous, or embarrassed about my body. My social worker is the only person who reads my log.

Date and Time	Situation	Who Was Present	How I Felt
Feb 5, 10:30	Science	Teacher Classmates	I hate it when we pick teams because I'm always the last one picked. Because I wear braces on my legs, people think I can't participate. Today we were just doing a stupid experiment. I don't need to walk to do a stupid science experiment.
Feb 6, 9:00	Science	Teacher Classmates	I'm really nervous because the teacher asked me to be the group leader. I'll have to pick 7 people to be in my group. My feelings will be hurt if they don't want to be in my group.
Feb 7, 8:30	Homeroom	Teacher	Today I was assigned to a gym class for handicapped people. Why me? Why do they have to put all the crippled people in the same class? Some of the people in my class are mentally retarded. They don't belong in a class with me.

FIGURE 12.3 Sample client log

often represent the intensity of some feeling, but they also can relate to behaviors or cognitions. Examples are ratings of anger, depression, self-worth, pleasure, pain, or affection. In developing the scale, the client can improve the quality of the information yielded by providing specific examples of each of several levels of the behavior. For instance, the degree and intensity of anger vary considerably for any two clients. One adolescent may feel hatred and malice toward others while another describes feelings of irritation and annoyance. A self-anchored scale can accurately represent the intensity of these emotions for both individuals because each individual is involved in defining the anchors. Generally, self-anchored scales should have five or more points. If there are too many points, clients may have difficulty discriminating between the different levels. Using too few points yields insufficient information about client change. At a minimum, the first, last, and middle points should be defined with anchors (Bloom & Fischer, 1994). The practitioner and client also need to determine when and how often the measure will be completed.

A variation of the self-anchored scale is the rating scale, which differs only in that it is not completed by the client but by someone closely affiliated with

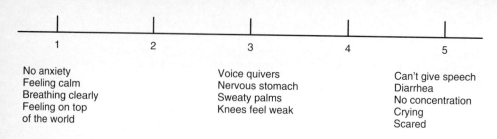

This scale was designed to measure speech anxiety in an adolescent male who was required to take a high school speech course. The client was instructed to rate his level of anxiety before giving his speech.

FIGURE 12.4   Sample self-anchored rating scale

the client, such as the practitioner, a teacher, a friend, or a parent (Gingerich, 1979). As with the self-anchored scale, it is important to involve the person completing the measure as the scale is developed.

Interviewing is perhaps the most common vehicle for collecting self-report data. Both structured and unstructured interviewing help workers collect information from clients. With a structured interview schedule, the same questions are asked on each occasion. For instance, a probation officer may ask a juvenile offender a standard set of questions about school attendance, peers, family life, substance abuse, and reoffending. Unstructured interviews address the same problem areas, but the sequence and format of the questions vary from interview to interview.

Collecting data through self-report offers practitioners many advantages. First, self-report measures can be tailored to individual client problems (Barlow & Hersen, 1984; Bellack & Hersen, 1977). Clients often come to practitioners with multiple, somewhat unique problems. Rarely does one single measure address all the various problems or even all aspects of one problem. The ability to individualize measurement strategies for clients offers flexibility. A second advantage of self-report measures is that they provide practitioners with a means to capture covert thoughts and feelings, as well as behaviors.

Practitioners should also be aware of the limitations of self-report measures. First, they are less standardized than any of the other measures discussed here. Therefore, they may yield less reliable and valid information which must be interpreted more cautiously. Care in defining the information to be gathered and in outlining recording procedures can mitigate these problems. Whenever possible, multiple measures should be administered for the data received through self-report. A second disadvantage is that self-report measures may produce biased data if the client is attempting to please the practitioner. An adolescent girl keeping a journal about her relationship with her parents may begin to fabricate diary entries because she believes that her practitioner wants the relationship to improve. Finally, all self-report measures except interviewing require the client to have enough motivation to collect data on a regular and consistent basis, even when the task becomes tedious, time consuming, and monotonous.

Problems of Measurement

Although measurement appears to be a straightforward process, practitioners frequently encounter problems that inhibit data collection. One set of problems stems from lack of worker experience in collecting data from clients. Practitioners often feel awkward or uncomfortable introducing the concept of measurement to the client. In these situations, neither the importance and value of data collection nor instructions on how to collect data are communicated effectively. A client may leave the session feeling confused and therefore fail to collect the necessary information. When introducing measurement to a client, it is important to explain why the information is being collected, how it will be used, and who will see it. Moreover, clients should receive explicit instructions in data collection procedures; and when appropriate, they should rehearse these procedures before actually collecting the data. Following these guidelines will enhance the likelihood that clients consistently collect accurate data.

Another problem involves fabrication of data by a client. Typically, the client wants to show more improvement than is actually occurring. This problem highlights the importance of collecting multiple measures whenever possible, because it may take time for the worker to detect that data are fabricated. If a worker uses more than one method of data collection, the contrived data become evident from comparison with the other methods. If a worker suspects that a client is fabricating data, concern should be expressed to the client in a straightforward manner. The worker should not adopt a blaming posture but express concern about the importance of accurate information and give reasons inaccurate data are undesirable.

A third problem involves getting incomplete or inaccurate information because the client lacks the skill or ability to follow data collection procedures correctly. This problem can be especially prevalent with young children and with children and adolescents with disabilities. Workers are encouraged to review data collection instructions and rehearse them with clients (Shelton & Ackerman, 1974). If problems continue, the workers should revise the procedures or enlist others to assist in the data collection process. Frequently, parents and teachers are willing to assist in data collection.

DESIGNS FOR EVALUATING PRACTICE

Practitioners use evaluation designs to organize data gathered during assessment and intervention phases. Case studies, A/B, multiple-baseline, and pretest/posttest, are examples of designs. They assist workers in establishing relationships between intervention procedures and client outcome.

Evaluation designs vary considerably in their ability to control for variables other than the intervention that might influence client outcomes. To a large extent, designs are determined by what occurs normally in practice. For example, the baseline is usually defined by the length of the assessment phase and how soon intervention begins. The number and sequencing of interventions defines the remaining design phases.

The following section discusses case studies, single-case evaluation, and experimental and quasi-experimental designs in terms of their usefulness for evaluating practice.

Case Studies

Symbolically, this design is represented as /B where B includes both assessment and intervention. Case studies are generally used when practitioners have little or no time to collect baseline data, although opportunities for repeated measurement during intervention are possible. For example, a practitioner is likely to begin intervention immediately for a physically disabled child who displays such self abusive behavior as biting or scratching. After the intervention, the parents could record the frequency of subsequent self-injurious episodes every hour. In another example, a practitioner counseling an eight-year-old boy in jeopardy of being expelled from school for disruptive behavior in the classroom is likely to begin intervention without a baseline. Again, after implementing the intervention, the worker could collect daily information from the teacher on the frequency of further class disruptions (see Figure 12.5). The failure to collect baseline data does not prevent the worker from collecting assessment data although it precludes establishing stability in the baseline prior to implementing an intervention. In the above examples, the practitioner would collect data from the parent and teacher on such items as the history of the problem, precipitating events, level of intensity, and duration of each episode as a part of the assessment process.

Case studies make an important contribution in the evaluation of practice. They provide a framework for collecting continuous data on a target problem during intervention and at follow-up. Also, with a simple modification of the basic case study, /C or /BC, a practitioner can implement multiple interventions and continue to collect data on the target problem. For instance, in the example of the eight year old, the practitioner might suggest that the teacher use time-out for disruptions. After collecting data for one week, the practitioner learns that the child has reduced his disruptions from 18 to 12 per day. Nonetheless, the teacher wants the disruptions reduced further. In addition to the time-outs, the practitioner suggests that the child be given ten minutes of computer time for every hour he is free of disruptions. This revised case-study would be represented symbolically with the notation /BC.

The major disadvantage of the case-study is the inability to establish a causal relationship between intervention and outcome. The fact that no systematic baseline is recorded precludes such an inference. However, the case study remains an important and viable option for monitoring change in target problems.

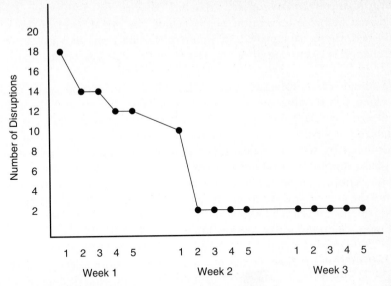

FIGURE 12.5   Number of disruptions per day

Single-Case Evaluation

Single-case evaluation includes the systematic assessment, intervention, and outcome evaluation of a single individual or system (Jayratne & Levy, 1979; Hayes, 1981). Bloom and Fischer (1994) identify seven characteristics of single case-evaluation, including problem specification, measurement of the problem, repeated measurement, collection of baseline data, design selection, clear identification of the intervention, and analysis of data.

Problem Specification.   Problem specification includes conceptualizing and articulating the target problem in clear, observable, or measurable terms. The target problem might include individual, family, or environmental change. Target behavior can be overt or covert.

Measurement of the Problem.   By utilizing observational, self-report, or standardized measures, practitioners are able to categorize and quantify the target problem so that change can easily be monitored.

Repeated Measures.   One of the fundamental characteristics of single-case evaluation is repeated measurement. Repeated measurement involves collecting data at several intervals throughout the intervention process. At a minimum, the practitioner must collect data at the beginning of, during, and at the end of the intervention. Depending on the target problem and the measurement package, however, data may be recorded either continuously, or repeatedly throughout the intervention period.

Collecting Baseline Information.   Baseline data are data about the target problem collected before intervention begins. Once the initial level of the problem is established, these data provide a point of comparison, or a gauge, to determine if change is occurring after the intervention plan has been initiated.

Design.   Single-case evaluation offers the practitioner several types of designs to use when determining intervention effectiveness. Bloom and Fischer (1994) define designs as "arrangements for collecting data." That is, data are collected and organized in a certain way dependent upon the design phases, which in turn are determined by what is occurring in practice. In single-case evaluation, each design phase represents a different activity either for the practitioner or for the client. For example, phase B may represent the first intervention while phase C represents the second intervention presented to the client. Practitioners will need to consider the target problem, the type of measurement package, and the sequencing of intervention when deciding on a design.

Clear Definition of Intervention.   The intervention phases are the most important phases of the evaluation process. Here the practitioner attempts to make an impact on the target problem by implementing the intervention plan. There are three basic reasons for clear definition of the intervention. First of all, a worker needs to define the intervention so that he or she will know that it is actually being implemented. Second, workers who have clearly articulated their interventions find it easier to change or modify them if they are not having the desired impact. Finally, the clear definition of an intervention makes replication easier. That is, if an intervention worked with the first client, it can be tried with another client who presents with a similar problem under similar circumstances (Peterson, Homer, & Wonderlich, 1982).

Analysis of Data.   Practitioners can determine the impact or effectiveness of their intervention plans by analyzing outcome data. Although single-case designs offer statistical approaches to evaluating outcomes, the most common approach is visual analysis. Data from repeated measures are graphed, with demarcations indicating the beginnings and ends of various phases. By "eyeballing" the graph, a practitioner determines if there has been change in the target behavior and if this change corresponds with the intervention phases. If the change is in the positive direction, the worker has some reason to believe goals are being achieved. If the amount of change seems sufficient, the worker may decide to discontinue intervention on a particular goal. Guidelines for visually analyzing data are available elsewhere (Blythe & Tripodi, 1989; Bloom & Fischer, 1994).

Single-Case Designs

AB.   The AB design is the basic single-case design. In this design, A represents baseline and B represents intervention. The primary difference between the case-study design and the AB design is the presence of a baseline (Bloom & Fischer,

1994). In the AB design, practitioners systematically collect data before intervention is implemented. For example, a practitioner working with a family on communication issues found that the 12-year-old daughter was shy, withdrawn, and
unusually quiet during home visits. The practitioner designed a reinforcement
procedure to increase the number of verbalizations made by the child during each
family session. During intervention, the worker made positive and supportive
statements following any verbalization by the daughter. As shown in Figure 12.6,
verbalizations increased from two per session to eight to ten.

A baseline can be reconstructed when the client or a significant other can
recall the necessary information (Bloom, Butch, & Walker, 1979). In the case of
a sexually assaulted girl, intervention could not ethically be withheld—the young-
ster was suffering from depression and from painful flashbacks of the
attack. The worker helped the client recall the number of flashbacks for the three
days preceding the intake. At this point, the girl was unable to report the flash-
back episodes accurately, and the worker discontinued further attempts to recon-
struct a baseline.

There are many advantages to the AB design. First, it complements what
normally happens in practice. When possible, collecting baseline data should be
a regular part of the assessment process and therefore should not place any constraints or unusual burden on the worker. Second, the AB design is adaptable to
many different situations, problems, populations, and settings (Bloom & Fischer,
1994). It can be used to organize data on a child's thoughts, behaviors, and, feelings, as well as organizational variables.

FIGURE 12.6   Verbalizations and home visits

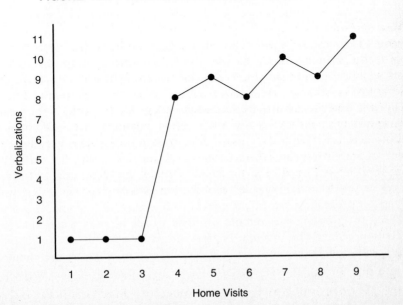

The greatest disadvantage of the AB design is that it cannot establish a causal relationship between intervention and outcome. A direct cause–effect relationship is impossible to verify because workers cannot control for a variety of other variables that impinge on the client during intervention. These variables might include maturation, school stress, physical illness, knowledge gained by reading a self-help book, advice from a friend, new boyfriend or girlfriend, and so on. While other designs also must contend with these variables, they offer additional procedures that establish a stronger association between intervention and outcome.

The ABAB design, a variation of the basic AB design, is sometimes called the withdrawal or reversal design (Leitenberg, 1973). In the ABAB design, the second A represents a return to baseline conditions and the second B a reinstatement of the intervention. The power of this design lies in the second baseline: If the intervention was responsible for the change in the behavior, withdrawing the intervention should cause the behavior to also return to baseline conditions. Once this association is determined, the intervention is reinstated in its original form.

Although the addition of the second AB phase seems simple, in actual practice the design is difficult to implement. First, the design is not appropriate when the intervention involves learning or awareness on the part of the client. New skills or understanding cannot be unlearned or forgotten, even if the intervention is withdrawn during the second baseline (Rubin & Babbie, 1993). A second problem with the ABAB is the ethical dilemma presented when the practitioner must withdraw an intervention that seems to work (Nelson, 1993; Kratochwill, Mott, & Dodson, 1984). Although this is the only way to determine that the intervention is responsible for the change in behavior, many practitioners believe it is unethical in light of a client's progress. This is especially true when the behavior has potential for danger or injury to either the client or a significant other. Occasionally, interventions are withdrawn naturally when a client misses several sessions or is unable to use an intervention procedure for a period of time.

Changing Criterion Design.   The changing criterion design offers a possible solution to the dilemma posed by the ABAB design. This design involves establishing a stepwise performance criterion for the client that ends when the final treatment goal is achieved (Bloom & Fischer, 1994). The practitioner begins by establishing a baseline for the target behavior. The intervention is implemented and continued until the client reaches a preset criterion. After the client stabilizes at the new criterion level, a more difficult criterion level is established. This sequence of stabilizing the client at one level and increasing the difficulty for the next level is continued until the client reaches the target goal or an acceptable level. As an example, consider a probation officer meeting with a juvenile in a diversion program. A treatment goal is to decrease his cursing. The problem is measured by counting the number of curse words he uses when talking with the probation officer. The juvenile begins with a baseline of 69 words per session. The practitioner's intervention is a reward system whereby the client earns a pass to the YMCA gym each time he meets the criterion level. The first level

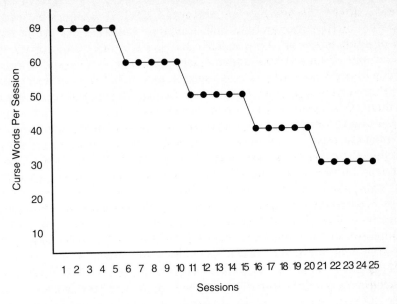

FIGURE 12.7 Curse words per session

was 60 words. When he stabilized at that level and earned his reward, he then had to reduce the number to 50 before he could earn the next gym pass. The third criterion level was 40, and the fourth level was 30. The target goal was 20 or fewer profane words during a treatment session (see Figure 12.7).

The changing criterion design is especially helpful when treatment goals involve targets that lend themselves to shaping or need a gradual increase or decrease in the frequency or intensity (Barlow & Hersen, 1984).

Multiple-Baseline Designs.   Because it is more likely to fit with practice as it occurs, the multiple-baseline design is a good choice for a worker who wants to look for a causal relationship between the intervention and the target behavior. As its name suggests, the multiple-baseline design requires more than one baseline. The practitioner can gather baseline data from several different people with the same problem (multiple-baseline across persons), from the same client but in different settings, such as school, work, or home (multiple-baseline across settings), or from the same client but with several different target problems (multiple-baseline across problems) (Kazdin, 1982). In all cases, the same intervention must be used with each client, setting, or problem.

The practitioner begins by collecting data for all baselines. After the baselines have stabilized, the practitioner initiates the intervention on the first baseline while still collecting data, with no intervention, on the other baselines. The practitioner does not begin the intervention on the second baseline until an effect is demonstrated with the first baseline, and so on, until all baselines have received the intervention. The real strength of the multiple baselines lies in the repeated impact of intervention on the respective baselines. In effect, the intervention is replicated one or more times, and the same outcome is achieved during each replication. Hersen and Barlow (1984) suggest that multiple-baseline designs have at least three or four baselines to establish the effectiveness of the intervention.

A multiple-baseline design across persons was used with a child welfare worker trying to improve school attendance in three middle-school boys. The intervention consisted of a planned recreational activity with each individual child if he attended three consecutive days of school. Recreational activities included going to the movies, to a park, to a video arcade, or to a college basketball or football game. The worker obtained baseline data for the previous month from the boys' teacher. Intervention was begun with child 1 while baseline data continued to be collected on child 2 and child 3. After two weeks, the worker saw marked improvement with child 1 and implemented the intervention with child 2 while continuing the intervention with child 1 and still collecting baseline data on child 3. After two more weeks, the worker implemented the intervention on child 3, but only after she saw improvement on child 2 (see Figure 12.8).

FIGURE 12.8 Days per week at school

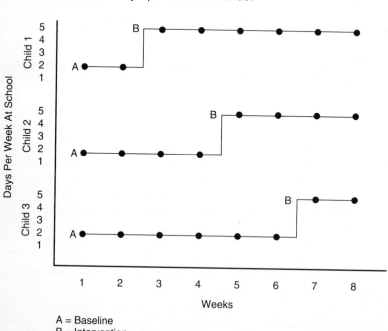

A = Baseline
B = Intervention

Group Designs

It is undeniable that single-case evaluation adds an important dimension to the evaluation of practice. It provides practitioners with techniques that can be employed when working with individuals, families, or small groups. These techniques are scientifically valid and have the potential to demonstrate a causal relationship between the intervention and the target behavior. At a minimum, they facilitate routine monitoring of client progress toward goals. Single-case evaluation, however, is a relatively new approach to evaluating practice. The more traditional model of evaluation is the group design.

The group design provides a systematic approach to evaluating the impact of an intervention on larger groups. There can be thousands of participants in a group design, as occurs when the Food and Drug Administration tests a new drug. An individual practitioner, however, is not likely to have access, time, or resources to conduct such large-scale evaluations. More likely, a practitioner has access to 25 to 50 participants for an evaluation.

One advantage of group designs is that the practitioner may be able to make some inferences about causality, in other words, to suggest that the intervention is responsible for the clients' change. A second advantage involves the ability to generalize findings to a larger group of individuals. Presumably, group members are representative of some larger population. Group designs can be further divided into two categories, experimental and quasi-experimental designs.

Experimental Group Designs. Experimental group designs are more sophisticated designs that include several precautionary measures to control for bias in experimentation. The most important of these precautions are randomization and the presence of a control group (Campbell & Stanley, 1966; Cook & Campbell, 1979; Rubin & Babbie, 1993). In experimental designs, it is necessary to have at least two groups. The experimental group receives the intervention while the control group does not. Each group is compared on the same outcome measures, with the expectation that the experimental group will show more progress. It is important that the experimental and control groups be relatively equivalent in terms of relevant client characteristics before the intervention begins. Random assignment, which involves an unbiased assignment to either the intervention group or the control group, assures that important characteristics will be equally distributed between the groups (Grinnell & Stothers, 1993). Random assignment allows the practitioner to rule out competing reasons (or threats to internal validity, as they are called) for the change observed in the experimental group but not in the control group.

An example of an experimental design is the evaluation by LeCroy and Rose (1986) of strategies for enhancing social competence among adolescents in which 73 seventh graders were randomly assigned to one of four intervention groups:

Group 1: Social-cognitive and social skills model—intervention consisted of problem solving and social skills training

Group 2: Social problem-solving model—intervention consisted of problem-solving only

Group 3: Social skills training model—intervention consisted of social skills training only

Group 4: Control group (attention placebo)—no intervention, leader contact focused on educational rather than interpersonal task

Dependent measures included standardized measures of moral development, locus of control, problem solving, role taking, and skill acquisition.

The results of this experiment indicated that groups 1, 2, and 3 made significant gains, on all measures as compared to the control group. Groups 1, 2, and 3 increased their scores in problem solving, while Groups 1 and 2 realized about equal improvement on the social skills component and both showed greater improvement than Groups 3 and 4.

A number of different variations of the group design have been developed and tested, but they all share certain basic characteristics. First, baseline data are collected from both experimental and control groups. As with single-case designs, this information is compared with post intervention data to determine the impact of the intervention. Second, only experimental groups receive well-designed interventions. Control groups receive placebos (very weak intervention) or no intervention. Last, experimental and control groups both receive post-intervention measurement. Readers are referred to research texts (Grinnell & Stothers, 1993; Tripodi & Epstein, 1980) for a more detailed discussion of experimental designs.

Experimental designs are difficult to implement in practice. First, many practitioners believe that withholding treatment from clients is unethical (Barlow & Hersen, 1984). Experimental designs, however, require a no-treatment or placebo-treatment control group as a necessary condition of experimentation. Second, finding a homogeneous group of participants large enough to satisfy the requirements of the design is difficult if not impossible. This problem is exacerbated when the subjects are children with severe or extremely rare problems, such as childhood psychosis, severe panic disorders, or head trauma. In general, at least 25 subjects are needed for both the experimental and the control groups.

Quasi-Experimental Design. Quasi-experimental designs differ from experimental designs in that randomization is not required. Practitioners using the quasi-experimental design often do not have the opportunity to assign participants randomly to a control group (Rubin & Babbie, 1993). Instead, this design uses a nonequivalent control group. To illustrate, a practitioner developing a specialized adoption program for an agency might select a quasi-experimental design. Rather than randomly assigning families to an experimental group (aftercare) or a control group (no aftercare), the worker would provide intervention to all families adopting children with special needs in the primary agency and seek a similar agency for the comparison group. The children in the second agency are not likely to be the same on all personal and treatment characteristics, but both groups are likely to be similar in that the children being adopted have special needs. Only families served by the first agency will receive specialized services.

EVALUATING PROGRESS

Once a practitioner has collected data on a client or client group, the data must be organized and analyzed to determine the effectiveness of the intervention. Practitioners can use a variety of techniques to draw conclusions about intervention outcomes; but the analysis will depend largely on what type of design was selected, single-case design or group design, and what type of data were collected (Tripodi & Epstein, 1980). The three types of analysis include visual display and analysis, statistical analysis, and analysis of clinical significance.

Visual Analysis

Visual analysis is most often associated with single-case research. It involves analyzing and interpreting data by visually inspecting (or "eyeballing") a graph of the data (Jayarante, Tripodi, & Talsma, 1988; Kazdin, 1981; Parsonson & Baer, 1978). The practitioner first looks to see whether the data go in the direction indicated by the goal statement. If the purpose of the intervention was to increase a behavior, feeling, or cognition, the data should indicate an increase. If the purpose was to maintain the behavior, feeling, or cognition, the data pattern should be stable. If the purpose was to obtain a decrease, the data should show reduction. The practitioner then looks for a change in level and trend. Changes in level refers to a sharp increase or decrease in a data pattern immediately following intervention (Kazdin, 1982). Suppose the goal of intervention was increased verbalizations during sessions with a reluctant adolescent client. The teenager began with a baseline of two statements; immediately after intervention, the level increased to 12. This jump is obviously a significant change in level that suggests a very strong and powerful intervention.

Trend refers to the direction of the data pattern. Obviously, the trend can be an increase, decrease, or fluctuation in the data. No change (i.e., a flat data pattern) indicates absence of a trend. In the above example, if the client had a baseline of 2 but after intervention gradually began to verbalize more, this would illustrate an increase in trend.

Finally, during visual analysis, the practitioner examines the stability of the line. A flat line across phases suggests no change and qualifies as an effective intervention only if the goal was to maintain the behavior. A highly variable data line is difficult to interpret as all of the data points include either a slight increase or a slight decrease, with no discernible pattern.

It should be noted that the first item of concern for the practitioner is to determine if the baseline is stable before the intervention is implemented. It is difficult, if not impossible, to make any judgment of progress if the baseline is unstable.

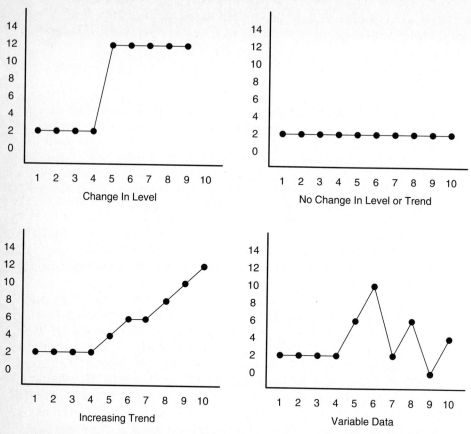

FIGURE 12.9   Change in level and trend

Statistical Analysis.   Statistical analysis is most frequently used with group designs, but it also can be approximated with single-case data (Jayrantne, 1978; Kratochwill, 1983). Statistical techniques provide a framework for practitioners to organize and interpret data gathered from participants. Statistical analysis can involve detailed mathematical computations more easily carried out by computers. The two major approaches to statistical analysis are descriptive and inferential. This section will provide only an overview. More detailed discussion, can be found in statistical texts such as Blalock, 1972; Jendrek, 1985; Weinbach and Grinell, 1991.

Descriptive statistics analyze important characteristics of the participants in a particular group and make comparisons between groups. These statistics are usually expressed as percentages or averages. Here is an example:

Problem Behaviors in Special Education Classroom

Problem Behaviors	Percentage of Total Problem Behaviors
Out of seat	25%
Failing to attend to task	40%
Disruptive talk	15%
Inappropriate verbal outburst	20%
	100%

They include such statistics as means, ranges, and frequencies (Rubin & Babbie, 1993). As noted previously, statistical analysis is primarily used with group designs, which generally include a large number of participants. Descriptive statistics allow practitioners succinctly to describe such characteristics of the population as age, educational level, ethnicity, target problem, and marital status and to communicate information about treatment outcome without presenting data on each individual client. Descriptive statistics are also helpful when making comparisons between experimental and control groups or even pre- and post-intervention comparisons with the same group.

Inferential statistics are used in conjunction with descriptive statistics. Complex mathematical formulas are used to determine if the difference in scores between a group that received treatment and a group that did not are significantly different from what might happen by chance alone. They include such statistics as t-tests and analysis of variance. Inferential statistics also can determine characteristics of a larger population on the basis of outcomes from a representative sample (Rubin & Babbie, 1993). For predictions to be legitimate, practitioners must be sure that participants have been randomly assigned to the treatment group or the control group. In addition, the number of participants must be large enough to be representative of the larger population.

Clinical Significance. Clinical significance is a relatively new concept in the practice evaluation literature. In general, clinical significance has to do with whether the change achieved by an intervention makes a meaningful difference in the well-being of the participant (Risley, 1970). For example, a practitioner designs a program to encourage a teenager to attend school regularly, starting with baseline attendance of four days per month. With the intervention, attendance increases to 13 days per month. This is a large increase, and both visual and statistical analysis would indicate significant improvement, but in reality the practitioner must ask if 13 days per month of school attendance is enough for significant learning to occur? Is the student really benefiting from his educational opportunity if he still misses more than one-third of the required time? After considering these questions, the practitioner would probably conclude that because the client is still at risk the intervention is not clinically significant.

Deciding about the clinical significance of an outcome is primarily a subjective task that requires the worker to address the notion of social validation (Wolf, 1978) which encompasses ways of evaluating whether intervention effects produce changes of clinical or applied significance. Was the change important, or did it have significant impact on the client's life? Is the client (or client's family) satisfied with the changes that have been achieved? Have the problems or situations that prompted the initiation of services been resolved? The practitioner also observes others who are in circumstances similar to the client's and seeks to change the target behavior in a range compatible with the behavior of a desirable model. For example, a practitioner working with a developmentally disabled adolescent seeks to teach and shape skills to be consistent with those of other developmentally disabled adolescents, and not those of adolescents with no known disabilities. Finally, a practitioner might ask another objective person to rate the behavior of the client in relation to what would be expected if there were no problem. For example, a school counselor might be asked to rate a child's social skills based on his or her expert knowledge of the appropriate social skills level for a school-age child.

SUMMARY

This chapter presents basic concepts in the evaluation of practice with children and adolescents. Although methodology has improved immensely over the past ten years, there continue to be many unanswered questions and issues that need further research and development. Following is a brief discussion of several of these issues.

Influence of Developmental Stages on Practice with Children and Adolescents

Children and adolescents will undoubtedly grow and mature during treatment, particularly when it is a lengthy process. Many questions remain unanswered about the impact of these developmental changes on the intervention process and outcome. Practitioners must be mindful of the normal developmental process for children yet realize that many children will not proceed through the stages of development in a linear fashion. How then can practitioners plan and adapt interventions and evaluations when changes are unpredictable? Another basic question lies in the behavioral and emotional manifestations of children and adolescents as they proceed through the developmental stages. What are these expectations?

Practitioner–Researcher

This chapter suggests a model of combining practice technology with the close monitoring of client progress. Many schools of social work have been training students in this practitioner–researcher model for several years, yet the data suggests that many social workers continue to provide services without systematically examining their impact on clients (Richey, Blythe, & Berlin, 1987). Future research must address the personal and organizational barriers that prevent practitioners from evaluating their practice. Personal barriers might include lack of skills and knowledge to appropriately apply the research technology. Agency barriers might include lack of resources and lack of agency support for conducting research on practice.

Rigor of Design

All research designs have been developed and tested in their current format. Adaptations of these designs may produce unreliable results, yet the reality of practice is that workers cannot always collect measures and provide interventions in a highly structured manner. This raises two points of conflict for workers. First of all, to what extent is the integrity of the intervention and evaluation jeopardized when the research design is not followed rigorously? Second, the larger issue of the potential for conflict between research and practice must be examined.

Development Research

Developmental research methodology is a newly emerging approach to developing and evaluating innovative interventions that seems relevant to many practice settings. The methodology, developed by Thomas (1984), includes five phases. In the first phase, problem analysis, the worker defines the problem and collects pertinent information about the scope, severity, and nature of the problem. In the second or design phase, the practitioner develops a blueprint or plan for the intervention. The third phase, the development phase, is perhaps the most important aspect of this research schema. It involves field testing, refining, and redesigning the intervention. The fourth phase, evaluation, employs the more traditional single-case and group designs to evaluate the effectiveness of the newly created intervention. Finally, dissemination involves the marketing and distribution of the newly created intervention. Developmental research appears to be highly compatible with practice. Especially in the early stages of the model, the practitioner is not limited to a highly structured intervention or design and is thus free to use creativity and imagination in developing the new intervention.

Need for Agency Supports

It is perhaps ironic that agency support is presented as the final issue confronting practitioners as they strive to evaluate practice. Without agency support, the ability and motivation to evaluate are lessened. This support can range from moral support from supervisors and coworkers to educational support in the form of workshops, conferences, and in-service training. Last, economic support is needed. Reductions in caseloads or volunteer or paid employees to help analyze data might encourage more practitioners to evaluate their services to clients.

QUESTIONS FOR DISCUSSION

1. One of the limitations of self-report data is the potential for clients "fudging" or fabricating data. Discuss strategies for minimizing the likelihood of manipulation of self-report data.

2. Introducing the purpose and instructions for data collection can be critical in getting cooperation and accurate data from clients. Develop a script for introducing standardized measures, client logs, and self-anchored rating scales.

3. Operationalizing target behaviors can be one of the most difficult and important jobs in the assessment and evaluation process. Think of behaviorally specific indicators of the following behaviors for a 15-year-old adolescent girl:

   - depression
   - loneliness
   - isolation
   - peer pressure
   - popularity
   - anger

ADDITIONAL READINGS

Adams, G. R., & Schvaneveldt, J. D. (1991). *Understanding research methods,* 2nd ed. White Plains, N.Y.: Longman.

Barlow, D. H., & Hersen, M. (1984). *Single-case experimental designs: Strategies for studying behavioral change.* New York: Pergamon Press.

Bloom, M., Fisher, J., & Orme, J. (1994). *Evaluating Practice: Guidelines for the accountable professional.* Englewood Cliffs, N.J.: Prentice-Hall.

Marlow, C. (1993). *Research methods for generalist social work.* Pacific Grove, Calif.: Brooks/Cole.

Rubin, A., & Babbie, E. (1993). *Research methods for social work,* 2nd ed. Pacific Grove, Calif.: Brooks/Cole.

REFERENCES

Barlow, D. H., Hayes, S. C., & Nelson, R. O. (1984). *The scientist practitioner: Research and accountability in clinical and educational settings.* New York: Pergamon.

Barlow, D. H. & Hersen, M. (1984). *Single case experimental design,* 2nd ed. New York: Pergamon Press.

Bellack, A. S., & Hersen, M. (1977). The use of self-report inventories in behavior assessment. In J. D. Cone & R. P. Hawkins, eds., *Behavior assessment: New direction in clinical psychology,* pp. 52–76. New York: Brunner/Mazel.

Blalock, H. M., Jr. (1972). *Social statistics.* New York: McGraw-Hill.

Bloom, M., & Fischer, J. (1994). *Evaluating practice: Guidelines for the accountable professional,* 2nd ed. Englewood Cliffs, N.J.: Prentice-Hall.

Bloom, M., Butch, P., & Walker, D. (1979). Evaluation of single interventions. *Journal of Social Services Research* 2: 301–310.

Blythe, B. J., & Briar, S. (1985). Developing empirically-based models of practice. *Social Work* 30: 483–488.

Blythe, J. J., & Tripodi, T. (1989). *Measurement in direct social work practice.* Beverly Hills, Calif.: Sage.

Bostwick, G. J., Jr., & Kyte, N. S. (1993). Validity and reliability. In R. M. Grinnell, Jr., ed., *Social work research and evaluation,* 3rd ed., pp. 111–136. Itasca, Ill.: F. E. Peacock.

Campbell, D. T., & Stanley, J. C. (1966). *Experimental and quasi-experimental designs for research.* Chicago: Rand McNally.

Ciminero, A. R., Nelson, R., & Lipinski, D. (1977). Self monitoring procedures. In A. R. Ciminero, K. S. Calhoun, & H. E. Adams, eds., *Handbook of behavioral assessment.* New York: Wiley.

Cook, T. D., & Campbell, D. T., eds., (1979). *Quasi-experimentation: Design and analysis issues for field settings.* Chicago: Rand McNally.

Corcoran, K., & Fisher, J. (1987). *Measures for clinical practice.* New York: Free Press.

Cormier, W. H., & Cormier, S. L. (1991). *Interviewing strategies for helpers,* 3rd ed. Pacific Grove, Calif.: Brooks/Cole.

Edelson, J. L. (1985). Rapid-assessment instruments for evaluating practice with children and youth. *Journal of Social Services Research* 8: 17–32.

Foster, S. L., & Cone, J. D. (1980). Current issues in direct observation. *Behavioral Assessment* 2: 313–338.

Gingerich, W. (1979). Procedures for evaluating clinical practice. *Health and Social Work* 4: 104–130.

Grinnell, R. M., & Stothers, S. (1993). Utilizing research designs. In R. M. Grinnell, ed., *Social work research and evaluation,* pp. 199–239. Itasca, Ill.: F. E. Peacock.

Hayes, S. C. (1981). Single case experimental design and empirical clinical practice. *Journal of Consulting and Clinical Psychology* 49: 193–211.

Haynes, S. N., & Horn, W. F. (1982). Reactivity in behavioral observation: A review. *Behavioral Assessment* 4: 369–385.

Hersen, M., & Barlow, D. H. (1984). *Single case experimental design: Strategies for studying behavior change,* 2nd ed. New York: Pergamon.

Ivanoff, A., Robinson, E. A. R., & Blythe, B. J. (1987). Empirical clinical practice from a feminist perspective. *Social Work* 32: 417–423.

Jayrantne, S., Tripodi, T., & Talsma, E. (1988). The comparative analysis and aggregation of single case data. *Journal of Applied Behavioral Science* 1: 119–128.

Jayrantne, S. (1978). Analytic procedures for single-subject designs. *Social Work Research and Abstract* 14(3): 30–40.

Jayratne, S., & Levy, R. L. (1979). *Empirical clinical practice.* New York: Columbia University Press.

Jendrek, M. P. (1985). *Through the maze: Statistics with computer applications.* Belmont, Calif.: Wadsworth, 1985.

Kazdin, A. E. (1981). Drawing valid influences from case studies. *Journal of Consulting and Clinical Psychology* 49: 183–192.

Kazdin, A. E. (1982). *Single-case research designs.* New York: Oxford University Press.

Kratochwill, T. R., & Mace, F. C. (1983). Time-series research: Contributions to empirical clinical practice. *Behavioral Assessment* 5: 165–176.

Kratochwill, T. R., Mott, S. E., & Dodson, C. L. (1984). Case study and single case research in clinical and applied psychology. In A. S. Bellack & M. Hersen, eds., *Research methods in clinical psychology,* pp. 55–99. New York: Pergamon Press.

LeCroy, C. W., & Rose, S. D. (1986). Evaluation of preventive intervention for enhancing social competence in adolescents. *Social Work Research and Abstract* 22: 8-16.

Leitenberg, H. (1973). The use of single-case methodology in psychotherapy research. *Journal of Abnormal Psychology* 82: 87-101.

Marlow, C. (1993). *Research methods for generalist social work.* Pacific Grove, Calif.: Brooks/Cole.

Nelson, J. C. (1993). Single subject research. In R. C. Grinnell, Jr., ed., *Social work research and evaluation,* 3rd ed., pp. 362-399. Itasca, Ill.: F. E. Peacock.

Parsonson, B. S., & Baer, D. M. (1978). The analysis and presentation of graphic data. In T. R. Kratochwill, ed., *Single subject research: Strategies for evaluating change.* New York: Academic Press.

Peterson, L., Homer, A. L., & Wonderlich, S. A. (1982). The integrity of independent variables in behavior analysis. *Journal of Applied Behavior Analysis* 15: 477-492.

Richey, C. A., Blythe, B. J., & Berlin, S. B. (1987). Do social workers evaluate their practice. *Social Work Research and Abstracts* 23: 14-20.

Rubin, A., & Babbie, E. (1993). *Research methods for social work,* 2nd ed. Belmont, Calif.: Wadsworth.

Shelton, J. L., & Ackerman, J. N. (1974). *Homework in counseling and psychotherapy.* Springfield, Ill.: Thomas.

Thomas, E. J. (1984). *Designing interventions for the helping professions.* Beverly Hills, Calif.: Sage.

Tripodi, T., & Epstein, I. (1980). *Research techniques for clinical social workers.* New York: Columbia University Press.

Weinbach, R.W., & Grinnell, R. (1991). *Statistics for social workers.* New York: Longman, 1991.

Wolf, M. (1978). Social validity: The case for subjective measurement or how applied behavior analysis is finding its heart. *Journal of Applied Behavior Analysis* 11: 203-214.

Index